On the Ropes

By the same author

SURVIVORS OF STEEL CITY

MAKING IT: THE REALITY OF TODAY'S ENTREPRENEURS

ALL TALK

ENGLAND AFTER DARK

WE ARE THE PEOPLE: JOURNEYS THROUGH THE HEART
OF PROTESTANT ULSTER

On the Ropes

boxing as a way of life

Geoffrey Beattie

VICTOR GOLLANCZ

LONDON

First published in Great Britain 1996
by Victor Gollancz
An imprint of the Cassell Group
Wellington House, 125 Strand, London WC2R 0BB

A catalogue record for this book is
available from the British Library.

ISBN 0 575 06224 X

Photographs on pages 168 and 171 © Geoffrey Beattie.
Photograph on page 275 © Empics Ltd.
All other photographs © Bill Stephenson.

Typeset by Rowland Phototypesetting Ltd, Bury St Edmunds
Printed in Great Britain by
Butler & Tanner Ltd, Frome, Somerset

96 97 98 99   10 9 8 7 6 5 4 3 2 1

This book is dedicated to
Brendan Ingle, professor of
kidology and maker of
champions

Contents

Acknowledgements

My main debt of gratitude must go to Brendan Ingle and all of the boxers in the gym who gave their time so freely. A number of pieces I wrote about boxing and the culture of boxers in the north of England appeared in the *Guardian*, particularly *Guardian Weekend* and *Guardian Sport*, the *Independent Magazine*, the *Independent on Sunday*, the *Observer*, and the *New Statesman and Society*, and I would like to thank Mike Averis, David Robson, Roger Alton, John Course, Bruce Miller, Ian Parker, Richard Askwith, Peter Wilby, Steve Platt and Michael Watts for their general encouragement, support and interest. I would also like to express my gratitude to John Gaustad for making some invaluable suggestions about publishers at a critical time in the development of the book, and to Neil Tunnicliffe who thought that this might be an interesting book for me to attempt in the first place. I am grateful to Weidenfeld and Nicolson for granting permission to use in a modified form extracts on dog fighting and championship boxing which first appeared in *England After Dark* (1990). Finally, I would like to thank Richard Wigmore and Katrina Whone, at Victor Gollancz, who have been excellent editors.

The verse quoted on page 1 is reproduced with the permission of Curtis Brown Ltd on behalf of Anthony Thwaite.

'Never contend with a man who has nothing to lose.'
(Baltasar Gracian, 1647)

Introduction

Nothing the critic said of tragedy,
Groomed for the stage and mastered into art,
Was relevant to this; yet I could see
Pity and terror mixed in equal part.
(Anthony Thwaite, *Home Truths*, 1957)

The Song and Dance Man

'Oooooooommmmmmppphh.' The noise erupted from the pit of my stomach. From way down low. It did not sound human. It was an involuntary response way beyond my control. Way beyond anybody's control. That's what I tried to tell myself. It was out before I could do anything about it, and there was no way to apologize or make amends now. That noise sealed my fate. Gary, standing at the side of the ring, laughed. I wanted to. I wanted to smile and to clown about to show that I wasn't taking any of this seriously. But I couldn't. It was all serious, and that was obvious even to the casual spectator. I was grimly determined. Just try saying that word 'grim' and watch how it makes your lips purse in an ugly manner. My lips wanted to hang open, bleeding, sucking in the air. It took all my effort to keep a face together. I was past caring whether it looked aggressive or like the face of somebody who should be respected. It was a grim mask.

To spare my embarrassment Gary kept glancing away, shouting to his mates still on the bag routines. But I could see him looking back towards me, looking out for little signs from my body. To see how I was taking it. To see what kind of a man I was. I covered up. I watched the eyes of my opponent. I was looking for signs from him. Of what, I didn't know.

But I was already starting to slide down the greasy, phylogenetic scale of respect. If I had started the morning at the gym on my first day of boxing at the level of hamster or dormouse, I was now fast approaching the level of amoeba. I had been warned, you see, not to make any noise when hit. 'We have lads who've come down to train once or twice and they've taken a good shot and then they're down on the canvas,' Gary had warned me before we started. 'The rule down here on a Saturday morning is if you're hurt you box on. If you're hurt, you don't make any noise – you don't make a song and dance about it.' But it was too late. I had made a noise, and not just any noise. I had managed to produce a low moan that had played its own tune on the way out. I had never heard that noise before, although I had seen it written down several times in comics when the filthy Bosch had been butted in the stomach with the handle of a gun by some Tommy or other. I was the filthy, cowardly Bosch. Or an amoeba. I didn't much like the thought of being either.

I was now watching my sparring partner's face for a sign of recognition of my rule infringement. I had broken the rule, I had violated the code of manly conduct in the ring. But there was no such sign, just that quiet look of satisfaction from Mick 'The Bomb' Mills of work well done. My song, which had started so softly and which had risen to some sort of crescendo, was music to his ears. There was a sign at the side of the ring that read 'Boxing can damage your health'. It was meant to be funny. I now knew it wasn't. I was trying to remember where my spleen was, and trying to imagine how it would feel burst. Or merely ajar, leaking. Seeping.

I was more determined now. It might have been just the impetus I needed. Sweat dripped into my eyes. It stung. I tried wiping it away with the edge of the glove. It left my stomach exposed. My vest was soaked with sweat. My biceps ached. Never had I imagined that a man, even a complete novice at boxing, who had been performing bicep curls more or less continuously from the age of eleven upwards, would ever have to endure biceps that ached. Not biceps, for God's sake; those curious muscles that run up the back of your arm, maybe, but not the obvious bicep. But just try that movement – out and back, out and back, out and back with the left arm – a hundred times, now a thousand times. Continuous defensive movement. I ached. All of this effort expended on my jab was meant to be effective. It was meant to keep my opponent at arm's length. But it was no defence at all. Mick walked right through them. His jabs, on the other hand, landed with great dull thuds on my upper arm and forearm with hypnotic regularity. My arms were stuck rigid in a defensive covered posture.

He bobbed and weaved as I tried to land one good punch on him. Just one, Lord, just one. I wanted him to respect me. I was desperate for some respect. But I knew that I was going to have to earn it. I wanted to start scrambling up the other side of that deep hole I had managed to dig for myself through my whimpering. But I was telegraphing my shots and he didn't even have to block them – he just

4

had to bob and weave. He was about my height, five foot eight, but his forearms were of similar dimensions to my thighs. My shots were landing harmlessly on those great slabs of meat. And by the time they had landed they had no power whatsoever. As Mick had said earlier: 'Boxing looks easy enough, especially on the telly. You may even be able to land a good punch on a bag. But connecting well with someone who's moving is a lot more difficult.' It's all in the timing, and my timing was off. It was as simple as that.

The problem was that I always thought that *I* could have done a lot better, even with a moving target. I had always fancied myself in the ring, you see, although for the life of me I couldn't remember why. I had been brought up on boxing. My uncle had been an amateur boxer in his younger days, and on Saturdays when he and my father got back from the pub I would be invited to box him. Me and the dog both. Spot, our black and white fox terrier, would only ever attempt to bite him on a Saturday night, when he reeked of Guinness. Spot would be on his shoulder biting his neck, I would be clambering over the back of the settee boxing his ears. My uncle was by then about five stone overweight, but it didn't matter. My aunt was always very proud of the fact that I had managed to give my Uncle Terence a black eye, never mind the scars that Spot managed to inflict. My uncle would sit hunched up in his suit, sweating, with the Guinness coming back out through his pores. The dog would distract him and then, 'wham', I got one in. My uncle would hurl the dog to the floor. 'You have to show them who's the boss,' he would say. My mother would agree. 'Your uncle's very good with animals. Your father's too soft. You have to be cruel to be kind.' We always worked ourselves up into a great lather, all salty sweat and sickly foam from the mouth of the dog. The dog would have to go and lie down in front of the electric fire afterwards to cool down, and then it would sneak round the back to drink the porter out of my uncle's glass. Only on a Saturday night. But all that was a lifetime ago. It was no preparation for this. A one-on-one. Man-to-man. No Spot to help me out.

Mick never stopped moving – this way and that. Impossible to pin down. My punches left my body hard and determined, but they fizzled out somewhere in the gap between us. Mick's glory days in the ring may have been behind him, and I say 'may have been' because there were still some people in Sheffield who were talking about a comeback

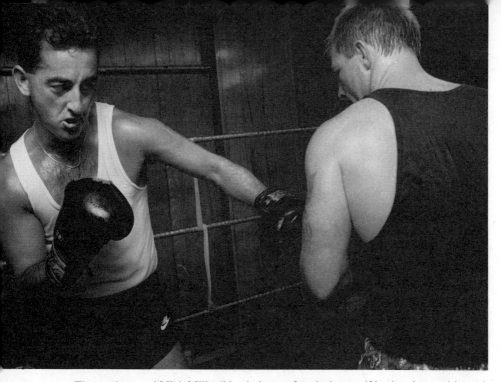

The author and Mick Mills. 'I had always fancied myself in the ring – although for the life of me I couldn't remember why.'

for this ex-fighter, who was now a bouncer, but he was streets ahead of me. Untouchable. He was always a good crowd pleaser, and his punch had not left him – the boxer with the hardest punch since Randolph Turpin, Harry Gibbs the referee had said. They had warned me on the way to the gym that Mick could be a bit heavy-handed. I thought they'd meant he wasn't very tactful. Now I knew that it was meant in altogether a more literal sense. 'But,' they told me, 'he won't hurt you. He knows that you're a nobody. He'll have nothing to prove.'

Sweat was closing my eyes. I was working in the ring. Voices from within. Nothing to prove indeed. A nobody. Work! Acidic little drops in my eyes. Narrower and narrower. Imaginings. 'So the countdown for the end of the first and the steam is already showing now.' The steam was showing, rising from the solid thick torso in front of me. Steaming bulls on a cold winter's morning. No, raging bull. Majestic. How would I look in the ring if the camera was on me? How was my footwork? Just try a little shuffle. I looked down, and another heavy jab nearly broke my shoulder. Careful, steady now. Blocking. The raging of the beef brigade, steaming bulls. Steaming. Steam. Two steamtrains speeding towards a head-on collision. A clinch, our heads collided. He compressed my arms at the elbows. Locked in tight. My breathing slowed. Like an animal caught in a trap. I didn't want to breathe on him. I didn't want my breathing to tell him anything. I felt his forehead grinding against the side of my head. I could hear the wet hairs rubbing. Short spiky, wet hairs grinding against my temples. I tried to pull back. Then again. Stuck fast. Just that noise in my ears, and my elbows feeling as if they were about to shatter. No referee in this sparring. Just one-on-one.

Then the trap flew open; he let me go. Bored.

Everything on the proximal horizon was now a blur. He was the only focus, the sole figure on which my attention was directed, and when he moved, which he did continuously, his whole body was a great white blur. Out of this haze, for that is what it had become, I just felt these slow, methodical blows. A man at work. Not sharp stinging blows that might leave you annoyed or irritated but great, solid, dull thumps. Every time they landed on my chest I thought they might stop my heart. I had never heard of a boxer's heart being stopped by a punch before, but in those moments in the ring I thought that this was a real possibility. My heart was racing and then, boom, it slowed. The involuntary noises coming from my body, as I was winded, reassured me that I was still alive. A sudden surge of energy. The body in full flight. Adrenaline pumping. A strange feeling of optimism. Noises from within and without. Alive and working now. Harder! Faster! I was listening for the bell that had to come, and hearing other voices. 'This is the most professional that I've seen Beattie.' 'Beattie was never intimidated, he got on with the job.' 'I'm proud of Geoffrey Beattie, because he did the job fantastic.' Gary stood there saying nothing, too embarrassed to watch.

Out through the haze and way out somewhere in the corner of my eye I could see that we were now being watched by another bouncer with a t-shirt that said 'Kiss my ass'. I had dreaded this moment. I thought I might be able to survive in the ring with Mick, as long as there was no one there spectating, or just Gary, who was only half watching anyway, but now there was a crowd of two to egg him on. My heart was sinking fast. My wave of optimism had broken on the shores of this grimy blood-stained ring. Paul, the bouncer in the 'Kiss my ass' t-shirt, and a black belt in jiu-jitsu to boot, who also happens to own a couple of fitness clubs, called across the room: 'You're not running, are you, Mick?' It was an inoffensive kind of question, really. My eyes told Mick to ignore it. They pleaded with him to ignore it. But his feet started to grind to a halt. My knuckles were already bleeding after the bag work. 'Left jab, left jab, right jab, left upper-cut, left hook' – the opening routine in the bag work. Ten times. It was the upper-cuts that had done the damage. It was they that had brought the knuckles of my two smallest fingers on my left hand into contact with the bag. After one routine they were bleeding. After six or seven routines, all of my knuckles were bleeding. My hands felt tender. What damage could I inflict on him with those hands?

I had been talking to a climber the previous day who had just fallen off a rock face. He had told me that it was the longest one and a half seconds he had ever experienced. As 'The Bomb' drew to a halt, I could understand exactly what this climber meant. I remembered what Joe Louis had once said: 'You can run, but you can't hide.' But I couldn't even run. At least not backwards. Mick had let me go after him. I now had a little experience of moving forward and defending myself, but none whatsoever of moving backwards and staying upright, with those jabs coming at me.

The first blow came to my shoulder. It jerked my body around, as if someone had rotated me in a dance. He squared up for a second punch . . . 'Don't forget, no head shots!' shouted Gary. I covered my stomach and started to make an involuntary but very quiet 'uuurrrrggghhhh' sound even before the shot had landed – in preparation, I think.

'Time!' shouted Gary, laughing. 'We never time rounds here. We play it by ear, so to speak.' I wasn't sure whether he intended the pun or not, but I was relieved anyway. 'He was just playing,' said Gary reassuringly. Mick and I touched gloves and I climbed slowly out of the ring. My legs were trembling. Mick started to shadow-box the air where I had stood. The air probably put up more resistance than I had. Steve climbed in beside him. Steve had also been a professional boxer, but he'd never had the same kind of talent as Mick. One of Brendan Ingle's old boys – a spoiler. He knew how to look after himself in the ring and that was about it. Now, he looked after himself on the door of a nightclub. He still had a full-time job as a sheet metal worker. He was no challenge to Mick. 'Bastard,' said Steve under his breath, as one of Mick's bombs landed within the first few seconds.

I had a chance to look round the gym. Old faded posters, heavy bags, sweat-stained floor. Everything hinted of work. There was a lot to be done. This was my first day of training. My sparring partners worked as bouncers at Josephine's nightclub, Sheffield's ultimate nite-spot, it called itself. They had been asking me for months to join them in the gym, but I had always managed to get out of it without losing too much face. I had said that I wanted to learn about boxing. They had told me there was only one way, and that was by stepping into a ring. This ring was famous. Herol 'Bomber' Graham, who had had two cracks at the world middleweight title but had never made it in the end, had bobbed and weaved in that confined space. Kids would queue up to try to land a punch on him. The old slippery Graham would stand with his hands behind his back, dodging every one. Johnny Nelson, an up-and-coming cruiserweight, was honing his skills in those same few square feet. Then there was a young Arab boy, called Naz, with buckets of talent, or so they said. And here was I. The song-and-dance man with leaden feet. The ring was in Brendan Ingle's gym in Wincobank in Sheffield. An old church hall – St Thomas' – with a great wooden door. A few rusty weights, and huge punch bags everywhere. One speed ball looked forlorn in the corner. On Saturdays Brendan let Mick and the lads borrow it for a workout. 'We all come from different backgrounds,' said Gary. 'Professional boxing, karate, jiu-jitsu, and then there's Lloyd, who's been a professional heavyweight boxer and is now a body-builder. He's currently "Mr Central Britain". Mick Quirke is also a body-builder and he owns his own fitness club. Oh yeah, and then there's the DJ from the club where we work. That's him trying to skip over there. After the bag work today he took off his gloves and his hands were all red. He thought they'd been cut to pieces. It was the dye from the bag gloves! But it's good for us all to get together and know what we're all capable of.' Or not capable of.

Mick now climbed into the ring with Paul, the black belt in jiu-jitsu. Paul had something to prove. Mick winded him in the first few seconds. Unlike myself, Paul made no sound. Gary watched this bout with me. 'Everybody here has a lot of respect for Mick. You don't appreciate how good he is until you step into the ring with him.

Although we only play at boxing down here on a Saturday, you've still got to think very carefully about what you're doing. It's a very good way of finding out what it's like to be hit. It's also a good way of getting rid of aggression. Working on the door of clubs, you rarely get called upon to do anything, and then when you do it's usually out of the blue. Some kid managed to get my coat over my head and put my head through a glass door in Dinnington a while ago. The kid had a big reputation in the area. Mick was working with me at the time, but he didn't help out. In fact, he was standing taking bets on who was going to win. But it was important for me to get the better of this kid. Mick knew I had to come through it on my own. It was like an initiation ceremony. It must have been harder for Mick to stand there and watch than join in. Mick could have punched holes in the kid. He's still very good. Although Lloyd is good and very, very big, he doesn't have the same kind of talent that Mick has. These regular training sessions down here let you get all of that kind of stuff sorted out. You soon get to know what kind of talent everyone has, and who to respect.'

I kept thinking of deer rutting, and status hierarchies in the animal kingdom, but what had any of this to do with mating, for goodness' sake. The DJ, who had trouble skipping and even more trouble with his upper-cuts, had his girlfriend and new-born baby along to watch, as if to emphasize the point.

'I've never done any boxing in the past, but Mick has taught me everything,' continued Gary. 'I regret not taking up boxing earlier. The nightclub where we work recently put up a glass case with photographs from all the door staff's fight days. They had boxing photos of Mick and Steve, boxing and wrestling photos from Big Jim, and boxing and body-building photos from Lloyd. I had nothing to put in the cabinet. Mick says that although I'm thirty I should try a few fights in the ring. He says I'd be OK. It'd be something to look back on, something for the glass case.'

In the changing room with the paint hanging off in great dollops sat another Gary, an up-and-coming heavyweight boxer who works as a bouncer in a club in Nottingham. He was wearing a black t-shirt with 'Rhythm Killers' on the back. 'When you face up to guys like Mick Mills on a Saturday, then you know you can handle whatever comes off the streets the rest of the week. Training always makes me

Mick Quirke and Lloyd. 'Some of these boxers had been described as a bit heavy-handed. I thought that it meant they were not very tactful.'

feel very calm afterwards.' I wished I could agree with him. I had by now realized that there were people out there who could punch holes in me. I think I had been happier in my ignorance, but I kept my mouth shut.

This was my initiation. I sat in the changing room examining my body. My upper arms and forearms were black and blue. Bruises were appearing on my back as if the pain and injury had been conducted right through my torso. Mick laughed. I promised faithfully that I would become a regular down in the gym on a Saturday. I told them I wanted to understand boxing – what it felt like, where the boxers came from, why they did it. Mick told me that I had started well. 'You mean I now know what it feels like?' I asked. He wiped his face with the back of his glove and looked at me with little expression in his eyes. There was no sparkle there, no real warmth, certainly no respect. Perhaps just a little curiosity. He had a good look at me before he replied. 'I wouldn't go that far, but at least you know what a sickener it is to get one in the stomach. Boxers have to get used to sickeners. So at least you've made some kind of start.'

Setting

I wanted to write about boxing by focusing on just one gym, St Thomas' in Sheffield, or, to give it its proper title, St Thomas' Club for Boys and Girls – Brendan Ingle's place – a place to train, 'for life', Brendan always likes to say.

Ingle has been there since 1961. 'My brother Peter left Dublin for Sheffield in 1957,' said Brendan. 'He came home at Christmas with two hundred pounds in his pocket and three new suits. I wasn't working at the time in Dublin, but I was boxing. I went back with him in the January. When we got to England he told me that I'd have to stand on my own two feet. He told me to go round the steel works knocking on doors, asking for a job. He told me to say that I'd be prepared to do anything. I was eighteen. They were asking, "Now then, thee, what's yer name?" I couldn't understand what they were saying. They said to me, "What's the matter? Don't you understand English, thee?" I got a job with Alfred Beckett and Sons in Green Lane. They were blade manufacturers for the paper industry. I went to work with Ted Tag and Johnny the Pole. Johnny the Pole was supposed to come from Poland, but he was really a Lithuanian. They asked me to "mash" the tea, but I didn't know what they meant. They said, "You silly Irish git. Don't you even understand English?" We had to put whale oil on the blades to stop them from rusting, put a band of wire underneath and fasten the blades together. We had a big contract for the paper industry in India. The lads asked me my name. When I said, "Brendan", they thought I'd said "Brenda". "That doesn't sound right," they said, "we'll call you Bennie." I told them that they could call me whatever they wanted. I wasn't bothered. So Bennie it was. Then I got a chance to do some smithy work with this big hammer in the steel works to build me up for boxing. The blacksmith said to me that it would suit me because "the Irish are strong in the arm, but weak in the head". Today that would be classed as racism, but they were the most wonderful people you could come across.'

St Thomas' is the old Church of England village school in Wincobank. Brendan married the church secretary, Alma, in 1961. He met Alma in a jazz club on London Road in Sheffield. The vicar of St Thomas' then asked him if he would be interested in doing some youth work in the club. 'The only thing I knew anything about was boxing, so I put a heavy bag in one corner,' said Brendan. The original sign, 'Blows for heavy bag', was still there – 'seniors ten blows each set, juniors five blows'. This sign was Brendan Ingle's first contribution to the science of boxing. 'I used to run dances on a Sunday night as well, and a bit of keep fit,' he explained. The equipment was added to over the years, 'most of it scrounged'.

St Thomas' is a Northern club, a place to work rather than pose, and work hard at that. A club with basic facilities – four heavy bags, twelve ordinary bags positioned every few paces, three speed balls, all suspended from girders that run across the ceiling of the gym. 'Jimmy Childs gave me those girders out of his demolition yard,' said Brendan. Old-fashioned weights there since the gym opened ('some fella gave me those as well'), a skipping rope lying in one corner, the ring itself, a tarnished mirror propped up against the wall on the far side of the gym. Boys would skip in front of the old mirror, not for any reasons of vanity as far as I could see, but just to check their arm action. It was that kind of place. A place of work. 'You can have twenty-one people working in this gym,' Brendan pointed out; 'that's assuming that you only have two sparring in the ring at any one time, but I usually have six or eight in at a time.'

The paint was peeling off, and bits of the tired walls were covered with posters and newspaper cuttings reminding the young men who trained there of past boxing glories, and giving them hope of glories yet to come. Herol Graham in his prime looked down from one poster at the new boys in the gym. A few old cuttings about Graham and Johnny Nelson clung precariously to the wall, and a set of old articles about an elderly man with loose skin, stripped for action, posing with Graham and Nelson, was displayed in a glass case screwed to the wall. 'This is Denis,' said Brendan. 'A great character. He did a bit of boxing for me in the sixties. He came along to see me one day in the eighties and he was very, very upset. He told me that he'd got cancer. He told me that he didn't know what to do. I said that he could do one of two things: either he could go home and worry himself to death and die in a few months, or he could come back to the gym and start training again and get on with it. Anyway, he came back to the gym and he got nearly twelve years out of it.' The screws holding the glass case to the wall had been loosened. 'They'd nick anything that wasn't nailed down,' said Brendan. A dishevelled-looking brush locked one door from the inside. It was probably the brush that Brendan had used to sweep up in Beckett's in the early sixties. The gym was last renovated in 1978, when Brendan had got a job looking after a gang of kids on a Youth Opportunities Programme, called 'Starting Point'. He was teaching them, in his words, 'life and social skills, including a bit of painting and decorating, bricklaying and gardening, and, of course, a bit of boxing.' He had the necessary qualifications – after Brendan left the steel works he worked in the Parks Department and then on various building sites. 'Some of the old park rangers didn't much like the Irish,' said Brendan. 'They thought we were full of TB, and born trouble-makers. The Irish were the original blacks in this country.' He and the kids renovated the gym. Brendan says that he has always been into ducking and diving.

The notice above the ring reading 'Boxing can damage your health' was repeated a few steps to the left. The signs had been there since the club opened. The gym smelt musty, it made you sneeze. Sweat had been worked into the fabric of the building. The dust on the hard wooden floor resembled beads of sweat that had somehow become solid over the years. They lay there as a testament to what this place was all about, to what this place was for. The gym smelt of hard work from years gone by. The floor was marked out in a mysterious array of lines and circles, so that Ingle could teach the 'science' and the 'art' of boxing to his eager apprentices. The bell in the corner sounded every three minutes throughout the day, whether there was someone in the gym or not. Time was measured not in hours and minutes in this hard, dusty place, but in rounds. The bell made an irritating, buzzing sound. The gym was always packed – a bustling, vibrant, multi-ethnic community training, working, dreaming. Somebody had scrawled 'National Front' on the wall of the garage that runs alongside the gym. It didn't stop them coming here. Nothing would. They came here to dream. Ingle knew that and he nourished the dreams of each and every one of them. He worked on that. He lived just opposite the gym with Alma and three of their five children, in a house in a permanent state of crisis of being extended. Except for Saturday mornings, when you would go over to their house to get the key, the front door of the gym always seemed to be open, as if Brendan was inviting any lads passing through Wincobank just to walk in and have their lives transformed. There was something vaguely religious about it. The work on his house never seemed to progress from one week to the next, or from one month to the next. Brendan said that he liked to work on his house with some of the lads in his spare moments. But there weren't many of those. There were more important things on the go. It was 1993. Herol Graham, who had almost become the World Middleweight Champion and who had put this gym on the map, may have just retired from boxing, but now there were Johnny Nelson – an up-and-coming cruiserweight – and a new star emerging from the gym. They called the new star 'The Prince'. A little Yemeni boy whom Brendan had been dragging around since he spotted him scrapping in a school playground when he was seven. 'Five foot nothing, but phenomenal,' said Brendan. The next Herol Graham, most were saying at the time. The next Muhammad Ali, Brendan always liked to say, in a pointed sort of way. Then there were all the rest – all ages, all colours and all shapes. Ingle's soft Irish lilt would tell the boys just what they could be with some dedication. And dedication he got – day in, day out, in great dollops.

St Thomas' offered me the diversity I wanted. I wanted to train down in the gym on a Saturday morning with the club bouncers, the men who were over the hill, the men who were past it but still hard and still 'in the know'. I wanted to go down there during the week to watch the young lads turn up full of high hopes and big dreams, and those awful yearnings to be a somebody. I wanted to see something of their lives, and how they would cope if they did not make it, and most surely wouldn't. Then I wanted to watch the Prince, the one with all the skill, the lad who was growing up in that gym. I wanted to see what would become of them all – the hard men and old pros on the way down, the one or two on the way up and those who were destined for a life stuck right in the middle, training, training, training for a few hundred quid a fight every few months, which got harder and bloodier as the years passed.

18

Mick 'The Bomb' Mills – still able to demand some respect.

It does, of course, take a special sort of place to produce boys and men able to step into a ring and trade punches toe-to-toe with another athlete, let alone fighters who nearly become world champions. Fighters from the Bronx in New York, the Gorbals in Glasgow, the Markets in Belfast. They punch their way out of the slum, they dance their way out of the ghetto. That's what they say, anyway. After training one Saturday I asked Mick Mills what sort of a place Sheffield was. What made it so special that it could produce great boxers? The Bomb looked at me with that slightly lopsided quizzical expression that could look both funny and threatening at the same time. 'I'm not from Sheffield. I'm from Dalton in Rotherham. Dalton's as 'ard as fuck. But I don't know about Sheffield.' 'What about Wincobank, then?' I enquired. That quizzical look remained on his face. 'It's all right.' 'But is it hard?' The Bomb started to grimace. 'What do you mean by 'ard?' 'No, what do *you* mean by hard?' I said, interrupting him.

'Don't play fuckin' games with me,' said Mick. 'If you want to find out if Sheffield's 'ard, you'll have to go out and find out for yourself.

Take a walk about after dark. Go up to the Manor. Try mithering the lads up there. See where that gets you.' And Mick slammed a punch into the heavy bag that my weight was supposed to be behind. The bag and I both went flying.

I realized that writing this book was going to be full of challenges and that I would have to meet these challenges as best I could, because boxing was about saving face as much as anything else. You can't lose face in the ring or on the street. I told The Bomb that I would start my research by finding all the action in the City of Steel for one full weekend. I would be there in the thick of it. I'd then be able to tell *him* how hard it really was. He asked me how I planned to do that. 'Have you got a cape or something? You're not Superman, by any chance? You're not going to fly over the place, trying to spot lads scrapping?' I told him that how I did it was my business.

I slipped off from the gym and rang the press office of the South Yorkshire Police, and asked whether I could sit in the back of a panda car for a weekend. The Bomb would certainly not have approved. But then again, he didn't have to know.

A Hard City?

We had passed the 'For Sale' sign on the corner seven, maybe eight times. 'It's dead tonight,' said PC Mayle almost apologetically. The radio crackled away in the background. We began another circuit of Sheffield city centre on a warm Friday night in summer. Everybody was dressed up with somewhere to go. Everybody except us.

'We may just get some action later on from the BBC.' I stopped counting the recession's 'For Sale' signs for a moment and looked round in surprise. 'They're the real threat. The BBC, by the way, are the "Blades Business Crew". They're so-called supporters of Sheffield United who manage to keep active out of the football season.' At that very moment we swept down past the Sheffield United ground and on to the London Road. The warm air or the cramped conditions inside the pubs had drawn the clientele on to the pavements. Everybody was supping. The PC scanned the faces on the pavement. They scanned ours. 'They've got a bit of a reputation for causing trouble at one particular nightclub in Sheffield. They let off some CS gas in there recently. They then went up to the City Hall and let some more off. It wasn't directly at the police, but there were police in the vicinity.' The police had obviously taken this extremely personally.

'The BBC have got a bit of a reputation, but basically they're just a gang of daft lads who're all out associating with each other.' The PC scowled at one lad on the pavement. 'Their reputation far exceeds who they are, if the truth be known. They wander around in large groups causing small disturbances all over the city. That's why they're very difficult to deal with.' The big daft lad on the pavement scowled back even harder. 'We keep a couple of police horses in reserve to deal with them. Police horses seem to have a very soothing effect on them.'

The panda car took a sharp left and drove up a very tight alleyway at the back of some pubs. Two young men in neat white shirts and fashionably cut trousers stood with their backs to us urinating against the low wall. The panda crept silently behind them. The PC wound his window down. 'Can I have a word with you, *please*?' The young men looked round. I recognized one of them from the gym, but I kept my mouth shut. There was a brief pause that stretched to eternity. '*Shit!*' shouted the one on the left – the one I vaguely knew. 'Now don't run off chaps, please.' There was then a moment's hesitation. The men looked at each other as they put their offending tackle away. Then bang! They were off. Sprinting down the alleyway. The PC quickly reversed the car. We were in hot pursuit. He was almost apologetic again. 'You see, the problem is that I have to work out why they ran off. Have they run off because they think I'm going to do them for being drunk and disorderly? Or is it because they're wanted for something else? I have to chase them now to find out.' The panda bumped and weaved down the narrow, rough alleyway. We didn't lose sight of them. At the bottom of the alleyway they turned and ran up a one-way street. We started off round the block, to try to cut them off. Suddenly a call came in that there was a fight in a pub near the bus station. We had to give up on our pursuit. Our panda accelerated away, its blue light flashing.

'We'll keep an eye out for them later on when the pubs close. If our luck's in we may spot them again.' A line of cars slowed our progress. PC Mayle sounded his horn. 'Though we have flashing lights on the panda cars, we don't have any sirens. Probably because they're too expensive. But you'd think these motorists would notice the blue light.' Slowly, one by one, they pulled over to the side of the road to let us past.

'This could be it,' said the PC. 'The big one of the night. It might be the BBC.' We pulled up at the far side of the bus station. The dog handler was there. So too was the public order van with a sergeant and five officers inside. Two other panda cars had beaten us to the fight. A small male group were standing outside the pub looking towards the police. In the middle of the ring formed by the public order van, the pandas and the dog handler's van stood one lone blonde female. She was in some distress, screaming across at the group in the doorway of the pub. There was no sign of any injury. 'If I lose this baby you're dead. I'm pregnant, so why do it?' Occasionally the group by the pub shouted back. You couldn't really make out what they were saying, but it sounded conciliatory. It sounded like a vague explanation shouted across the carriageway separating the police and them. With the police at her back, the woman felt brave enough to approach the group from the pub. 'You started on me with a pool cue.' The warm summer's night had attracted some curious onlookers and they wandered in and out of the frame, confusing the picture. The police dog was yelping in the background. 'Why did you pick on me? Eh? Well, he's *dead* for a start,' she shouted, pointing at one large, bearded fat man. The group from the pub did not budge. The bearded fat man came across to explain. The distraught woman was led away for a moment. Our panda moved back towards the town centre. There were more than enough officers to sort the disturbance out.

Back to the endless circling, to counting the 'For Sale' signs. One lone WPC seemed to be facing up to a group of five young men all dressed up for their night out in the very heart of the city. Reluctantly they moved off. But you could see from their facial expressions that there had been some aggravation. They sloped off slowly, frequently glancing back. 'What's been going off here?' asked our sergeant. 'I caught them pissing in that shop doorway,' answered the diminutive WPC. 'So I said to them, "What would you do if you caught some-body pissing in your doorway?" So this big lad says, "I'd kick the shit out of them." So I said to him, "What's to prevent me from doing that to you?" And he said, "Because you're in uniform." "Precisely," I said.' I didn't quite understand the logic of her last quip, but I didn't feel like querying it. She went back to her lonely sentinel at the corner of the street. We drove off.

PC Mayle shook his head. 'Some people have a real attitude problem when you stop them. You can tell that some will get violent. But a lot of officers are very good at talking people down. The only problem is if they've had so much beer that you can't reason with them.' There was a moment's pause. 'Or if they've got a certain kind of character. I believe that you can tell with ninety per cent certainty when someone is going to hit you. If people are shouting threats at you, then they're not going to do it. The ones that you have to watch out for are the quiet ones with a little smile on their face. They'll go along with you so far, and then bang. It's the ones who say or do nothing that are the real risk. The ones who are all mouth are getting rid of their aggression by mouthing off. That's my theory, anyway.'

The radio was crackling again. The next call sounded foreign. I asked how he could possibly make out the message from something that sounded as if the people were speaking a different language. 'That's because it is a different language. We pick up Norwegian trawlers on our radios. It's something to do with the fact that Sheffield is built on a whole series of hills and valleys. The reception is poor. You can hear the men talking to their wives on shore. It's just a pity we can't make out what they're saying.' The message from the Norwegian trawler was cut short by the report of an accident in Bridge Street. We got there before the ambulance. An elderly man lay half on and half off the pavement. He lay quite still. A policeman from another panda car tried talking to him. He did not respond. An elderly woman leant into my ear. 'They'll get no sense from him. He's drunk as hell. He'll be all right in the morning, but I bet he'll have a hell of a sore head. My daughter works for the police, by the way, as a switchboard operator. And do you know something, she hates drunk men. She says that it's drunk men that cause all the problems in this town.' I wasn't sure whether 'man' was being used in its generic sense here, because the elderly woman herself appeared to be quite inebriated, as she leant right into my ear in the road. 'That's the thing about people when they've had quite a bit to drink,' said PC Mayle when we had climbed back into the panda car. 'They tend to bounce a bit when they've been struck by a vehicle. They're not hurt half as bad as you would expect. The drink relaxes their bodies.'

The night was dragging. Then another call came out – a domestic disturbance on the Wybourn Estate. 'Could be serious,' said the PC. We went hurtling across Sheffield city centre, our blue light flashing. They were all already there: the public order van, two other pandas. Only the dog handler hadn't made it, and the horse. 'You can tell it's quiet tonight,' said the PC. 'Everybody's present at every incident.' A woman in white leggings was directing the police cars up to her house. 'She's obviously the complainant,' said the PC. Two men had been fighting over her. She had had enough. One man was having trouble controlling himself. He wanted to talk to the woman.

'Get the fuck in here now. Come here.' She stayed where she was. 'Get here now.'

The constable standing beside him told him repeatedly to calm down. It had no effect.

'Get here, now.'

When it came, it came without warning. 'You're under arrest for causing a breach of the peace.'

'What's that?' The man looked confused and a little hurt.

'All right!' said the officer, taking him in a headlock. 'Just go, my friend. You're not obliged to say anything unless you wish to do so. Anything you do say...' The rest trailed off as the officer frog-marched the man to the public order van. The man looked more surprised than angry, more hurt than irate. He sat in the back of the van with his head in his hands. Four local children – still up though it was well after midnight – came to stare. We got back into our panda. PC Mayle offered a gloss on this tiny fragment of life. 'You see, the woman obviously rang up requesting the police to arrive. She obviously felt she needed someone there, and that the situation was out of control. By removing that particular man when he's probably had a drink, you are removing the problem from the area.' There was obviously a script for this type of incident, but then again it probably happens so frequently that the script becomes indelibly etched on your brain. The man, however, was clearly surprised by the role written for him. The PC was ruminating on the incident. 'One of the biggest problems, of course, with domestic violence of whatever sort is that people are likely to withdraw their complaints after the situation has cooled off. You end up being the bad guys.'

Down in Bridge Street cells, the man arrested for breach of the peace sat on the low board which functions as a bed. It could well have been his very first arrest. 'For nowt!' he kept shouting. In the cell next to him sat a convicted rapist brought to the station for an ID parade. The rapist had tried to kill himself with some electrical leads the last time he was in a police station. So one officer was assigned to look after him throughout the long quiet night. He had to check his cell every ten minutes. The night was dragging down there as well. Pairs of trainers lay outside the occupied cells. There were only a couple of pairs that night. 'The breach of the peace will be let out when he cools off. He'll just get a verbal warning. It might make him control his temper a bit more,' said PC Mayle. We hit the streets. A call came through that two youths were breaking into parking meters just off the Moor. The panda sped across the pedestrianized part of the street. Two men stood at the bottom chatting. It was after 2 a.m.

'Excuse me, did you see two lads run off down here a few minutes ago?'

'Why?'

'Just asking.'

'Fuck off.'

'OK, thanks.'

On that note, PC Mayle headed back to the station to catch up on his paperwork.

The great thing about the British summer is its unpredictability. My first night out in the panda might have been warm and balmy; tonight was like mid-winter. It was wet and misty. But the lads and lasses were still out in their summer clothes. 'Last night was quiet, but tonight there's a lot of action about,' said Michael Hope ('my nickname's "Bob", by the way'). 'We've had some pre-season football matches and we've got a crew in from Barnsley. A load of them have been locked up already.' It was only 10 p.m. 'You can expect to see some violence.'

Nevertheless, our first call was a reported burglary on Park Hill flats, just behind the big roundabout as you drive into Sheffield from the M1. The lift stank of urine. 'Try not to breathe in,' said Bob Hope helpfully. The burgled flat had no carpets. The floor was strewn with soiled clothes, cigarette butts and bits of food. Holes had been punched in the door of the toilet and the door of the cupboard. A Treasure Trail map hung on one wall. Just. 'God, they've really made a mess in here,' said the WPC. The complainant looked confused. 'Yeah, they smashed a bottle in the kitchen.' 'But what about all this?' said the WPC, pointing at the floor of the lounge. 'It's always like that. I'm not the tidiest of people.' Bob Hope took a statement. The flat looked empty, apart from the debris, but the only thing reported missing was the telly. The complainant knew who had taken it. In fact, he confessed that he had burgled a neighbour's flat to check that his telly was there. 'The problem here is that the flat is so dirty you couldn't lift fingerprints from it,' explained PC Hope. 'The other problem is that he got the telly from a friend of a friend in the first place. Therefore he hasn't got too many details about it.'

The WPC visited a flat a few doors away. An elderly woman had been complaining of harassment by local children. The WPC knocked at the door. 'Hello, it's only the police.' There was no response. She turned to me. 'You see, the elderly are scared stiff of opening the doors in these flats. They're terrified, in fact.' An age later an old woman made it to the door. She was housebound, she explained, and steep stairs led down to her living room. The contrast with the previous flat was stark. This flat was totally spotless. Children were tormenting the old woman by dropping lit matches through her letterbox. 'It takes me ages to get up the stairs, and my mother is bedridden. She's ninety-five. What happens if one of the matches doesn't go out? How am I going to get her out of the flat? I wouldn't be able to carry her up the stairs. They pick on me because I speak differently to them. My father was a major in the British army. I was born in India. I speak proper English and they don't like it. They say that I'm not one of them. But it was my family who fought in the last war to keep them here in luxury.' The old woman went to attend to her mother. 'I can't blame the children,' she said. 'Their mothers and fathers are in the pub all the time.'

Her mother was calling in the background. She was thirsty. Age had taken its toll. The old woman was now shouting about her greenhouse. A greenhouse from some far-off days. Perhaps a greenhouse back in India. You couldn't really tell. But certainly before all this. I noticed the calendar on the wall. It was from 1984. It read 'Bless this house/O Lord we pray/Make it safe by night and day.' The WPC, Vicky, said that she would sort out a smoke detector for the old lady, and told her that she would ask the community policeman to keep an eye out for her. 'It's the best we can do with the available manpower.' It wasn't enough and she knew it. When we got outside the flats the WPC looked up to check that nobody was going to drop something down on us from above. Bob Hope noticed one fourteen-year-old with a brand new haircut. 'That's better than your last haircut, Brett.'

'Shut up, you fucking twat,' replied Brett before turning his back.

We stopped outside Bizzie Lizzie's fish and chip shop for Bob to leave a note for the community policeman. A drunken woman insisted on getting into the car. 'Me mum died last Christmas day. Let me tell you this little tragedy . . .' When Bob eventually got back she agreed to get out. 'I love you,' she said to the WPC. She gave her a big wet kiss on the cheek. 'Jesus, she smells all of Persil. You smell lovely.'

We left Bizzie Lizzie's for Sheffield's red light area. A very thin, white-faced girl stood on the corner, holding an umbrella. It was a miserable night for anybody to be out and about. Let alone to be out hanging about the streets. The panda pulled in just by her.

Bob Hope wound down his window. 'All right?'

'Yeah.'

'You're a braver girl than me on a night like this.'

The white-faced girl did not smile or respond.

'Take care.'

After the panda, the public order van looked impressive. It moved slowly, almost stealthily through the town. He was spotted a mile off. 'He's watering!' came the cry from the front of the van. The van pulled to an abrupt halt. Two officers jumped out. The forty-year-old man in the cream trousers chomping at his doner kebab looked shocked. When the two officers got back into the van they were both laughing. 'He said that he was standing there because he was lost. He'd got a big stain down his trousers. That's his fine for the night. He denied that he was having a slash, but it was still hanging out as we were talking to him.'

We had just stopped laughing when the van pulled in behind a Volkswagen driven by a large black guy. The car was wanted in connection with an assault reported earlier in the evening. The black guy was having none of it. He shouted about police harassment before disappearing into a nightclub. The public order van parked opposite, waiting for him to return to his vehicle. Ten minutes later his friend emerged from the club and tried to move the car for him. The police stopped him so he went back into the neon shadows of the club. 'This one might take a while to sort out,' said the sergeant in charge of the van as he slumped down on the front seat. 'It could be a very long night.'

It was an opportunity for me to reflect on what I'd seen. I learned that it was a hard industrial city, like many others, and hard not just for the young men who may turn to boxing for a living. Whether it was as hard as fuck, I couldn't say. But I could see that boxing might help. It might get you off the streets and away from all of this, some of the time.

The Highs and Lows of the Fight Game

The Comeback Trail

Then

Herol Graham had been more than just a champion. For a while he had been the hope, some would say the only hope, of this once-proud industrial city. It wasn't just the success – the thirty-eight straight professional fights without a single defeat under his manager, trainer and mentor Brendan Ingle – it was the manner of the success. Graham was the master of defensive boxing. The media may have called him 'boring', and some rival boxing camps may have referred to him disparagingly as the 'limbo dancer', but his opponents never managed to lay a glove on him, and he always won. They used to say that Graham had been sacked by Alan Minter as a sparring partner in the summer of 1980, as Minter prepared to defend his world title against Marvin Hagler, because Minter just couldn't hit him. Roberto Duran was also said to have sacked him for the same reason. Eddie Shaw, once trainer to Barry McGuigan, was quoted as saying that 'Good defensive boxing is a poetic art, and Graham is a master at it. Trouble is, nobody ever knocked anyone out with a poem.' But Graham did. Poetry in motion. It wasn't just that he avoided taking punishment. His slippery defences bamboozled opponents. As Brendan Ingle used to say: 'It did their heads in.'

Brendan had identified this unique feature of Graham early in his career. 'What caught my attention when I first saw him as an amateur was his amazing ability to destroy opponents without landing a blow.' There was magic there – a magic in survival, which was a tonic to Steel City, decimated by the rationalization and decline of steel and then of coal. Here was the man from Sheffield who could survive in the ring. (In fact he was from Nottingham, but he had moved in with Brendan Ingle's family in 1977 at the age of eighteen to be opposite

'Good defensive boxing is a poetic art, and Graham is a master at it. Trouble is nobody ever knocked anyone out with a poem.' But Herol Graham did: poetry in motion. Over a decade ago.

Brendan's gym in Newman Road, and from then it was always Shef-field.) The fact that for years the London promoters seemed uninter-ested in him because of his style made him more the local hero. What did London know about anything in the North? Boxing? Industry? Character?

Brendan and Bomber were a double-act, one doing the business in the ring, the other doing it outside – training, whipping up support for the fights, bamboozling the media with his charm, touring Sheffield city centre with a loudhailer telling the shoppers to get themselves down to the Sheffield United ground in Bramall Lane to watch Herol in action in the open air, making deals, hustling, ducking, diving, getting up for the early morning runs, motivating his protégé. 'Making myself busy,' as Brendan himself likes to put it, 'and important.'

Then things went badly wrong. The father–son relationship with Brendan Ingle, the leprechaun from Wincobank with the twinkling blue eyes and the smile and all the blarney in the world, was torn asunder. They say money is the root of all evil, but in boxing it is the root of all greatness, too. Otherwise why would they be there? Any of them? Herol was number four in the world at that time, but still the world title chance eluded him and his management team. It was then that Barney Eastwood offered him that chance. The Eastwood entourage had arrived at Leeds–Bradford airport in Eastwood's private plane. It was a world away from the gym in Newman Road, Wincobank. Brendan Ingle sold the Graham contract for seventy-five grand, and invested the money so that, he said, for the first time in his life his family would have a guaranteed income. At the time it was all smiles and handshakes. Herol was quoted in the *Sheffield Star* as saying, 'It's great. Mr Eastwood has got Barry McGuigan up there and I hope he can do it for me as well. Brendan has done a marvellous job to get me to number four in the world. He just needed a bit of help to go the rest of the way. I'll still be working with Brendan in Sheffield and he'll be in my corner at the Albert Hall tomorrow. It's not a split, it's more of an organized consortium.'

The real split with Brendan came later, in April 1987, when Graham announced that he felt he should have received something financially from Brendan with the Eastwood deal. Personal reasons were also mentioned, but nobody ever went into them. The fact that Thomas Hearns and Marvin Hagler were making their millions at that time could not have helped. A month later, in May 1987, Graham fought Kalambay in London. It was the first time in Graham's professional career that he did not have Ingle in his corner. Ingle's place was taken by Barney Eastwood and his Panamanian trainers. Graham went into that ring as the 7–1 favourite to retain his European title. Most of his Sheffield fans looking to make a few quid on the betting were naming the round Graham would finish it in. The fifth was where the serious money was. Graham went out that night full of confidence; he brought the fight to Kalambay. But Kalambay countered ominously well. By round nine Kalambay looked the stronger of the two. Herol Graham, the old slippery eel, the man with the lightning reflexes, the cunning boxer who could slip and slide his way out of any trouble, looked tired and very, very ordinary with his bleeding nose and his puffed eyes. It all came down to the last round and Graham went in for a scrap, to fight rather than box. A right hook from Kalambay rocked Graham's tired frame. His legs turned to jelly. It was an image most Sheffielders will not forget – Graham staggering back, his right arm out groping for support, eventually finding the rope. Like a blind man mugged in the dark. The mandatory eight count cost Graham his title. Ingle was ringside and went hoarse through shouting instructions. There were a few tears in Sheffield that fateful night.

Since then there had been one comeback fight at the Adwick Sports Centre, near Doncaster. Graham's opponent was Ricky 'The Brick' Stackhouse, a twenty-nine-year-old journeyman ranked thirtieth in the world. Nobody knew a lot about 'The Brick' in Doncaster, but he did his job – he got Graham up and running again. Ingle and Graham patched up their differences temporarily and Ingle was back in the corner. That night Graham did the biggest victory leap in his career. Relieved to be back winning again.

In June 1988 the hero returned to fight James Cook for the vacant British Middleweight Championship. He was to fight in Sheffield for the first time since 1986, on which occasion he had taken the European Middleweight title from Ayub Kalule. I went along to cover the fight for the Grassroots page of the *Guardian*. The night was wet and miserable, so I turned up at the City Hall carrying an umbrella. Now this might not seem to be a problem, but I went to watch the fight with Paddy, a well-known local bouncer, his girlfriend and her dad, Harry, an ex-boxer. All were ardent Graham fans, delighted that he was on his way back. The last thing they expected was a man carrying an umbrella. 'Did you get that free with Aramis?' suggested the girlfriend helpfully. 'Are you carrying it for some bird?' asked Paddy. Harry 'Boy', the ex-boxer, just shook his head.

The steward who looked at our tickets was wearing a dark suit and hob-nailed boots. He spoke with a peculiarly middle-class accent. 'Look at the state of him, for goodness' sake,' said Paddy. 'Are you expecting a bit of trouble, then?' The steward told him that he was wearing the boots just in case there was a stampede to get near Bomber Graham at the end of the fight. 'Not very professional, is it?' said Paddy. We made our way to the balcony of the City Hall. We were above the ring, which had been placed right up against the stage of the hall. It was 8 p.m., but the hall was virtually empty. The balcony was emptier still, except for three kids – one black girl of about twelve and two thin white boys sitting some way off. Kids from Ingle's gym, where Graham used to train and dreams were nurtured for all those years, who had sneaked in to watch the hero return. 'If they mess about bring them downstairs,' said one steward in his shirtsleeves to the steward with the hob-nailed boots, who was now starting to look a little perplexed. Paddy just grunted, 'He hasn't got a clue, has he?'

We went off to the bar, passing the waifs on the way in. Paddy recognized them immediately. Lisa Bailey, the twelve-year-old girl, told us how she coaches down in the gym. 'I help with the pads and things, I do proper coaching with the young boys down there.' The two thin boys were nodding in agreement. I asked what Brendan Ingle's gym was like. 'Magic,' said Lisa. We eventually got into the bar, past the waifs and the steward in the hob-nailed boots. Paddy, all six foot four of him, was on Coke. I was still carrying my umbrella. The fight fans made way to let us through. The talk in the bar wasn't about boxing at all. It was about pubs and the sizes of lunchtime crowds and reminiscences about the days when certain pubs near the steel works were so busy at lunchtimes that you had to bring your own glass with you. One customer, who was obviously a pub landlord, was telling his friend that he knew a pub down by the iron foundries where they used to get so desperate during lunchtimes that they had to use jam jars to serve the beer in. He was also moaning about the fact that there were no cigarettes on sale in the City Hall. Ice cream was on sale in the auditorium, but no cigarettes. Perhaps the organizers knew all about the fight fans from Brendan Ingle's gym, like Lisa.

It was time to get back into the hall, where the first two supporting fighters were making their way into the ring. Somehow you always expect the grand entrance – the theme from the film *Rocky*, the corridor of stewards, the silk dressing gowns, the audience roar. You don't expect two fighters with towelling dressing gowns to amble towards the ring, admittedly from different directions, climb in, do the business and amble off again, in a hall only one quarter full. The boxers were substitutes as well, not even on the official programme. There was more response to the girl that carried the card than to the boxers themselves, even if the boxers did put on a good show. During rounds the girl sat motionless with her legs crossed and her hands placed on her knee, registering no discernible emotion. At the opposite end of the stage was a man in a wheelchair, but lying right back, unable to see any of the action, with his elderly grey-haired mother acting as commentator on the fight for him. Harry, the ex-boxer, could not stop himself offering me a commentary on the fight: 'That was a slip, not a knock-down'; 'He hit him when he was down, disallow that punch'; 'He's holding too much.' All the fights on the undercard looked a lot messier than I expected, and a lot noisier. Perhaps it looked messy because I was watching it from above – it was a strange angle.

The crowd were very subdued, in fact so subdued that at one point when the referee shouted 'break' very loudly, a largish section of the crowd could be seen to jump quite noticeably in their seats. Paddy was looking bored and went in search of the steward in the hob-nailed boots. 'What did I tell you?' he said when he returned. 'Talk about professionalism. The stewards are from a local rugby club. Someone just rang them up. They don't even know what money they're on until the end of the night. They've just been promised a meal.'

Paddy then started to work his way through the personnel gathered around the ring, filling me in on some personal details. 'That's Brian Anderson, the ex-British Middleweight Champion, he's training to be a referee at the moment. He used to be my apprentice when I worked at Brown Baileys, the steel works. And can you see that little black guy on the stage with the steward's badge, standing just beside the ring? I got him a job doing some security work in shops. He was no good, he was always walking around the shop shadow-boxing. He didn't exactly blend into the surroundings. He asked the manager of one shop whether he'd got a receipt for his cigarettes. All the stewards near the ringside are boxers from Brendan's gym, not like the clowns up here from the local rugby club.'

My attention started to slide towards the fight that had been continuing in the meantime. The two boxers had been slugging it out for the full eight three-minute rounds. The referee awarded the fight to a short, stocky white kid whose name hadn't appeared on the programme. Harry 'Boy' stood up and shouted, 'No, never! There was nowt in it, but the coloured kid just had it.' There was little applause for the winner, but the audience suddenly came to life to applaud the loser. They clearly agreed with Harry 'Boy'. The black boxer told the MC that he had taken the fight at very short notice – at 12 o'clock that day, to be exact. For that he got even more applause.

The next fight on the bill was between Rambo Loughran of Bally-mena and Tony Britland of Cardiff. Rambo was from Barney East-wood's stable and it showed – he wore a silk dressing gown and he approached the ring with his seconds bathed in the glow of a spotlight. His opponent, meanwhile, walked across the floor to the ring with nobody taking a blind bit of notice of him. The kid who looked as if he had just wandered in off the bus was stopped in 1 minute 20 seconds of the first round. The third fight was also stopped. This time the crowd voiced their disapproval, with shouts of 'Give him a chance, ref,' and 'Rubbish!' There was a slight gap in the boos from the audience, during which one punter from the balcony decided to articu-late the views of the crowd – 'You're a tosser, ref!' – to considerable applause.

The fourth contest had one local lad, Nigel Bradley, appearing for the first time, and you could see the atmosphere of the place suddenly changing. The referee warned Brendan Ingle twice for shouting instructions into the ring. There were chants of 'easy' when Nigel's victory was announced, but it was anything but easy; he won by fifty-nine and a half points to fifty-seven and a half.

Then it was time for a long intermission, occasioned by the fact that the main fight was being broadcast live. You could see Harry Carpenter drumming with his pen to while away the minutes. The hall was filling up, as assorted characters from the Sheffield underworld entered to take their seats. One was wearing a steward's badge. 'He never pays for anything,' said Paddy. 'The last time I saw him at a fight a steward asked him for his ticket and he just knocked the steward aside. I suppose it's easier to give him a badge and let him get on with it.' When I spotted the kids from Brendan Ingle's gym move into position near the ring I knew that the waiting was nearly over. I saw a young Arab boy of about fourteen down there as well. Paddy told me that he was Naseem Hamed, Brendan's latest discovery, his latest protégé. A huge barrage of boos greeted James Cook as he made his way out to the stage, only eclipsed in volume by the cheers that greeted Herol Graham. The hero had come home. As Harry Carpenter said in his commentary: 'I don't think that Peckham would have turned out in quite the same force for James Cook.' Or he might have added – sung with quite the same force – 'We love you, Bomber/Oh yes, we do/We love you, Bomber/Oh yes, we do.' Lisa had now climbed on to the stage right beside the ring and was chanting loudly.

The start of the fight was fierce. Herol came tearing out and threw Cook to the canvas. The referee cautioned him for this. I always found this aspect of Graham quite surprising. Graham the eel could also bundle his opponent over whenever it was necessary. His slipping and sliding on the ropes was often accompanied by physically hoisting his opponent round and hitting him on the turn. I always think the Shef-field crowd liked that – there was the magic of Graham and deep inside there was a certain toughness, a good old-fashioned physical foundation to the whole thing. There was iron in the soul. Graham put Cook down in the first round with a left hook. The crowd started chanting: 'Are you watching, Nigel Benn?' after each of Bomber Gra-ham's assaults. Suddenly someone from the balcony shouted that he'd spotted Nigel Benn in the audience. 'There he is, down there!' All eyes were riveted on this black man in the main body of the hall with a partially shaved head and a green tie. 'The bastard with the green tie.' 'That's him down there.' Paddy, however, was looking quite sceptical. 'That's not Nigel Benn, that's Slugger O'Toole, the black Irishman. I should know – I got him a job on the door of a pub this week.' But it was no good, everyone was trying to spot that bastard Benn with the green tie. Some of the audience seemed more intent on eyeballing Benn than watching the fight.

In the fifth round Graham was up on his toes, dancing, slipping, his arms dangling by his sides – his favourite routine for all those years in the Wincobank gym, inviting anyone to lay a punch. Cook managed to land one good right-hander and Graham responded by sticking his tongue out feigning a right, and landing a left to cut Cook's left eye. Sid Nathan, the referee, stopped it in the fifth. But Graham gave them all they wanted: a characteristic show of brilliance and much, much more – the return of a hero. Despite the fact that Harry 'Boy' had told me not to blink in the fifth round, I nearly managed to miss the final punch, as Cook crumpled and the crowd went wild.

Even the card girl was jumping in the air; the indifference she displayed with such sang-froid during the fights on the undercard had long gone. Brian Anderson had forgotten all about his practice refereeing and was on his feet cheering for his pal. But I'd seen enough. I left the City Hall as the kids from Brendan Ingle's gym tried valiantly to scramble into the ring to stand beside Bomber Graham, their hero, back in the spotlight again. The middle-class chaps from the rugby club, who had been acting as stewards, were meanwhile trying desperately to keep them out. Without much success. The hero had returned. The City of Steel was winning again. It was on its way up.

For a while.

Now

But the wins did not continue. They were now as elusive as Graham himself once had been. I went to talk to him at his house in October 1993, nine months after he had announced his retirement from the fight game. This was to be the end of an illustrious career in boxing, and the beginning of a new one in the media, in TV, in something glamorous and exciting. Fourteen years in professional boxing had made him many contacts. Graham had the personality and the charisma to go with being a public sporting figure. He was confident of finding new avenues through his contacts. 'The phone used to be buzzing all the time,' he said. 'Now it's silent. When I was boxing I had hundreds of friends, I could go through lists of names – he's a friend, he's a friend, he's a friend. I had friends everywhere. Now, since I've retired, I can tell you that I have four friends – exactly four; three of them are or were professional boxers.' He was sitting in his living room on his pink leather settee bought when things were going well, mentally going through the long list of friends who have simply gone. 'You don't know your true friends until the going gets rough. And the going got rough with me. All of a sudden all my friends started scattering. I hit rock bottom psychologically. My girlfriend and I split up. I loved her. I was devastated. I was really depressed. I was on my back. I went through hell and back. I wouldn't put anybody through it.'

He was sitting in some old work clothes. He had been clearing out the basement of his house so that he could sell the house and move on. He needed a fresh start, he said. He glanced over towards the telephone; it was a practised glance, a habit of nine months' standing. The look said it all, mild expectation trampled by disappointment that he tried to hide. He attempted a smile. 'The phone was always ringing in the good old days, now it doesn't. It makes me laugh, really. The money's gone now, and so have the friends.' So, he might have added, has the car. He drove a sponsored Toyota for nine years. 'Now, it's an XR2i. I've started at the bottom again to work back up. One day I want a BMW, not because it's a black man's wheel, but because it's a great car. It doesn't date.'

These were the dreams of a novice, not one of Britain's finest boxers, who did it all. Or nearly. They always called him 'the nearly man' – nearly a World Champion, just one punch or one duck away. During his retirement he had stayed with boxing. He had been coaching part-time in a local gym. On his birthday on 13 September however, he got a letter from the management board of the gym, terminating his contract. He read the letter out loud. 'In no way does this reflect your abilities and skills as a coach. You are always welcome to train here.' This hurt the man who was nearly champion of the world.

Herol had just announced that he planned to make a comeback to the ring. 'It's not just the money. I need the money, don't get me wrong. In fact, I desperately need the money, but it's not just that. I'm hoping to get about five grand for my first fight back, which isn't bad for a comeback situation. It's not that I'm up and coming, after all. I've been there, and the tickets will still sell. The name still carries on. Surely,' he added after a pause, in which you could see by the expression in the eyes that he had been looking inwards. He has had a lot of time to do that recently. I nodded. He was Sheffield's greatest boxer. 'They don't forget that quick,' I added. I'd started to sound like one of those hangers-on from the good old days. But he needed reassurance. 'People will still remember the name and turn up to see me getting beat up. But it's not just the money, I still have to prove to myself what I can do. Since I started my boxing campaign my goal was to win the world championship and that is the only one to have eluded me. I want a second chance. My opponents haven't been named

Herol Graham today. 'The phone was always ringing in the good old days, now it doesn't . . . The money's gone, and so have the friends.'

40

yet, and to be honest I don't even know when I'm fighting yet – probably October or November. The later the better. It gives me more time to prepare.'

But had he not been advised to retire? Had he not taken one or two big punches that the Graham of old would have seen coming? I looked into those eyes again. 'My friends had mixed views about my return. Brian Anderson hasn't warned me not to return, but his advice is "don't-ish", because when he retired from boxing, he retired for good. He says that I've got nothing to prove. Well he's right in a way, I've nothing to prove to other people, but I've still got things to prove to myself. It's for myself I'm doing it. Johnny Nelson wasn't surprised that I was going to make a comeback. He had a dream that this was going to happen. It was a sort of omen in a way. My dream would be to fight for the championship of the world in Mansfield in the summer of 1995. Mansfield Council sell tickets like I don't know what. Tell Mansfield that I'm on my way.'

Bomber Graham in his long, illustrious career in the ring never really got used to being on the deck. He was the former British and European middleweight champion, and the former British, Commonwealth and European light middleweight champion, who made a career out of avoiding being hit, who for years did not know what it was like to go down. He would stand in Brendan Ingle's gym in Wincobank with his hands behind his back, and a long line of kids and enthusiastic amateurs would be led in to stick one on him. Of course, they never could. Graham's reflexes were the stuff of legend. In professional fights the same reflexes kept him out of trouble. Most of the time. He seemed to go on for ever without a single defeat. Some purists did not like his style. Of course his critics said that it was not aggressive enough, and that it was too defensive. But he never got hit, and it was noticeable that the likes of Nigel Benn and Chris Eubank never fought him. He never had to take any punishment, so when the big bombs eventually did land, they did some real damage to him and his fans. But he still only lost to the best.

His defeat by Sambu Kalambay in 1987, where he lost his European title, was his first defeat in thirty-nine professional fights, and Kalambay went on to a world title. At the Albert Hall in May 1989, Graham had lost by one point to Mike McCallum in a contest for the WBA world middleweight title. Just one foul by Graham cost him his world crown, although in Sheffield they are keen to point out that the referee missed a blatant low blow from McCallum, or 'the Bodysnatcher' as he's called. Then in 1990 Graham met Julian Jackson for his second crack at the world title, this time on the Costa del Sol. Graham outboxed and outpunched Jackson over three rounds. The fight was about to be stopped because of Jackson's cut eye, then Graham got caught when he walked on to one of the most powerful right hands in boxing. If you can ever hope to identify a single moment from the great flux of time that changes all of the future time and events in a person's life, then this was the moment for Herol Graham. A momentary mistake that transformed Graham's future, for the worse. An event that signalled the end. Graham told me that he has never watched the video of this particular fight, and, he emphasized, he never will. As promoter Mike Barrett said at the time, 'Boxers just don't recover from that kind of punch.' A rough bruising rematch with Kalambay in 1992 was his next defeat. Here, the Graham reflexes were clearly not what they had been, and the fight that went the distance left Graham with severe damage around the eyes. One cut required twenty-six stitches.

But it was still a fine record. Graham had lost only to the best in the world, to those in the middleweight division, who had or would subsequently hold the world crown – until his last defeat, that is. He lost the British Championship in September 1992 to the unfancied Frank Grant. In the fight against Grant, it was not the Bomber Graham that everyone knew. Here was a boxer who now took punishment as well as gave it out. Nevertheless, at the start of the ninth round, Graham was judged to be well ahead on points. So much so that his manager at the time, Mickey Duff, was to joke that if it had been a cricket match, Graham could have declared. But in the ninth, Grant put him down. There were flashes of the Graham of old when he stuck his tongue out at Grant after the knock-down, but it was not the Graham of old in terms of the proportion of punches finding their way on to his tired body. More punishment followed. The referee stepped in and stopped the contest in the ninth.

It was time for a rethink for the man who had been untouchable at the domestic level for all those years, who had watched Benn and Eubank somehow get to the top without having to fight him. Over the Christmas holiday back in St Thomas', it was clear to all the regulars that something about Bomber had changed. Graham had decided to think positive, to go up a division, and box on as a super-middleweight (the 12 stone division) rather than as a middleweight (11 stone 6 pounds), so that he would no longer have any problems making the weight. They were already pencilling in potential world-class opposition for the championship fights to come. But the speed and reflexes that were the foundations of his boxing style had gone, drained away that night in the plush setting of the Torrequebrada Hotel in Benalmadenas on the Costa del Sol by Julian Jackson, and in that bruising battle in Pesaro in Italy by Sambu Kalambay. But the plans and the dreams were still going ahead. It was only when an unknown thirteen-year-old schoolboy called Steve Akers, who had recently won the South Yorkshire Schoolboys title, started to land punches on the great, untouchable Bomber Graham, that Graham knew it was time for him to call it a day.

In Brendan's gym they had always thought that the end would come with the world middleweight title, or perhaps the world super-middleweight title, in Bomber's hands. The pessimists among them had nightmares about another KO from the big hitter Julian Jackson, but every dream and every nightmare still had Graham going out in a blaze of glory on the world stage, competing with the very best in the world. Nobody had anticipated it would be like this on a cold January day back in Wincobank, where it had all started. Back in the old gym where the amateurs and the professionals, against all the rules, still sparred together. Back with the kind of kid who would once have been led into the gym to demonstrate that Graham was a boxer like no other, a silky-smooth boxer who could duck and dive and who could not be touched. Back with a thirteen-year-old amateur who was now demonstrating that the champ had feet of clay.

Nine months into his retirement, Herol was clearly down on his luck. The money had gone. 'I was very foolish the first time around. I won't make the same mistakes twice. I aim to make a fresh start, and the first thing I aim to do is to leave Sheffield. All through my boxing career I was advised that there were more opportunities down in the Smoke, but although I was born in Nottingham I was Sheffield's own. But this time I have to go to where the money is.'

I asked him to reflect back on the night he decided to announce his retirement. What had been going through his mind? 'I was just fed up with the game, all the squabbling, whether it's about money or . . .'

His voice trailed off. 'I was just pissed off, to tell the truth. I don't remember much about the last fight. It just seemed as if I wasn't there, even before I got into the ring. It was outdoors. It's so funny, so funny.'

His voice had a dreamy quality, like someone weary to the bone, especially when looking back. 'In the first round I was just feeling him out. I knew that it was going to be a hard fight. But he wasn't in my class – he should have been a sparring partner for me really. We shouldn't have been in the same ring. But I was proved wrong in that he was strong, and I wasn't mentally prepared for the fight. It was all mental rather than physical. A very close relative of mine had been attacked at the Notting Hill Carnival just before the fight. I had to go to see her at Guy's Hospital. I took her back with me to Sheffield. Subconsciously you say to yourself "Nothing's happened, nothing's happened," but it was happening. I wasn't mentally prepared because of this. Also my girlfriend and I had split up. My mind just wasn't on that fight.'

Graham had also changed manager. The fight against Frank Grant was his second under Mickey Duff. 'At one point there was a possibility of me signing for Barry Hearn, but he had Eubank, so I don't think he would have wanted to jeopardize Eubank with myself. And when I lost the fight to Julian Jackson, Hearn was quoted on TV as saying that I should retire. So he couldn't really have wanted me. This was the fight I came closest to taking the world title, then he landed one. So I went to Mickey Duff, after my contract with Barney Eastwood ran out. Mickey said to me "Are you ready for the fight?" and I just said "yeah".

'The first couple of weeks of my retirement were good. The Lonsdale Group in London organized a retirement do for me. I didn't miss the boxing. It was a big weight off my shoulders. There were no more early-morning runs, although I did get up to have a run now and again. I didn't have to train at specific times, I trained when I wanted to. My weight didn't shoot up. I was walking around at twelve stone four, my boxing weight at super-middleweight was twelve stone two, so I was just two pounds heavier. I had time for the first time in my life to sort out my personal problems. I started sorting them out by talking and talking and talking. Before, I hadn't had time, I used to always leave them to later. I got a job training some boxers in a local gym, and I was spending more time in the gym than I did when I was still boxing. Things were going OK.'

When he retired he was often quoted as saying that he was looking forward to a new career as a children's TV presenter. He had, after all, done some showbusiness work in the past, appearing in panto with Larry Grayson at the Civic Theatre in Mansfield in Aladdin, and had been looking forward to the TV offers pouring in. I watched as his frown knitted those famous features into a tight, unyielding mask. 'Nothing happened, nothing came of it. It's too cut-throat a business. I didn't have the credentials or anything like that. It's best to work in radio first. I did start working for Radio Crystal, which is the radio station for the Children's Hospital, but that was just to get into it. I did it for about five weeks on a voluntary basis. But it's hard getting a permanent job, so I was going to go back to college to do teacher training, with the intention of becoming a physical education teacher. The only problem was that I don't have any 'O' levels. So I signed up at a local college to do two 'O' levels in English and Maths. That was just before I announced my comeback. I still want to do this when I've finished with boxing. In the meantime, I've got a play coming up. I'm playing a Northern busker in a play called *Old Father Time*. I play the part of a man who goes to London to make his fame and fortune with his dad, Dodger. Something I should have done myself years ago. I'm Bodger, he's Dodger. It's not going to be on the telly or anything, it's just going to be in the university drama studio.

'My problem basically was that I wasn't a very good keeper of money. When I'd got it, I spent it – clothes, record players, furniture – necessary items, well, not exactly necessary. If I liked it, I bought it.' He motions around the room at the evidence of money spent some time in the mid-eighties – state-of-the-art hi fi's already obsolete.

'I also loaned a lot out, and I'm still waiting for it to come back. I loaned one friend fifteen grand to set up a cleaning business. This time around it'll be different. The money's going into the bank. I'm going to invest it well. A lot of money went through my hands. I don't know how much exactly, but I know that I made a lot. The most I ever got for a fight was ninety grand. But don't forget that out of that your manager gets 25 per cent, your trainer gets 10 per cent, then there's your own expenses. I squandered it. I put sixty grand into a jewellery business. I never got the money back. I was always mad on jewellery.' He showed me a diamond-encrusted gold bracelet on his wrist, in the form of two leopards. 'I used to wear a diamond ring, but I just gave that away. The bracelet's one of the few things that I've got left. I thought about other businesses as well, like sports shops, but that's too cut-throat. I went into jewellery because I like looking at jewellery, and it's a luxury item. Everybody likes a bit of jewellery. I thought that the business was going to be a dead cert, but it wasn't.'

It seems that Herol Graham just never had the luck running for him. 'Eubank was just in the right place at the right time. I don't resent his success. I was never at the right time in the right place, or it would have happened to me. I say "good luck to them". I'm not bitter about other people's success. The only thing that does annoy me is when they call themselves "the best". If you want to call yourself that you need to prove it. It's like football. To win the football league the teams have to play each other. I would have fought any of them, but they didn't want to. Then it got to be too late. But my comeback won't just be for two fights. I want to get back to the top by 1995. OK, I'll be thirty-six then, but I'm still going to make it. A year to get back into it, a year to win the world championship. Then a year defending it to make a bit of money.'

There was almost a note of desperation in his voice. It seemed that he needed to convince himself as much as others. 'This time around I'm going to get it right. I'll know what to do with my money from day one. This time I'll know who my friends are, I'll know who the hangers-on are. The hardest thing when you're coming up is knowing who to accept. I'll be a bit wiser second time around. Everybody deserves a second chance, don't they?'

Brendan's New Boys

They were standing in his parlour in front of a pair of scales. A grey-haired man in his fifties stripped to his underpants and a small, slight Arab boy. On one side of the room was a large bookcase. There were a lot of books on Irish history. Black covers with the green of the shamrock. Serious reading. It could be the parlour of a minor academic or a priest. On the other wall was a large framed photograph of Herol Graham, the Graham of years ago, the Graham of eternal optimism and promise. Not the Graham of the moment. Not the Graham of 1993. The grey-haired man got on the scales first. 'Twelve stone dead. Now it's your turn, and don't forget I've been warning ye.' His Irish brogue was as thick as buttermilk. The small Arab boy stepped forward in a mock swagger. 'It'll be all right, Brendan, don't worry.' His was a cocky Sheffield accent. 'I'm young, fit. I *am* the business.'

Brendan averted his gaze from the scales just for a moment. He felt that he needed to explain. 'The problem with Naz or Prince Naseem Hamed, as he's known in the ring, is that he knows he's good. At that age it's bound to go to your head. He loves himself and why not? I've had the lad since he was seven; he's nineteen now. His father is from the Yemen. I was passing on this bus up the road here, and the bus stops outside a school. It's three o'clock and the school is just getting out. There's this little kid who I thought was a Pakistani pinned up against these railings fighting these three white kids off. All three of them are kicking and punching at him. My first thought was that life doesn't change. I can remember getting into scraps in Dublin when I was a kid. Sure, they always had some reason to pick on you for a fight – "You're not proper Irish – your grandfather's English." "What kind of a name is Ingle, for God's sake?" They could always find something. And if it wasn't that, it would be "You think you're great because your brothers are boxers." I was from a big family – I had

48

The Prince at sixteen. 'The greatest thing since sliced bread. The greatest boxer since Muhammad Ali,' says his trainer and manager Brendan Ingle.

ten brothers and four sisters. But I was impressed with this young Pakistani kid. I can spot talent a mile off. I'll go anywhere where there's a fight. I'll get me distance and I'll watch. I won't get involved but I'll watch them. I've always been interested in what goes off in confrontations between people whether they're arguments or fisti-cuffs. I'm interested in human nature, and that's what you see when people fight and argue. I like to see what starts trouble and how it goes on. I like to watch who's involved, who makes themselves busy, who's the matchmaker, and who's stirring the whole thing up. I watch and I learn. I could see this young Pakistani kid had talent. I ran home and told my wife Alma. I was right, as well. Naz has won seven British titles, and he's boxed for England as an amateur. Now he's a professional but even as a newcomer he's earning good money. But it's still only the start, now it's all about self-discipline.'

Naz climbed on to the scales.

'These scales never lie, Naz, remember that . . . Eight stone nine. What did I tell ye? What did I say? You were boasting about all the crap you'd eaten yesterday. Fish fingers and chips. Well, this is what you get. You're three pounds over the weight. I've said to you time and time again – you're eating all wrong and you're sleeping wrong. You're up far too late playing snooker.'

'But, Brendan, I'm beating everybody. I'm knocking them all out. You know how good I am.'

'You may be the greatest thing since sliced bread, but this is your come-uppance. Three pounds overweight two days before a big fight can be hard for any fighter to shift let alone a bantamweight. You've got less than two days. This will be a test of what you're made of outside the ring.'

'I always knew that young Naz would fail to make the weight some day,' said Brendan, exactly one month later. 'That lad could eat for England. I didn't allow him to eat anything for the remainder of the Monday or on the Tuesday morning. At lunchtime on the Tuesday I weighed myself again – I was twelve stone again. I explained to Naz that by the time we got down to London, with the stress and strain of me driving all that way, I'd have lost two pounds. It wouldn't be so easy for him. We were staying in a flat above the Thomas à Beckett gym. I'd brought my scales with me. When we got to London my weight was down to 11 stone 12 pounds, exactly as I'd predicted. Naz had lost a pound, but he still had two extra pounds to shift. Naz's room was cold. I took the blow heater out of my room to give to him. I also switched on the sunbed in the corner of his room. It's my job to see he's as comfortable as possible before a big fight. I explained to him that he'd lose nearly one pound sleeping. We were both starving. I hadn't had anything to eat or drink all that day either. It's no good me trying to motivate or inspire somebody else if they're trying to make the weight and I'm eating.

'It was a rough night. The bed was damp and somebody down below was playing some old Beatles records. By the next morning I was down to nearly eleven stone eleven pounds, I'd lost almost another pound. Now I was counting in ounces. I went to the toilet and I was now only six ounces over the weight I'd set myself – I had to lose three pounds just like Naz. Naz was less than a pound over the weight.

So I went to the toilet again. Naz accused me of having something to drink. He said that I must have sneaked a drink. I kept going to the toilet and my weight kept dropping. Naz couldn't believe that I was going all this time without having something to drink. But the proof was in the scales. He could see the ounces coming off. He knew I wasn't cheating, and that he and I were going through this thing together. But every time I went to the toilet I had to reassure him by stepping on the scales again to show that the weight was coming off, and that I wasn't sneaking a drink. We were watching each other like frigging hawks. I took him for a walk and by the time we got to the weigh-in he was half a pound under the weight. He hadn't had anything to eat or drink since the Monday, that's thirty-six hours without anything. I took him to a restaurant after the weigh-in, but he couldn't finish his soup or his spaghetti. His stomach had shrunk. But he felt good. I told him that day that he'd grown in my estimation. Naz has this little routine when he gets into the ring. He jumps over the ropes, just like Chris Eubank, but then he does a flip holding on to the ropes and then three flips across the ring. He's a bit of a showman. But I told him that night that I just wanted one flip from him, then he was going straight to work. I told him that he was going to mentally and physically destroy his opponent. Incidentally, his opponent was unbeaten before that night. Naz had him down three times in the first round. He knocked him out in the second. I told him afterwards that there is nothing to stop him becoming world champion. "Who's going to stop you now?" says I. "Nobody," says he. "Right," says I.'

Brendan's got a way with the boys. He must have. They come from all over Yorkshire to train and spar in his gym in Wincobank, although most, it must be said, come from the streets roundabout. This small gym has produced four British or European champions, and almost a world champion in Herol Graham. Now Johnny Nelson had gone the whole way (or part of the way depending upon who you listened to, because most fight fans seemed to regard his recent acquisition as a bit of a Mickey Mouse title), and taken the WBF world cruiserweight title from Dave Russell in Melbourne. The title was not recognized by the British Boxing Board of Control. It's the Irish blarney, they say. 'The blarney did all that?' I asked incredulously.

Matthew was twelve, with a round, open face. Brendan was perched on some wooden steps by the side of the ring. He called Matthew over. 'How long have you been coming to the gym?' 'Three years,' said Matthew. 'Tell him what it was like before you came to the gym.' 'It was terrible, I had no friends and I was being bullied all the time at school.' 'Tell him what it's like now,' said Brendan. 'It's great. I've got lots of friends, and I'm not bullied now.' Brendan squeezed his arm tighter. 'This lad here can't fight. He'll never be able to fight. I'll teach him to dodge a bit in the ring. I'll teach him to mess his opponent around, to make the other fella look bad. I'll build up his confidence. I taught him that if anybody comes up to him in the street and starts to bully him, that he should just shout "Piss off," and run away. I'm teaching him personal and social skills for life. My job is to get these lads through life as safely as possible, both inside and outside the ring.

'It can be rough around here. I was the one to bring the first blacks into this area to my gym. So the National Front put posters all over my house and scrawled their name on the walls of the garages outside the gym. You can still see their graffiti to this day. But they've gone and I've survived, and that's what it's all about. I knew this guy who was big in the National Front, and he ended up marrying a black girl. So it was all a load of bloody bollocks anyway.'

In the ring above us there were five boxers. Two were black. One was a powerfully built novice boxer, the other was Johnny Nelson. Two were small white boys, probably no more than ten, the fifth was a serious-looking Asian youth, dressed in a black polo and black tracksuit bottoms, who stalked his opponent before unleashing incredibly ineffectual-looking punches. They took turns at sparring with each other, with one always left out. Johnny Nelson with the muscled black novice, then Johnny with one of the boys. 'Only body shots up there. I won't stand for any boxer in this type of sparring giving his opponent one accidentally on purpose like to the head,' said Brendan. '*Time!*' he shouted, and all five boxers walked slowly around the ring in an anti-clockwise direction. 'In my gym the professionals train with the novices. They can all learn something from each other. Bomber Graham used to stand in the middle of this ring and the lads would try to land a punch on him. They never could. *Change over!*' The boxers touched gloves gently, as if they were in some barn dance, and started again with a different partner.

A sixteen-year-old stood by the ring bandaging his hands. Brendan called him over. 'How old were you, Ryan, when you came to the gym for the first time?' 'Six.' 'What did I say to you?' 'Do you know any swear words?' 'So I got him to tell me every swear word he knew: "fuck", "bastard", "wanker", the lot. So I says to him, "From now on you don't swear when you're in this gym and you do as you're told." It took him by surprise, you see. Then I says to him, "What do they say about the Irish where you come from?" and he says, "They're all tick bastards." But this tick bastard says that this lad will be winning a gold at the Olympics in three years. When the English shout "Fuck off, you tick Irish Mick," at me, I just remind them that they were riding around on dirt tracks before the Irish came over.'

He pulled out a book that he has been carrying around in the pocket of his anorak to show me. It has pages of nineteenth-century political cartoons on the Irish problem. 'This shows you what the English thought of the Irish. The Irishman was always portrayed as a wee monkey. Here's the Irish Guy Fawkes, a wee ugly monkey in a hat, sitting on top of a keg of gunpowder before setting light to it. The tick wee monkey bastard. But the Irish are too cunning for the English. I've had the British super-middleweight champion. When I was start-ing him off I called him Slugger O'Toole. The Irish are great boxing fans, so I reckoned that they'd turn out in force to see an Irish boxer with the name of O'Toole. Slugger would come into the arena dressed in green, and it wasn't until he'd taken his dressing gown off that they would see that he was black. So they'd all be shouting, "He's not Irish!" and I'd say "What's the matter with you? Haven't you ever seen a black Irishman before?" And then when they asked me his real name, I'd reply, quite truthfully as it turns out, "Fidel Castro Smith". They'd not believe me anyway.'

Brendan pulled Ryan closer to him.

'Who's the only person who's ever going to lick you?'

'Me, myself.'

'Who's responsible for you?'

'Me, myself.'

'Correct.'

This was a routine they had rehearsed many times. Ryan knew when to come in, and he knew all the unvarying responses. It was like the litany from a church service.

'Some people think it's easy to be a boxing trainer and manager.

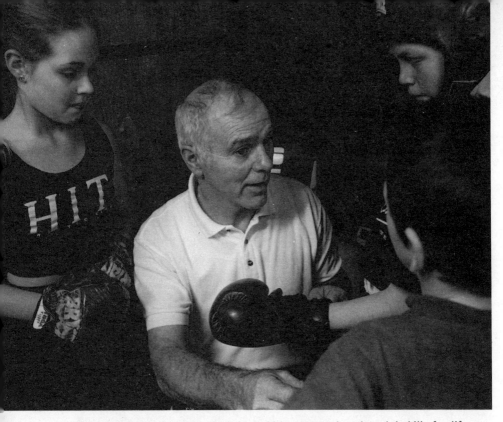

Brendan Ingle. 'I'm teaching these kids personal and social skills for life. Now concentrate: getting a job is like winning the . . . what?'

You just cream off your twenty-five per cent and the lads do all the work. But that's not how it is. I take these lads in when they're kids and I have to work on them. I have to build up their confidence. I have to teach them about life and replace all the crap they've learned. They come here and their heads are full of it.' He called over a somewhat shy-looking boy with a thin moustache and dull greyish shorts. His girlfriend had been sitting in the corner of the gym biting her nails all afternoon.

'What school did you come from, Matt?'

'Arbourthorne.'

'What kind of school is it?'

'Special needs.'

'What were you there for?'

'Because I was a thick bastard.'

'What are you now?'

'A clever bastard.'

The responses were instantaneous, starting almost before the question finished. He pulled Matt closer until their faces were almost touching.

'Who didn't you like when you first came here?'

'Pakis.'

'Pakis and blacks?'

'No, just Pakis. I always thought that the blacks were all right.'

'Who don't you like now?'

'Nobody.'

'When that lad came here he had nothing going for him,' said Brendan. 'Now he's a part of the team in here. There are a lot of Pakistanis in the team. He trains with champions. He'll be sparring with Johnny Nelson in a couple of minutes. I can identify with these lads. When I was a boy I had what you would call now "learning difficulties". Over in Ireland I was just a "tick bastard". I struggled with my spelling, my reading and everything else. I struggled with Latin and Gaelic. I can still say in Gaelic "What is your name?" "My name is Brendan Ingle." "Where do you live?" "Dublin City." "Do you have any money?" "No, I haven't." I can recite all these verses in Latin, but I've no idea what any of them mean. These verses were beaten into me. One of the nuns was a right bastard with her leather strap. I was beaten because I was tick. But this taught me a valuable lesson: you can't change people's attitude by mentally or physically abusing them. The only way that you can change people is by engaging in dialogue with them. Only dialogue.'

He shouted over to Matt. 'Who is the only person who can beat you?' 'Myself,' replied Matt across the crowded gym. 'My lads come to me with all their problems. I always say to them that if you haven't killed anybody, then you haven't got a real problem. I can sort everything else out.'

He turned to the boxers in the ring. 'Now, lads, before you get down out of the ring, I want to see you one by one jump over the ropes.' Johnny Nelson did it with some flair, the rest struggled to get over. 'I let them jump off the second rope, if they can't manage it,' said Brendan. 'I do it to build their confidence in all aspects of life. Boxing isn't just about punching and how to slip a punch. It's about building confidence and learning to survive.' He shouted up to Matt, now sparring with Johnny Nelson. 'Matt, what do you say if some dirty pervert comes up to you in the street?' 'I shout "Fuck off!"' 'What do you do then?' 'I run like fuck.'

'I'm teaching them how to survive inside and outside the ring,' said Brendan, 'which isn't that bad for a tick Mick.'

A Morning in Court

There were prams everywhere. Whole families were encamped in the reception area. It was a world of two cultures. Those waiting to go before the magistrates wore jeans, those waiting to represent them and sentence them wore suits. There was nothing in between. Two sixteen-year-olds swaggered in. They headed straight for the reception window. One wore a black baseball cap pulled low. Both had scuffed shoes. 'Darren.' 'Briggs,' said his friend without a pause, and without letting his friend finish. 'Downstairs,' said the voice from behind the glass. I followed them down towards the youth courts. The 'kiddie courts' they call them. 'More informal, the bench is lower. It makes the defendants less intimidated,' I had been told. It did not look that informal. Mark sat in the middle of the court staring at the floor. He wore jeans and a lumberjack coat. The man in the dark suit was offering an eloquent defence. Mark looked unconcerned. 'Mark has a girlfriend of several years' standing. She is now pregnant. At the age of seventeen he is entering a period of considerable responsibility. He has a record, but not an extensive one. His appearances before this court are getting less and less. Mark is effectively sorting himself out. This is just a hiccup.'

Perhaps musing on the hiccup, perhaps not, Mark sat there staring blankly ahead, on his own. The bench retired. Mark's solicitor sat reading a Dixon's catalogue. The prosecution solicitor picked at her fingernails. The magistrates may be out for as much as twenty minutes, I had been told. As the Clerk of the Court explained, the magistrates like to be thorough. They may have social work reports, school reports and psychiatric reports to consider. The bench returned. Mark was asked to stand and face the bench. 'You've got a history of stealing from shops,' began the chairman. Mark's face dropped; he had already served one custodial sentence and he dreaded going back. But the tone suddenly changed. 'In a few months' time you will have a child to support.' He was given a conditional discharge for one year. 'You are being put on trust. Go away, Mark.' Mark slowly left the court, a big smile lighting up his face as he reached the door. I followed him out. What did his girlfriend think of his court appearance? 'She doesn't know. I told her I was going out to town today. I'll tell her tonight, now that everything is all right. She's got a right good job in a bank. She'd have killed me for being so stupid. I only told my mum this morning. She went daft. She'd have come with me, but she had a hospital appointment.' What about the baby? I enquired. 'Well, my girlfriend did one of those do-it-yourself pregnancy tests, and that were positive, but she hasn't been to the doctor yet. We're both going tonight. I'm right looking forward to it now.'

The next boy in court, Philip, was sixteen but looked younger. His parents sat behind him. They mirrored his movements, with that same downward look. Philip was charged with taking a car without consent, and his solicitor spent most of his time trying to counter the media image of the joyrider. 'This was by no means a case of a person tearing around a city in a stolen car. This was slow, almost hesitant driving. He was tempted because he had seen others. He only took the car after they had abandoned it.' The theories came hard and fast from the solicitor. 'He is a young boy growing up. He is interested in motorcars and motorcycles. He wants to try cars out for himself.' The focus of the plea seemed to be that Philip was an extremely poor driver. He had a bump in the car, but only a little one, the magistrates were assured. Philip was sentenced to attend a special centre for twelve hours in all – two hours each Saturday afternoon for the next six weeks. The special centre was a local school, open at weekends. The chairman of the bench addressed his parents. 'You have to make sure that he's neat and tidy.' A social worker explained to me that at the school Philip will be required to do PE and make things, 'at least I think that's what they have to do. But it's a good punishment, if he's an ardent Sheffield Wednesday fan, because he'll have to miss the match.'

Samantha was next in. She had been in police custody for the night, and was led into the glass cage in the corner. She could hardly keep a straight face. She had been arrested for breaking bail conditions. She was residing at a bail hostel, and failed to return one night at 11 p.m. She had surrendered herself the previous day, but through some administrative cock-up had not come before the court, and for that reason had to spend the night in custody. The chairman of the bench apologized profusely: 'We're sorry the system failed you.' The magistrates' decision was that she could now reside at the home of a friend, but a strict curfew was to be imposed.

The next defendant, Lee, was altogether more serious. He had a history of shoplifting to support his solvent abuse. The effects of the solvent abuse were clear for all to see. On the day he was caught shoplifting for the offence for which he was now in court, he had been to a police station for a verbal caution for a previous offence. The three magistrates sat reading his psychiatric reports. Lee sat twisting his nose this way and that. He was not trying to be funny, he was just very self-conscious. His feet started off parallel and close together, but now the side of one foot was climbing over the ankle of the other. His hands were tightly clasped. Occasionally he glanced up at the bench, even the moderately low bench of the kiddies' court. The magistrates were a world away, with their soft rounded vowels and their superior tones. His mother sat behind him. Her skirt was a little too short. I sighed. Lee looked around for the source of the noise, and stared at me. His mother pleaded with the bench. 'A supervision order is no good. He's had every chance that's going. He's openly admitted to his psychiatrist that he's going to go on stealing. It's very hard for a mother to say this, but something needs to be done. It's me he steals off most of the time. There's only so much a body can take. I'll end up strangling him.'

The magistrates seemed desperate to help, but they could only sentence on the basis of the charge before them. The chairman of the bench addressed Lee: 'Is there anything you can tell us about your life to help us? Your mother says that you steal a lot to buy Calor gas and Butane gas. Is that true?' 'That's not true.' Lee was indignant, and for the first time all morning it looked as if there was going to be an argument in court. But then Lee continued. 'Butane gas, yes, but not Calor gas.'

I felt like laughing, but I was the only one to find it funny. Lee told the magistrates that his main interest outside school was rugby. 'I can't understand why a rugby player would want to damage his health by sniffing solvent,' said the chairman of the magistrates. The funny thing was that Lee did not look as if he understood it either. Lee was granted another supervision order. His mother looked extremely angry.

The morning sitting was jam-packed. There were no tea breaks. The next defendant was led in. He had been in custody for a week. The chairman asked him to take his hands out of his pockets. The prosecution had opposed bail, because it was argued that he would commit further offences. He was charged with one offence of actual bodily harm and one of attempted grievous bodily harm. The prosecution alleged that the defendant had hit a man with a stick and then tried to attack his house with a petrol bomb. The attacks were said to be racially motivated. The defendant had just turned sixteen. He had no previous convictions. The defence solicitor, who was trying to get his client out on bail, claimed the attacks were encouraged by adults, and insisted that David 'was ill-at-ease with hardened criminals'. The solicitor recounted an anecdote which he said would tell the court a lot about David's character. David had apparently held the door open for another solicitor. 'My colleague was amazed that David was in prison.' The boy, despite his good manners, was not granted bail. As he was led up to the cells his father walked up the stairs and out into the spring sunshine. He looked devastated.

The morning session, meanwhile, was running over. The young boxer, charged with assault, whom I was waiting to see, still had not had his turn in this never-ending queue. He had told me that this particular incident had happened out of the blue, and he was now sorting himself out with Brendan's help. Brendan was teaching him to direct his aggression in the gym, to use it rather than allowing it to use him, perhaps even to make a few bob out of it one day. 'Brendan's a lot more use than anything the court has to offer,' he told me. Having sat there for just one morning, I could see his point.

Big Fight Special

There is something special about world championship boxing. A mystique. It draws the celebrities. The names alone have a certain magic. Ali and Frazier, Tyson and Ruddock, Hearns and Sugar Ray Leonard, the rumble in the jungle, the thriller in Manila. Milestones down the foggy road of memory. Where were you the night Ali beat Sonny Liston or Tyson lost his title? You may not remember much about the days or months around that time, but you will remember that night in all its detail.

I had never met a world champion, but here I was having lunch with the new cruiserweight champion of the world, just after the weigh-in and hours before his first defence of the title. It was to be a world championship contest on home soil. Johnny Nelson had gone all the way to Australia to take the title, but then again that's not far when you're going for the championship of the world. But now he and I were sitting closer to home, in the Buttercup Café in the Water Meadows swimming complex run by Mansfield Council. The lasagne and chips were on the house. I assumed that I would remember those chips all my days. I surveyed the scene. Large inflatable pink elephants hung from the ceiling, dummy wind surfers clung to the wall for all their life was worth. What were we doing here, of all places?

Frank, a fanatical fight fan, who had gone 'on the sick' from work to be present at the weigh-in, perceived my quizzical look. 'The food here's terrific,' he explained. 'I've been to Las Vegas, France, Italy, you name it, to watch the boxing, but believe me Mansfield Leisure Centre is not a bad venue for the boxing.' 'Even for world championship boxing?' I wanted my tone to be searching. The chlorine from the pool was making my eyes close. The accompanying facial expression was making my question sound incredulous.

Johnny was starving. He got up to fetch some cutlery, and coughed into his drink. 'We always do that in my house to stop people touching our drinks when we're away.' He had arrived that morning at Brendan's house a few pounds overweight. Brendan's son, John, had taken him out for a good walk around Wincobank, in a large thick padded suit and boots to make him sweat. While he was out, Brendan's small living room started to fill up with the fight faithful: Frank, who had arrived in his work clothes and changed in the front room; Bill, who despite looking well past retirement age still ran a fruit and vegetable shop in the city centre; Nigel, another boxer from the same stable who had recently got out of prison after serving a one-year sentence for assault. ('These lads picked on me, and I ended up knocking one of them out. The problem was that I wanted to humiliate the guy, so I pissed on him. The judge wasn't impressed by that. I thought that he was going to give me community service, but he ended up sending me down for a year. It's just as well I didn't have a curry – I'd have crapped on him as well.'

Bill has watched the fight game for years. 'We call him Uncle Bill,' explained Brendan. 'Or Billy the Bag Man – he carries the money. We get him in for nothing by pretending that he's one of the family. He's been to all of Johnny's fights.' 'I've watched Johnny from the very beginning,' confirmed Bill. 'His best performance were against Marcus Bott in late 1991. Bott were a right hard case. I remember him standing eating a sandwich after the fight, and the blood were dripping from this cut in his eye right into his sandwich. It didn't bother him one little bit. If Johnny hadn't fought hard that night he'd have been killed.'

Johnny arrived back from his walk with a thin film of perspiration on his face. Brendan set up the electric scales in the living room. He looked pleased with the result. 'The drive down will take off the last few ounces.' We made our way out to Bill's old Mercedes saloon. Another car drew up just outside Brendan's house. It was Clifton Mitchell, whom Brendan had christened Big Paddy Reilly, a heavyweight boxer from Brendan's gym, currently ranked sixth in the heavyweight division in the British rankings. Johnny got in beside him. They were going to make a detour to Pittsmoor to pick up another friend to bring to the weigh-in. Bill did not look pleased. He

Johnny 'The Entertainer' Nelson and Ali, Naz's younger brother, in 1990. 'In Australia one guy asked me if I was related to Azummah Nelson because he said that we were both the same colour and we had the same surname.'

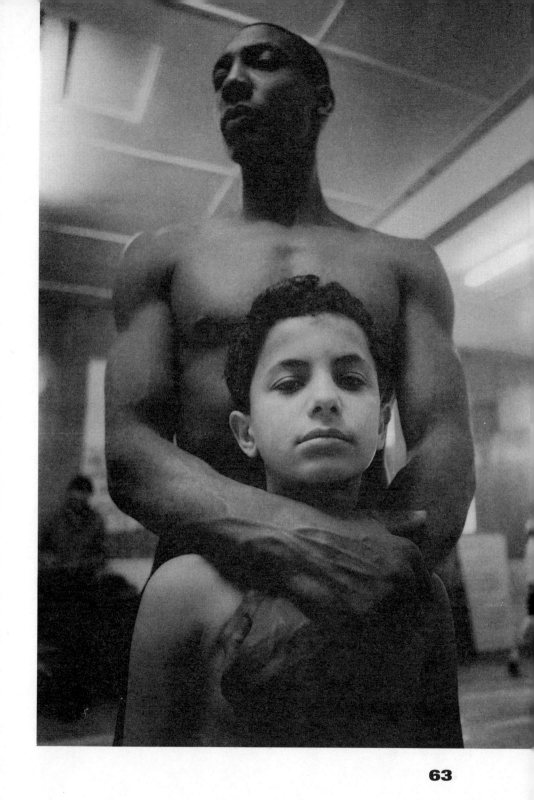

had been looking forward to travelling down to Mansfield with the world champion in his car. He was shaking his large pendulous head. 'When they get to Pittsmoor that other bastard won't even be out of bed. They're going to be late for the weigh-in.' Bill limped slowly to his car, obviously disappointed. 'I've burst a blood vessel in my leg. I stood on a cherry in my shop and ended up doing the splits.' He started up the car, Brendan in the front beside him with the electric scales on his lap. 'Don't get me wrong,' continued Bill. 'I've been in the market game for fifty years. I've played every trick under the sun. But you've got to have principles. The problem with some of these lads today is that they have no principles. None. They'd let you down as soon as they'd look at you. They've no sense of responsibility. Not like the old days, Brendan, not at all like the old days.' Nigel let out a very loud yawn in the back seat. The old saloon shambled out of Newman Road. Nigel pretended to go to sleep. Clifton swerved round the other corner of Newman Road with Johnny Nelson beside him hanging on to his seat.

Johnny Nelson was the reigning WBF champion of the world. WBF stands for World Boxing Federation. Once there was just the WBC and the WBA, then came the IBF and the WBO; the WBF was the latest title. As *Boxing News* said, 'Boxing's parlous state means that anybody who thinks up some initials can sanction a world title fight now.' Brendan had defended the world championship claim stoutly earlier that morning. 'Look what they said about the WBO until Chris Eubank came along. We'll have to wait and see what Johnny can do with the title. The WBF is big in Australia where Johnny beat Dave Russell. Don't forget in Australia the WBO doesn't mean that much.' Johnny nodded in agreement. 'The Australians were really mad about me taking the title. At the press conference afterwards they were saying, "OK, you won the boxing, but what about the cricket? England aren't doing very well at that. Are they?" One guy asked me if I was related to Azummah Nelson, because he said that we were both the same colour, and we had the same surname. The Australians weren't pleased that they lost such a prestigious title.'

Others, however, were not so impressed with the title. 'A Mickey Mouse title at a Mickey Mouse weight,' suggested one ex-boxer from Brendan's gym. 'That's why there won't be any live TV coverage.'

'So you'll not be going?' I asked. 'Oh yeah, I'll be there. I've always thought that Johnny Nelson had real talent. He's just not shown it in the big one yet.' Nelson was better known for his two failed attempts to win more recognized titles than for his success at winning the WBF title. He drew with the fading WBC champion Carlos De Leon in Sheffield in 1990, and lost a twelve-rounder with the IBF champion James Warring in Fredericksburg, Virginia, in 1992. Both fights were seen as rather tedious affairs, with Nelson refusing to show the necessary commitment. Many fight fans assumed that Nelson would simply vanish into obscurity. But now Johnny had bounced right back. Exactly how far depended upon how you rated the WBF. Some obviously did not rate it that highly. He was sponsored by Toyota cars for four years and got free meat from a butcher down the market, but not any longer. Toyota withdrew their sponsorship and the butcher went bust. Currently, he was hoping for a sponsored car from the Huddersfield Accident and Repair Centre, but that was still to be finalized. He was sponsored by a health shop, which supplied him with free vitamins. 'It can mount up to thirty quid's worth a week, so it's well worth having,' Johnny had explained.

Bill's old Merc chugged along the M1. 'This isn't a diesel, by any chance, is it?' asked Nigel, waking up from his slumbers in the back. 'It bloody well feels like one. It would send you to sleep.' Bill kept his eyes firmly on the road. 'Scoff all you like. You can't beat the old cars with real quality.' 'I don't know why you don't buy a new one, Bill. You can afford it.' Nigel turned to me, now whispering. 'He's a bloody millionaire. He owns this old people's home. He's got loads of property and yet he lives in a council house in Parson's Cross. If I had his money I'd spend it.' 'That's the problem with young people,' said Bill, as if he had somehow managed to get the gist of the whispered conversation. 'All they want to do is spend money. Spend, spend, spend, including money they haven't got. Brendan gives them their purse for a fight, and the next morning they've blown it. No principles, no discipline. That's their basic problem.'

The weigh-in had been set for 11 a.m., but with five minutes to go Johnny still had not arrived. Bill, the fruit and veg man and obviously something of an expert on the exact weight of things, had found a good seat just by the scales. 'What did I tell you? No sign of Johnny.

I wouldn't have let him drive off to Pittsmoor. Brendan is too soft with some of his boxers.' The room to be used for the weigh-in was filling up: a couple of boxers, one of Brendan's other sons who was going to be acting as corner man, with his five-month-old son, a few fight fans, Pat Brogan, the promoter, a few Mansfield Council employees, a TV camera crew, some Belgian promoters with waxed moustaches carrying posters advertising Nelson's next world championship defence to be held against an unknown boxer called Wanyama in October in Belgium. This had me a little puzzled. 'How come the posters have already been printed? What happens if Johnny doesn't win tonight?' Even the council employees were looking at me as if I was a little daft. They were passing round the poster. 'Does anybody know who Wanyama is?' asked one of Johnny's closest friends. 'This guy doesn't even look like a cruiserweight. He looks more like a super-middleweight. Look at the size of his gloves compared with the rest of him.'

Tom Collins, Johnny's opponent, was standing quietly in the corner, along with his manager. He looked around at this small group milling aimlessly about. 'I hate all this crap,' he muttered. He pulled down his jeans and stepped on to the scales. Johnny's little coterie were not impressed. 'Look at the fat on him. My daughter's got more definition than him. What's old Ten Bellies here going to do against Johnny?' They started passing round the official programme with photographs of Nelson and Collins on the cover. 'Just look, he needs three championship belts to hide his belly.' Johnny and Clifton arrived then, with their friend from Pittsmoor. The friend, another black boxer, headed for the nearest chair. Bill was still tutting. 'What did I tell you? You can see by his eyes that he's only just up.'

Things were warming up. Johnny stepped out of his padded suit and the young lady from the television news nearly fainted. 'He's got a rather nice body,' she enthused. The contrast with Collins was stark. Brendan was, by now, clearly excited. 'It's a sell-out. There are a lot of guys in the fight game who said that Pat Brogan and Alma were mugs for staging this contest between Johnny and Tom Collins. They were saying that Johnny is too boring a fighter and that Collins is past it. But they've been proved wrong. Johnny got rid of his allocation of two hundred tickets with no problem. He's on a percentage of the gate. It's going to be a cracker.'

66

A cracker or not, was it a real world championship contest? I asked Johnny whether he really did feel like the champion of the world. 'Well, I don't feel like an *international* world champion as such.' Implying presumably that there is such a thing as a national world champion. He went back to swigging out of the large jug of orange juice that had been left out for him. He had brought a Pyrex dish of chicken and rice with him. He tore into that. The man was clearly hungry.

I sat back in that little room in Mansfield Sports Centre and tried to put the contest into some kind of perspective. Given that Collins was also from Yorkshire, Brendan Ingle had perhaps hit the nail on the head when he was quoted in the official programme as saying, 'Remember the championship of Yorkshire is on the line.' But calling it a world title fight clearly sold tickets. But why Mansfield? I let the TV interviewer from the local BBC news station, the one who still had not recovered from the sight of Johnny's torso, ask that one. 'But, Mr Ingle, Mansfield is not exactly the most glamorous location in the world.' Brendan took a sharp intake of air. 'Some people might not think that it's the most glamorous of locations on this earth, but then, you see, I've travelled round Mansfield, and I've seen it for myself. It's an absolutely fantastic place. There are also fantastic sponsors for tonight's world championship contest: British Coal, local business-men, Mansfield Council . . .'

Brendan Ingle has the gift of the gab. He understands the power of language – to persuade, to direct, to bamboozle. If you listen to him long enough you will hear him describe himself as a professor of kidology. He may be a brilliant boxing trainer, but he's also a hustler. You have to be in his game. He calculated carefully when he renamed Fidel Castro Smith 'Slugger O'Toole' and Clifton Mitchell 'Big Paddy Reilly' to pull in the Irish boxing fans, and when he covered their well-muscled black torsos with the green of the shamrock in their dressing gowns. He also knew that the title 'World Championship Boxing' would sell tickets. And he was right. It was a sell-out. On the big night itself I sat ringside with a professional couple from Lincoln. The husband had watched some amateur boxing before but had never attended a professional fight. He'd brought his wife along for a night to remember. They had read in their local paper that world championship boxing was to be staged in Mansfield. I watched their faces as the celebrities drawn by the event climbed into the ring to be introduced to the crowd: Mick Mills, Glyn Rhodes, Herol Graham, Prince Naseem Hamed, all local boxers, past and present, whose names and faces meant something to a large section of the crowd, but nothing to the couple from Lincoln. 'Where's Muhammad Ali?' I heard the woman from Lincoln ask. She really had been bamboozled by the title of the event.

As for the fight itself, if Nelson had been criticized in the past for being a boring fighter with little commitment, then he upset his critics that night. A punch on the opening bell staggered Collins, who was then put down three times in the first round. But Collins looked throughout as if he hadn't got the heart for it. It might have been that first punch. The couple from Lincoln thought not. The referee stopped the contest in the first round. But as Frank, the ardent fight fan, had said at the weigh-in, Nelson was in a no-win situation. If he won easily they'd say that Collins (whose reported age varied between thirty-five and forty-four, depending upon who you asked) was past it. If Nelson needed a lot of rounds to win they'd say that he was no good.

The couple from Lincoln, tempted out by those magic words 'World Championship Boxing', were bitterly disappointed. This was not a night they would remember. The wife had already forgotten what she had had earlier that night for dinner.

One of Brendan Ingle's other fighters, who had fought on the undercard that night, bought the gloves that Johnny had used from the promoter. He used his entire takings from the fight. He was going to get them signed by Johnny, presumably in the hope that these gloves, used in the first defence of a world title, might be worth something one day.

On the way back to Sheffield I kept thinking to myself that he wouldn't make much from his enterprise if he ever tried to sell them to a couple from Lincoln.

On the Make

Selling Jewellery on the Never Never

Mark was looking for a job. His career had 'levelled off', that's how he liked to put it. Once there were just wins, then a few narrow defeats. He was amazed to find that he was more marketable than ever. He said that some of the big London promoters liked a lad who would put up a good fight then lose. But the statistics were mounting against him. A string of narrow defeats, no matter how narrow, made him look less appealing. He was becoming predictable. The prize money was starting to dwindle. It was time to get out. He always said that he wouldn't stay in boxing a moment too long. It was a friend who told him about the jewellery business on your doorstep, the jewellery business on the never never – 'A bit of a nobble for a lad like yourself. Just right for someone like you, Mark. A lad who can take it, and give it.' What had he to lose? I asked him if I could tag along. 'Just as long as you don't try to edge in,' he warned. 'There's only room for the best in this game. That's what I've heard.'

We drove to a suburb that Mark wasn't at all familiar with. Inside the shop – the nerve centre of the operation – you could hear the laughter out the back. Behind the jewellery, behind the glass cases, behind the gold and silver. Somebody was telling a funny story. The laughter dampened down. Then it erupted again. Great guffaws of laughter. Bodies curled up in spasms of mirth, behind those four walls. Behind the thick, blue velvet curtain. I edged closer. The voice had a Black Country accent. 'I've sold vacuum cleaners to people without a carpet in the house.' The laughter started again slower this time, but quickening. The pitch rose in volume. 'I sold a woman two ironing boards – one for upstairs. She only had a hundred-pound credit limit, so she couldn't have the iron.' This time the laughter sounded harsher; it came out like 'tak, tak, tak'.

'I've sold a woman velvet windows for every window in the house including the toilet.'

This time there was no response. 'Velvet windows?' 'Velvet curtains, I mean.' He had fluffed his lines, and the laughter never came. I could see in now. The man with the Black Country accent had a ruddy complexion. Too much time out in the biting wind, knocking on doors, canvassing – as they put it. His partner sat in a leather chair. Balding with a paunch, wearing a brightly coloured shirt. A large Rolex glinted on his arm, thick gold rings on two fingers of each hand. Two women were doing the accounts in an adjoining room. Brian, the owner of the shop, watched as the fifty-pound notes changed hands. He listened intently to the tales from the field. His employees had been out there and survived.

It was his turn in the round of stories. 'I remember Ron telling us about having to go back to this customer who had complained about his carpet, which had a hole worn in it. He went into the house and said, "What have you been doing here, then? It's not for walking on this, you know." The punter said, "Oh, I'm sorry." So Ron said, "You've worn it out because you're supposed to pick your feet up when you walk. You're not supposed to shuffle along on it."' The laughter crackled as Brian shuffled along in his imitation of the gait of the hapless punter.

In the background you could hear the quiet but confident tapping of the calculators as the figures were being totalled. 'A very good week,' said Brian. 'A very, very good week,' said the bald man with the Rolex in a parody of the AA advertisement.

We were in the back room of a jeweller's shop in Sheffield. The jeweller's car, all fifty grand of it, sat outside the shop, looking just slightly incongruous in front of a shop that size. The shop, despite its tasteful jewellery, didn't look capable of sustaining a car of that sort. And it didn't. It was the back room that paid for the car, the back room with the little charts on the wall and the rows of noughts after each figure.

This little room was the centre of a highly successful company selling jewellery in what it called a 'direct sales operation'. In the past they had sold other items in a similar fashion – duvets, ironing boards, sheets, hi fi's, carpets, vacuum cleaners, even frying pans. But now they were concentrating on jewellery. Brian explained to Mark how it all worked. The company worked hand in glove with a credit collection company. The idea was simple and very neat. Agents from the credit company would go out on a weekly basis to collect outstanding debts from clients. They obviously got to know their clients very well. A representative of the jewellery company would then accompany the agents to certain targeted customers – customers who were paying off their outstanding credit. 'But only to the very good payers, or to the "crème-de-la-menthe" [sic] of the good payers, as we put it,' explained Brian. The jewellery would then be offered to the customer on the never never. They showed Mark and meself an attaché case containing all the gleaming, glittering merchandise. Rows and rows of gold horseshoes and coats of arms, and rings inlaid with semi-precious stones ('*Semi-precious* covers a lot of bloody things,' explained one of Brian's salesmen helpfully; 'it's better than saying the stones aren't real'). All this temptation to clients already in debt.

'We're doing a social service to the public,' continued Brian. 'We sell directly to some disabled customers who can't get out to the shops. We bring a jeweller's shop right to their own doorstep in some of these highrise flats they live in.'

'And don't forget that ninety-nine per cent of our customers couldn't go out and borrow a tanner from anybody else. And if a customer decides not to pay, there's not a lot you can do about it. If a guy's unemployed and you take him to court, the court won't have a lot of sympathy for the guys who've got him into debt. The court will end up telling him that he'll have to pay you off at fifty pence a week. We're in a business where we have to take a lot of risks. You can't go in with a hard edge, because they're your customers.'

Brian blew on his coffee. 'And believe me there are some right evil bastards out there, who just want to screw you for what they can get. They'll borrow money, they'll take your jewellery, they'll take anything that's going with no intention of paying any of it back. Then when the credit company says that they have to pay up, they'll try to return the goods. We had one of our agents ring up and say that his customer wasn't going to pay because she was dissatisfied with the ring we'd sold her – the stone must have been loose or something because the bloody thing had fallen out. So we got the agent to send the ring back in. The stone was still there, but the ring was so dirty that you couldn't see the stone. It was all misshapen as well. We've had rings returned when the punters have obviously punched somebody with the ring on their fingers. These are the kinds of people that we have to deal with.'

Two more salesmen arrived back. A case of jewellery lay open on the table. One of the salesmen stood well away from the attaché case, as if it might contain a hidden, unexploded bomb. 'I hope that's not the case that the dog tiddled on last week,' he said. 'Perhaps you should sniff it and see. How did you let a thing like that happen? The worst thing that ever happened to me with a dog was when this little Jack Russell ate one of my rings. I put the dog's name down on the voucher. My boss at the time went mad. But what else could you do? Anyway, we got the ring back after a week, although the label had disintegrated.'

They all laughed. These were people on a high. You could see that everyone here was a winner. The jewellery company had a group of customers targeted for it, plus the introduction from someone who was almost a friend of the family, and the credit company got its customers to continue to borrow. The jeweller got his money directly from the credit company, which in turn took a hefty commission. The credit company had, however, to collect the debt, but this was their business. Sweet. Very sweet. Everyone was a winner.

Except, perhaps, the customer.

A customer buying a £300 ring over 120 weeks would pay £204 on top of that for credit, and this is an individual on a low income and already in debt. 'But the customers themselves care little about the interest rate being charged. All they're interested in is how much per week the ring or the gold chain or whatever will cost them,' explained Brian. 'This one-hundred-pound ring will cost them £1.60 a week over two years, this gold horseshoe ring, on the other hand, will cost them £2.80 a week over two years. We always say in this game that we leave all the multiplication up to the customer. It's not our problem, after all. But you couldn't walk into a High Street shop anywhere in the world and get a ring like this for a fiver a week.'

I looked at the ring with the horse's head on it. 'It's Red Rum, I think,' said Brian. 'You see, many of our customers are unemployed. But we always say that the unemployed are often better managers of money than those in work. They know exactly how much is coming in. They might be paying between ten and thirty quid a week to the credit company, for all sorts of things – household goods, car repairs, plus, of course, to clear previous debts – but they know they have to meet the repayments, because they've nowhere else to go for credit.'

'We're basically salesmen, we're not their financial consultants,' explained one of his salesmen. 'Our customers often tend to be the very bottom of the heap. You should see some of the houses that our men have to go into. I've been in a house in Winsford in Cheshire where the mother was selecting a £300 diamond ring and the six kids were sitting around having dinner out of a jumbo tin of processed peas. I've been to houses where you can see piles of disposable nappies chucked out the back and left to dissolve in the rain.'

'I've been to houses where I wouldn't crap in the bog,' said Brian, not wishing to be left out of all this. This notion that the customers are somehow different from themselves, somehow alien, is very important to maintaining the spirit of the team. 'It's a different planet out there,' added Brian unselfconsciously.

Mark and I left that cosy little office with Brian for a look. It was a bitterly cold night on the other side of the town. Brian parked his jeep at the end of the street. Some teenagers on the corner eyed us suspiciously. This was a regular call. Brian was on his own tonight. He was pleased that Mark, with his boxing skills, was with him. He poked his head in through the broken window between the kitchen and the living room. The house may have been poor, but still it had a colour TV, a video recorder and a library of videotapes, including, incongruously, *Jane Fonda's Workout*. Brian was welcomed into the house like an old friend of the family, which he undoubtedly was. Angela's husband was not about. 'He's off again,' said Angela. Brian told her not to worry. 'You've got some new curtains since I was last here . . . I've got some goodies here for you to look at.' Angela's father sat beside her. Things, you could say, were not going too well for the family. 'I was married forty-nine years, eleven and a half months. If she'd just lived another two weeks we would have made our golden wedding anniversary,' said the father. Brian was settling in – 'It's like coming home, you know, coming here. When I sit down on this settee I don't want to get up again.' 'I always have a right good laugh when Brian comes round,' said Angela. 'It's one of the few good laughs I ever have.'

Angela's son woke up at this point. He ate some ice cream out of a plastic bowl. A pile of coins had fallen into the bowl; the coins remained there as he ate the ice cream. Angela said she wasn't interested in any jewellery, until the case was opened. The rings sparkled brilliantly in those surroundings. 'Ooooooh, come here, let's have a look, then.' 'Try it on,' said Brian. 'Now let me tell you how much that would be a week if you were to buy it. That would be four pounds eight pence a week. Very reasonable, eh?' Brian turned to Angela's father. 'We've got some nice men's tackle here, if you're interested.' He unfurled the gold chains in their velvet case with a practised flourish. The old man sat up straight for the first time. 'Try it on,' said Brian. The old man fingered the chains as Angela started pouring her heart out to Brian, mainly about her financial worries.

'I'm more like a social worker sometimes,' said Brian as he climbed back into his jeep. 'Some of our customers are really decent people in hard times, and it's all very sad, but what can you do?'

If Brian was the social worker, Billy was the clinician. 'You can't afford to get involved,' he said. His technique was quite different. 'I'm a master at this game. It's all done as a series of moves. Watch me.' The frost was worse the following night. The punter looked as if he had just been roused from a deep sleep. He looked like the sort of man you wouldn't like to upset. Probably early forties, but could in real time be younger. 'What are you trying to sell me this time? Not more bloody rubbish, I hope.' This was Billy's cue. Mention 'rubbish' and Billy is right in there. 'Not rubbish, sir. Certainly not rubbish.' Billy had explained to me previously that selling works on objections. 'I've got some smashing jewellery for you today, sir, and a little bit special it is.' Billy was now ushering the punter, the agent and myself all into the front room of the little house. This house was a good deal more orderly than the previous one. Billy was in charge, and we could feel it already. The wife emerged from the kitchen. Billy had told me that the first thing you must do when selling is to assess the situation – see what priorities the customer has got. The wife had obviously just finished washing up, so there were no problems there. The telly was blaring in the background, but they'd obviously only been half watching it. The situation was 'ripe', as Billy liked to say.

As the agent sorted out the financial transaction, which was ostensibly the real purpose of the visit, Billy started to open his attaché case. All that glittering gold. He had their attention, their undivided attention – well, almost. 'Is anyone watching that?' said Billy, pointing at the television, and then without waiting for an answer he nipped across and switched it off. There was a stunned silence for a moment. The television probably acted as a backdrop to every conversation that had ever taken place in that front room, at least since the time when someone like Billy had last visited.

'Now, madam,' said Billy, 'if I said to you that you could have whatever you wanted from this box free of charge, what would you have?' There was another slightly stunned silence as everyone in the room tried to work out whether this was a genuine offer or some elaborate ploy. 'I'd have one of those rings. I love rings and so does Frank there.' Frank nodded enthusiastically. If there were any rings going free, he wanted to be in there as a potential recipient of any largesse. So Billy now knew that it was a ring they were both after, and he knew exactly what they could afford. 'Ripe,' I thought I heard him muttering, but he may just have said 'Right'. Billy guided them through the rings. Rings were no longer £180 or £220, they were just a couple of pounds a week over two years.

It was now just a case of selecting the items. 'What job do you do, Frank? Lorry driver? Right, then. You don't want anything with a stone in it, that's for sure. It'll make your finger go black.' Frank nodded and his gaze shifted to the solid gold horseshoe rings.

Billy started to chuckle. 'You know, I once said the very same thing to a blackie. It took me a few seconds before I realized what I'd just said. I apologized and told him that it was just a figure of speech. "No offence taken, mate," he said. You can't be too careful, though, can you, Frank? You have to watch what you say to them. Now, what about this smashing ring here with the horse's head on it. Are you a gambling man yourself, Frank? I like a bit of a flutter. I'm sure that's Arkle. Just think – you could be wearing a racing legend on your finger for years. It could be a family heirloom. Leave it to your kids, Frank, there's a little bit of history on that ring. And don't forget the price can only go up, especially with inflation. That ring's only £1.80.'

You could see that Frank was far from prepared to carry out the necessary mental arithmetic that would tell him exactly how much this nag's head ring at £1.80 a week over two years would eventually cost him. He didn't care. One look around the house told you that here was a family very short of heirlooms. Ripe.

It was now Alison's turn. 'I would have thought something with one of these ruby or emerald stones would be right up your street, madam,' said Billy. 'They are real, aren't they?' asked Alison nervously. 'A friend of mine bought a ring with fake stones in it a while ago. She'd been taken in, but I'd never fall for that.' Billy adopted a tone of some seriousness. He wanted to sound sincere, scholarly. 'They're what you call semi-precious, love. They keep their value very well, do semi-precious stones. They're a really good investment.' But it was time to get off that track double-quick. 'Here, let me try to guess your ring size, love. "P", I reckon. Is that pretty close? Now try this one. Didn't I tell you? A perfect fit. That one's only £1.20. What do you think of it, Frank?'

Before we had made the call, Billy had drawn Mark and myself a graph of the whole procedure from going through the door in the first place to finding the egress double-quick at the end. Even I recognized where we were now on the graph. We were, at that very moment, sliding down the hill, on the other side from the sale. Billy had now only to do the paperwork and then we were out. His rule was to talk about anything other than the sale at this stage. A little bit difficult with two customers still mulling over the concept of *semi-precious* on the very same settee as him. 'Aren't you going to put the kettle on, then, love? We're all parched in here, and I'm sure that Frank could do with a cuppa. Isn't that right, Frank?'

Friday was the day when all the salesmen came back from the field with their tales of survival out there with the punters. They swapped stories and compared sales. 'Now, Bob, are you going to explain to us all how you managed to lose an eighty-six-pound gold chain? I wouldn't have thought that a salesman with thirty-three years in the business would have fallen for something like that?' The rest of the salesmen laughed.

'Well, it was like this,' said Bob. 'I went to this jewellery party at this house, where there were fourteen scantily clad women. Now, you can't sell to all fourteen in one go, especially because they were all new to credit. So I had them in three at a time in the kitchen. I'd already sold a grand's worth of stuff when this eighty-six-quid gold chain suddenly went missing. One of the birds had obviously tried it on and then let it drop down her bra. What could I do? I couldn't very well line them all up for a strip search, now could I? Even if I'd wanted to. I've always believed, by the way, that you should never get involved with customers like that – even when I used to sell sheets and bedding. Business comes first, you have to remember that. Some of the reps I've known haven't been as disciplined as me. There was one rep I used to work with who had five kids in five different houses on the same estate. Straight up. But I've always put the sale first. My old boss used to say, "Never get your fishing tackle out when you're trying to make a sale," and I think that's a good philosophy of life. So I wasn't interested in any strip search at this jewellery party. So I played on their sympathies instead.

'I told them that it was a hundred-quid chain, and that the money would be coming out of my commission. Then I watched their reactions. One bird asked if it really was worth as much as that. You see that gives you a clue – she must have seen the price on the ticket by that stage. Then the same bird asked, "Aren't you insured?" That gives you another bloody clue. So I say, "For the whole case, madam, not for a single item. So who wants to hit me on the head and take the whole bloody lot?" You see, I'm still working on their sympathies. And it worked. One of the husbands, who had turned up by this stage, then ordered a three-hundred-quid chain. So I'm in profit, even if I have lost a chain.

'But this is small-time thieving. It's a dangerous game walking around some of these places with thirty-six grand's worth of stuff in an attaché case. I can tell you. I've had a few near misses over the years. I was in this block of flats in Birmingham one time and I was the only white face to be seen. My heart's pounding, and I'm gripping my case. There are these four big black guys in the lift with me, and I'm already thinking that I've been set up. There had been a single order, you see, from one of the flats on the top floor. So this big black guy turns to me and says, "Which floor are you going to, Doctor?" You see, I was wearing a pinstriped suit, a collar and tie, and was carrying this attaché case. So I played along with it.'

A close friend of Bob's, however, who also worked for the same company, was not so lucky. He had been mugged in Moss Side in Manchester. As he emerged from one house he was hit over the head with an iron bar and knocked unconscious. He was off work for a fortnight. 'And the worst thing about it,' said Bob, 'was that he was treated like a bloody criminal by the police for a fortnight. The police always seem to assume that it's an inside job, even if you're lying in the gutter with your brains smashed in. They think that you were involved in it somehow or other. My pal's carried all his jewellery in a sports holdall rather than an attaché case since the mugging.'

Bob had a theory about the violence that goes along with such robbery. 'The problem with muggings is that the people who do them always get so hyped up beforehand. They think that they're going to have to do you, so even if you offer to hand over the case of jewellery they end up doing you just the same. If anyone tried to mug me I'd hurt them, for the simple reason that I know they'd end up doing me anyway, so I might as well leave my mark on them. That way, they'd have to go to hospital sooner or later, and you stand at least some chance of getting your gear back. If you end up losing your gear, then you know that you're going to be the number-one suspect and that's not very pleasant, believe me. That's the negative side of the business, but on the plus side there's the thrill of selling, although you have to have a sense of humour for this job.

'I've got a joke for every occasion. OK, try this one: What do ostriches, pelicans and poll tax collectors have in common? . . . They can all shove their bills up their ass. I've been using this joke on some of the estates where the poll tax isn't too popular. Or did you hear the one about this fellow who went to the ticket office at the train station, and said, "Two tickets to Nottingham, please" (in that very nasal, blocked-up voice from the TV advert). So the guy from the ticket office says, "What you need is some Tunes." And the other guy says, "Why, do they cure cerebral palsy?" I use this joke all over the place. You need a good sense of humour in this business.'

Bob has spent a lifetime in direct selling, and telling jokes; it has not always been jewellery, although he reckons jewellery is easy. 'The basic argument with jewellery is that you have it for ever. It will give you years of pleasure, even after you've forgotten what you've paid for it. You buy it now and you even get two years to pay it off, so it's cheaper than it would be in two years' time. You get a new jacket, on the other hand, and the same time next year it's out of fashion. I've sold everything. I used to sell Calor gas heaters. They produced so much condensation that one woman rang the water board because she thought she'd got a leak. Then it was fitted suits. You should have seen the state of some of those suits – hanging right off the poor

80

bastards who ordered them. One salesmen couldn't fill in the forms correctly with all the details. I put it to him, "Have you ever seen someone with a fifty-six-inch waist, and a forty-inch chest?" Then it was safety rings for children to wear in the water, which came in the shape of ducks. With these particular rings, when the kids went into the water the ring turned over. There were all these complaints from parents that their children had been nearly drowned with them. Then it was furniture, now it's jewellery. It's all the same to me, to be honest. But the truth is with jewellery we get a lot of respect from the police for carrying this much jewellery around with us. I was in an accident last year, when my car went down a ditch. You should have seen this copper's face when I told him what was in my attaché case. He climbed down and got it for me. When I told him where I'd been with the gear he told me I deserved a medal. Well, it's all a service to the public, I told him. Somebody has to be prepared to do it.'

I offered to take Mark back to HQ, back to the little room with all the graphs and all the noughts and all the laughter. I asked him if he fancied the work. How big a nobble would it be for him to work as part of this team? I was just about to turn on to the road that winds up to the shop when Mark said that he wanted to go to the gym instead.

Everybody's Favourite Uncle

It was spitting with rain and the pavement was already slimy. It was mid-summer. We were standing on a street, appropriately called Spital Hill, outside a pawnbroker's. I was with Derek, an up-and-coming middleweight with, some said, considerable promise. 'Brendan says that soon I'll be a big hit in Sheffield,' Derek would tell anybody who listened. I liked the way this sounded. For days I had been running round saying I was hanging out with a guy who was going to be 'a big hit' in Sheffield. Derek was between fights. Not so much resting as waiting. 'I'm training every day. I'm in great shape. I'm in better shape at the moment than I was when I was last fighting.'

Derek had bought a large gold chain with the purse from his last fight. It had cost him two hundred pounds, exactly half the total purse. He had bought it off a mate from the same gym. 'My mate told me that it would be worth twice that in the shops,' said Derek. 'I've always wanted a nice, heavy gold chain. One with real weight to it. I've seen them in the shops.' But now, exactly two months later, Derek had run out of cash. However, for the first time in his life he had got something of value. 'Some c-o-l-l-a-t-e-r-a-l.' Derek liked playing with the sounds of words. He liked transforming them, modulating them, giving them an almost onomatopoeic quality. 'S-o-m-e c-o-l-l-a-t-e-r-a-l.' Derek stood with his collateral compressed tightly in the palm of his right hand. I swear I noticed that the chain was making his palm black, but I couldn't say anything. I looked around instead. Some youths sheltered in a doorway, sharing a cigarette. They looked as though they had been sheltering there for a while. The rain was probably just a suitable excuse. One large black man ran out of the bookies into an extravagantly large red BMW. Its registration number terminated in a 'Y'. I had noticed the hoardings all morning.

'Business to let'. I had read somewhere that 900 businesses were going bust every week. And we'd been through it all before. That was the worst thing about it. The North recovered from the last recession quite a bit later than the rest of the country, and here it was back again. It wasn't just Derek with his back to the wall. This new recession was evident everywhere you looked, or nearly.

'What recession?' said Colin Brown. 'Business is booming at the moment.' Colin Brown was the owner not just of the shop on Spital Hill but also of the biggest privately owned pawnbrokers' chain in the country, Herbert Brown and Son. 'My first name is Herbert, and my oldest son is called Herbert. It's something of a tradition in our family, as is pawnbroking itself. Ours is a family business going since 1840; we're now in the fifth generation and we're still expanding. My father really built the business up. He belonged to the old school of business. He couldn't bear to see his employees idle. If he caught them doing nothing he would throw a tin of pawnbroker's pins all over the floor and get them to pick them up. Sometimes it takes that kind of attitude to make a success of things. Pawnshops had a bit of a bad period a few years ago, but now business has really picked up. I have twenty-one businesses in various parts of the country, and I'm in the process of looking around for several more. One of our shops is in Westminster, but we haven't had an MP in yet, at least to the best of my knowledge. Our policy is that we try to open our pawnbrokers in an already existing family jewellers. That way we can employ the same staff, use the jeweller's basic expertise in valuing goods, and we can even share the same burglar alarm! Some family jewellers are finding things a little tight with this current recession. It's obviously quite attractive for them to go into business with a pawnbroker's. We complement each other rather nicely.'

It was hard not to like Colin Brown – he had that air of a country gentleman about him. I was not surprised to learn that his hobbies included hunting and fishing. He peered into the shop with a look of very mild distaste. 'That's the office in there,' he said as if pointing towards some woodland bolt hole. 'That's where it all happens.'

In Sheffield his business was attached to a jeweller's belonging to Keith Laycock, a family business dating back to 1918. The pawnbroker's had been operating from the premises for two years. 'If you haven't got a friend you come to us,' said Colin. 'That's our motto,

really. They call us "uncles", you know. We're everybody's uncle.'

Evidently, I thought. It was a wet Wednesday afternoon and this afternoon there were certainly a lot of people going to visit 'Uncle'. The pawnbroker's shop was a small private cubicle, with mirrored glass on two sides of it. The glass used to form the back of a cabinet, but Keith the jeweller couldn't bear to throw the glass out so he placed it on the walls on either side of the cubicle. The intention may have been to make this small cubicle look bigger, but the actual effect is to reflect infinite images of the desperate and the needy trying to get hold of some instant cash.

Twenty-three-year-old Sara Wood sat on the other side of the armour-plated glass, in front of a cabinet of scissors. The pride of Sheffield – the scissors, that is. This cabinet also belonged to the jewellers, but there they now sit, just behind Sara. 'We're a bit short of space,' she said by way of explanation. Many of the customers think that the case of scissors has been pawned by some desperate tool maker, but in fact it's there for convenience. There's also a panic button beside Sara, just in case things turn nasty. That's not there just for convenience. Sara watched me make faces in the mirror; they were the kind of mirrors that unfortunately invited this kind of behaviour. 'A lot of our customers think that they're two-way mirrors. I always tell them that they are – perhaps that's why they behave themselves so well when they're in here,' she said. 'I love the work. I got it through a job club. This was the first full-time job I ever had. I went four years without a proper job. I did some bar work, and some Christmas work at Ratner's. We get a lot of their stuff in, by the way, but we only pay the scrap price for it. When I started I had no idea of what pawnbroking was about, but I've taken to it like a duck to water. Many of the customers are really struggling, but I know what it feels like because I've struggled myself. I was unemployed for two years.'

But those years are now firmly behind her. She had found her niche, and she was evidently well suited to the job. 'It's all about dealing with people. You have to be very professional with them. Generally

Sara Wood. 'Pawnbroking is all about dealing with people. We have one Indian gentleman who comes in here and he gets down on his knees when we loan him money.'

speaking, the customers are extremely pleasant. They're coming to you for something. It's as if you're doing them a favour. We have one Indian gentleman who comes in here and he gets down on his knees when we loan him money. You don't get that kind of treatment when you work in a shop.' I noticed that some of Derek's colour was draining from him; he looked as if the same kind of behaviour might be expected of him.

Sara appeared not to notice. 'Some of the customers bring in chocolates and flowers and drinks. Well, I've been promised these sorts of things, but I haven't actually got any of them yet. Some people are extremely apologetic, they say that they've never done anything like this before. It's my job to put them at their ease. I tell them that it's not something to be embarrassed about. Plenty of nice, respectable people have to visit a pawnbroker's at some time in their life. That's what I tell them. One or two of our customers are really nasty. One bloke tried to make my life a misery, but I stood up to him and now he's as good as gold.'

Colin pulled me aside. 'Look at that nice young girl there in the purple shell suit. She's not embarrassed at all – she's probably an unmarried mum. She's just pawned a gold chain and a ring for fifteen pounds. If she gets it back in six months it'll cost her just twenty-four pounds. It's cheap instant cash, and a great service to the public that we're operating. Of course, some customers do try to pawn stolen goods. If they arouse our suspicions we quite simply won't accept the goods off them. The police are not entitled to come and look through our stock. They can only come here if they have a specific enquiry and there is something they're looking for. Some people think that pawnbrokers are full of stolen goods, but this isn't true. The reality is quite different. Ninety-four per cent of our pledges are taken out again.'

'A lot of our customers are regulars,' said Sara, 'pawning the same stuff month after month to keep themselves going until the next Giro arrives from the Social Security. They wouldn't try to pawn anything stolen, because they wouldn't be able to come in again, and that would be a disaster for them.'

The first customer that afternoon, apart from ourselves, was a thin lady, who looked in her late forties, but I had this sneaking suspicion that she was probably younger. She was pawning her engagement ring. I stood in this toilet of a pawnbroker's just behind her, trying to make polite conversation. 'What do you think of the mirrors?' I asked, to the back of her head. She turned round and looked at me as if I was daft. 'I don't notice them. I'm not in here to look at myself, you know. I'm in for my money and that's all.' Perhaps she thought that I was trying to chat her up. I hadn't got round yet to explaining what I was doing there. She turned her back on me and towards Sara, who was filling in the ledger with details of all the other engagement rings, wedding rings, gold watches and CD players and videos and power tools that had once belonged to the great citizens of Sheffield before they got desperate. 'Doesn't your hand get tired with all that writing?' asked the customer of Sara. 'Yeah, a bit,' said Sara, concentrating on her book-keeping. 'How much am I getting today?' the woman asked in a tone of slight irritation, and Sara by way of response handed over ten pounds, or rather ten pounds minus the six per cent ticket money charge. Nine pounds forty was all she was to get for her engagement ring, and on that nine pounds forty she has to pay ten per cent interest per month up to the sixth and final month. The APR on this borrowing is 175.56 per cent. The goods are sold on the eighth month. 'It's cheap, instant cash,' said Colin again.

'It's bloody expensive, but it's a lifeline,' said the woman who had just been divested of her ring.

Next into the pawnbrokers came a black guy in his mid to late twenties. He was wearing a smart black jacket, made of leather of the very softest variety, smart black trousers, and dapper, highly polished black shoes. He looked the part and rolled his shoulders in a confident manner on his way in. He wasn't put off by the fact that this far-from-large cubicle was already occupied. He'd come in for his gold watch. It was a make that I had never heard of but Sara told me that it was solid gold. He pulled a thick wad of notes out of his back pocket and peeled them off in front of her. I asked him if there was any chance of an interview. He said, 'No way. People only come here when they're under pressure, they don't want to be interviewed by the likes of you.' I was forced to agree with him. Behind him stood a man in work clothes, trying to pawn a chain which he assured Sara was solid gold. 'It was a present from my last girlfriend,' he explained. 'She had quite a lot of loot. It must be a really good one. She had plenty of money, plenty, and I meant a lot to her. It must be worth loads.' Sara examined it carefully. 'I'm afraid I can't loan you anything on this particular one.' 'You mean it's worthless?' Sara hesitated. 'Well, presumably it's of some sentimental value. Everything's worth something, you know. Everything, no matter what.' Despite all this home-grown philosophy, the workman shuffled back out again, avoiding eye contact at all costs. I thought that he might cry. Derek was now a ghostly white.

Next in was a young man in a smart, lizard-look jacket, and a classy modern tie. I'd noticed he'd got out of a white Honda Prelude with a personalized number plate. He was trying to pawn a watch and some other bits and pieces – all gold. The watch was a gold Omega in a presentation case, and he was looking for £200 for the lot. He had that kind of natural confidence that transcends embarrassing situations, and he was prepared to talk. 'I'm looking to pay off some personal debts,' he said. 'Basically, I'm mortgaged up to the hilt. I've got a car loan, a business loan, and a personal loan. The watch is insured for a grand, but I'm just looking for two hundred quid for it, a wedding ring and a brooch. I run a second-hand furniture business and basically I've got a cash-flow problem that I have to get through.' He had gone into linguistic overdrive to distance himself from the shabby position in which he now found himself. He said that he found the pawnbroker in *Yellow Pages*. He didn't look older than twenty-five. It turned out that his was a family business. 'The recession is hard at the moment but they say that it doesn't really hit the second-hand furniture trade, there's always a demand for what we're selling. That's what they say. I could have gone to the bank but I'm right up to the hilt with them anyway. It's basically quite a tricky situation.'

Sara took the gold Omega into the jewellers next door to be valued by Keith. She came back looking slightly glum. She explained that she could only go up to £100 for the lot. You could see that his pride was hurt. This was one upwardly mobile individual falling back to earth fast. He said that it wasn't enough. He didn't look so much angry as hurt and saddened by the whole thing. You could see that he was wondering what to do now. He couldn't decide whether to argue about the amount offered or leave with what remained of his dignity. In the end he just left.

'You can see for yourself that we get people from all over Sheffield in here,' said Keith, the jeweller. 'It's not just people from Burngreave and Spital Hill who come here, although we do have a good passing trade from the bookmaker's next door. We get people from the posh bits of Sheffield as well – Totley, Dore, Ranmoor and Fulwood – who want some instant cash but don't want to go to a pawn shop near where they live. Some of the people who come here are really desperate. It cuts you up when you see some young unmarried mum whose money's run out come in with her kid to pawn the wedding ring for five pounds, but that's how desperate some people can be. And to be honest with you, we get quite a few publicans in here. I'm not sure why that is, but I think that it's because the husbands and wives who run pubs always like to wear a lot of good jewellery and, because publicans pay for a lot of things by cash, they run out of money mid-week. We also get quite a few gypsies in, pawning their stuff for safe-keeping. We have a solid gold knuckle-duster in fourteen-carat gold at the moment. It's in the shape of a lion's head. It's pretty tacky, really. Some of the goods we take are quite pricey. We got a £2,700 Rolex in this week – the customer got £700 for it. But most of the stuff we take is bundles of gold necklaces and gold rings.'

'Electrical goods are also popular,' explained Sara. 'We loan twenty-five pounds on a video-recorder, and thirty pounds if it's got a remote control. The technology changes so rapidly that you can't loan any more. We also loan thirty pounds for a microwave. Of course, we can't tell whether such electrical equipment works or not. In the case of microwaves, we usually just check if the light goes on and the turntable goes round. Because we're based in Spital Hill we get quite a few West Indians in. Some of them like gold jewellery and like a flutter in the bookies next door. If they have a good win they can come into the jeweller's and buy something nice, which they can always keep for a rainy day to pawn. It's like taking out an insurance policy. They'll make jokes about it sometimes. And some of the enquiries are quite funny, as well. We had one lady ring up and ask would we take her portable jacuzzi. She said it would fit into a Ford Escort van. I had a word with Keith and he said that if she could get it folded so we could get it into our safe, then we'd take it. We had a good laugh about that one, but she never came in, after all.

'On the other hand, there are some really sad cases. We had one woman come in last week and pawn her gold tooth. She just took it out of her mouth right in front of us and handed it across the counter.

It was all hot and wet and had a bit of wire attached to it. Now she must have been really desperate. She got six pounds for it, minus the ticket money, of course. She came back to claim it after three days. You never ask why they need the money that desperately. Of course, some people get a bit surprised at what their valuables are actually worth. We had one lady in here, from the posh end of Sheffield, who brought in a bracelet she'd bought in Marrakesh. It was stamped eighteen-carat gold. She'd spent three hundred pounds on it but was told that it was worth a lot more than that by the man who sold it to her in Morocco. I had it valued by Keith, and to be honest it was worthless. She got very agitated when I told her because she said that her husband would kill her. Her husband warned her not to buy it in the first place. She was really terrified of having to go home to face him. And she was from the poshest bit of Sheffield. You wonder what goes on in some of those big houses, behind closed doors. I love this job, because you can learn a lot about human relations working here.'

Finally, it was Derek's turn. He handed over the gold chain, paid for with his blood in a bout in Mansfield. Sara shook her head slowly. I left before she said anything more.

Top-notch Gear

The first thing you see is the queue for the nightclub. It usually stretches out from the door down towards the steps and right along the glass office block. The queue starts early. It was long that night. Just the way the VIPs, with their gold cards, liked it. They say that it feels marvellous to walk right up past them – the respectable citizens of this fine old town – all queuing in the frigging rain. Soaked to the bloody skin. I just find it a little embarrassing trying to jump the queue. You can feel all these eyes in your back.

That night the door staff had got everything in hand. They had managed to get the ordinary punter right up against the wall, leaving a little space to the right. This space is important. It gives the doormen a chance to see past the ordinary punter. They can then watch you as you arrive, and nudge the ordinary punter even closer to the wall. Just enough room to squeeze in, in front of the paying customer – the mugs standing freezing in the rain. Sometimes the queue gets a little sensitive and the gap closes. The doormen peer over their heads looking out for the likes of me. Then you need a little deception. 'Er, Mr Beattie, there's a call for you inside,' said one doorman. I hurried in, winking at him as I passed. I could hear a female voice behind me, still waiting in the rain. 'Hey, is he a famous footballer or somebody like that?'

It's the 'somebody' that you can grow to like. They know that you must be a somebody, if you can skip the queue like that, even if you do it somewhat reluctantly. It may all seem a little pathetic, but it's still better than being a nobody.

That night the club was packed. The ordinary punter would walk in and get hit with all these bodies, all this noise, all this disarray. I could just see order. I walked slowly to the hallowed ground – the wine bar, but it was more than just a wine bar. There is an invisible line on the floor, which the ordinary punter feels unable to pass, and three critical steps. There was a doorman at the top of these steps. He was a pal. He shook my hand as I passed. He's there to spot any trouble in the club and to stop any punter passing with a pint mug in his hand, but his presence is symbolic. One observant manager of the club once told me that it took me three years to make it up those steps. And probably another three before I could order a drink. But that was then, when I was still an ordinary punter, when I was still a mug.

On a good night you can know everyone in this Northern nightclub. Tonight, Big Alex is in his favourite spot, just to the right of the edge of the top bar. I got my Tag Heuer watch off him. Nineteen quid, it cost. Of course, it's not real. But it looks the part in here, in this dim light. You can only tell that it's snide when you take it off. If you take it off, that is. It's as light as a feather. But I never take it off, except in bed.

You don't have to have money to have style. That's what they say around here. It's just as well. You get to know all the other VIPs – the big hitters and the rest. Bernard was by the pillar, he's big in fire insulation for factories. He was talking to Brian. Brian owned his own hairdresser's, or he did once. I heard that he was currently unemployed. But he can get in here for nothing, and he can make half a lager last a very long time indeed. Some other VIP will always buy him a drink. Perhaps things are a little vague sometimes. But here we're all superstars. For a while.

I was standing there enjoying the ambience. The ordinary punters were running around desperate for their three hours away from the wife or the husband. Their three hours of freedom. I was taking it nice and steady. Mick came up to me, Mick 'The Bomb', Mick the bouncer, or the security consultant as he likes to put it these days. He was wearing a sort of startled expression, as if he had just seen something truly awful. He asked me to turn around. I thought for a second that somebody had been sick over my back. 'Do you know that you've got creases all down the back of your jacket?' he said. 'Never,' I said, without any reflection. 'I know exactly what you need,' said Mick, taking hold of my arm. 'Some upmarket clobber. Some top-notch gear. Do you know I could get you an Yves St Laurent for a hundred quid, or a Louis Feraud for one hundred and fifty?' I may be a VIP but I had never heard of Louis Feraud. I thought it might be because of how he was saying it. He became a little defensive. 'You've never heard of Louis Feraud? You'll be telling me next that you've never heard of Bruno Kirches or Van Kollem? What about Armani, have you heard of that?' I said that I had heard of Armani. 'Thank God for that. I thought you might be into Man at C&A for a moment there.' He started smoothing the creases in my suit. The creases which, I have to confess, only he seemed able to detect.

'Look, you can sleep in the back of your car with the quality of suit I'm offering you. Wake up, give it a shake, and there won't be a crease in it. Not like that crap you're wearing.' He pulled my jacket open a shade aggressively, and peered at the label. 'Principles? Fucking Principles. What's a VIP like you doing shopping in Principles? How much did that cost you? One hundred and twenty quid? You were fucking well robbed. Feel the material of this jacket.' And he lifted my hand and placed it on the arm of his suit. I didn't know whether to stroke the material or squeeze the muscle bulging right through the suit that never creases.

'Marvellous,' is all I could think of to say.

'Where are the suits?' I asked, my voice descending into a whisper. 'They're in the toilet,' replied Mick at full volume. 'Just tell Tom that Mick sent you.' I pushed my way past the ordinary punters, now swaying gently in their alcohol-induced haze, and headed towards the toilet. Tom, the toilet attendant, was looking harassed, as the ordinary punters tried to spray themselves with the aftershave sitting out for them without paying the customary twenty pence. 'Come on, lads, it's twenty pence a shot. I've got plenty of change,' he said, as aftershave dispensers fired off indiscriminately into the surrounding ether. 'I'm here to have a look at the suits,' I whispered conspiratorially in Tom's ear. I didn't want the ordinary punter to get a hint of what was going on between the men in the know. I stood there wondering if Tom was going to direct me into one of the cubicles. Instead, he told me to stay where I was. He nipped out for a second and came back with three suits in a binliner. He unpacked them in front of everybody. Another VIP came into the toilet. 'Are you getting into the dry-cleaning business?' he asked helpfully. And then winked. He knew the score.

'Try them on,' Tom suggested. Unfortunately, you could have fitted two of me into the Louis Feraud. 'The arms need taking up a little,' said Tom. By now there was more than a little interest being shown by the passing trade of the ordinary punter in the toilet. 'Have you got it in a forty-four?' asked one punter, slurring every syllable as he did so. Tom told him that these suits were way out of his league.

'You can try on the trousers as well, if you like,' suggested Tom, as one pair of trousers landed on the floor of the toilet. When he picked them up, there was a wet stain on one leg. I didn't fancy being blamed for causing the stain, so I declined the offer. 'The trousers might be a bit long, but you can always have them taken up,' added Tom, continuing his sales pitch. Tom's prices seemed to be a little different from those mentioned earlier. The Louis Feraud had risen inexplicably to two hundred pounds. I pointed this discrepancy out to him. He told me to go back and check the prices with Mick. I then confessed that I didn't even have a hundred on me in cash. He assured me that the money would do tomorrow night. 'If we can't trust a VIP like you, who can we trust? After all, you are a regular.'

I went back out to look for Mick to query the prices. Mick explained that Tom had given me the price of the Louis Feraud for the ordinary punter. 'Not that I'd ever try to sell to the ordinary punter, you understand. I'm offering you the suit at cost.' My body language must have been leaking a slight reluctance. So Mick called over two other VIPs from the wine bar, Phil and Mark. Both were wearing immaculate suits. Mick asked them to do a twirl for me. Phil, the taller of the two, told me that the waists tended to be a bit big on these cut-price suits, but all I needed was a good trendy belt to pull the waist in. He told me that Mick might even throw one in for nothing. 'He can get you a shirt to go with the suit as well, if you like, for a tenner. All designer gear.' Phil stood right in front of me modelling the suit, running his hands up and down the lapels like some gentleman tailor. He even offered his own sales pitch. 'Do you know that you can sleep in the back of your car with this quality of suit, wake up, give it a shake and there won't be a crease in it.' The only problem with this spiel was that it did not sound very original. I started seriously to consider whether everyone in the club was working on a commission basis. After a while, I started to wonder how many of these VIPs habitually had to sleep in their cars at the end of an average night.

When Mick went off to tour the club to do some security con- sultancy, I asked Phil where he thought Mick might get the suits from. I wanted to know how hot they really were. Phil had a slightly different understanding from myself of their provenance. 'Working in a place like this you're bound to get to know people. And a lot of people remember Mick from his boxing days,' he said. 'He probably gets them at cost from the factory. All I know is that they're top notch and they're cheap. I don't ask anything else.'

It might have been my imagination, but the question seemed to have irritated Phil, dressed from head to toe in his top-notch clothes, which came from God knows where. He stood incessantly sipping his half of lager, gazing out into the great unknown of the ordinary punter. Finally, he turned to me. 'Look, if you want to pay full price for your gear, go ahead. The next thing you'll be saying is that you want to queue in the rain to get in here with the rest of the mugs. I'm sure Mick could arrange that for you, if you ask him.'

It was a long night. I eventually started to leave the club, with my new Louis Feraud clutched tightly under my arm. It was wrapped in half a binliner. Mick shook my hand as I departed. 'You'll look like a proper VIP in that suit,' he said, 'even if you do have to sleep in the back of your car tonight.' He laughed as he glanced at his watch. It was now four o'clock in the morning, and the birds were starting to sing.

Mr Big

Up in Rotherham, when it comes to the fight game, Bernard is Mr Big. Big fan, big benefactor, one day maybe a promoter. 'There'll be no dead bodies in the ring when Bernard promotes,' Mick Mills had told me. 'They'll be going in there to scrap. Bernard will make sure that the ordinary punter gets value for money.' Bernard is the self-made man of legend. From Dalton in Rotherham to Dallas-style housing. 'You wanna see his house. It's only half done but you wanna see it. If he brings a bird back there, she'll be easing her knickers down as she goes up the drive.' Up in Dalton there are few role models. You fight your way out one way or the other. Locally, they call it the Bronx. Bernard got out, now he wanted to put something back. The rumour was that Bernard wanted to transform the equestrian centre on his new estate into a training facility for local boxers. 'He wants to give the lads up here a chance. He wants to help others. He knows it's hard in Dalton, and harder now with all the pits closing.'

Bernard had come up the hard way. I was told that he had been shot when he was younger. But there was nothing glamorous about this shooting. He was shot by accident when he was out rabbiting, in a strange old-fashioned place where rabbiting still meant hunting rabbits rather than shooting your mouth off. 'But he can still fight like fuck,' I was told. Everyone was talking about Bernard as if their future depended upon it. For some their future probably did.

I was to meet him in a dark, dreary bar at noon. I recognized a colleague in the corner. I described Bernard to him. 'There's a couple of likely-looking lads here. Look at those two in the corner.' In a dark recess sat the two likely-looking lads – Chris Woods and Danny Wilson, then of Sheffield Wednesday. This was a lesson not to jump to hasty conclusions. Bernard was waiting patiently. The first thing to say about Bernard is that he looks the part. You don't have to look too closely to see it. Everything is out in the open. Everything is big and chunky and out on display on his thickly set body.

It's useful to get these sort of credentials sorted out at the very beginning.

'Is that a real watch?' I asked, trying to break the ice.

'Oh yes, that's real,' answered Bernard. It was a funny sort of opening. I laughed about it afterwards. We were not discussing the veridical nature of perception, or the philosophical problems posed by sense data. We were not discussing whether the watch was real or merely an illusion. We both knew what we were talking about.

'Of course it's bloody real. Feel the weight of the thing. That didn't cost me fourteen quid down in some shady club. That was about eleven thousand nicker. If I was walking the streets of Las Vegas or New York I might take it off because it is a little bit ostentatious, but if I'm walking the streets of Sheffield or Rotherham I leave it on. It's a Rolex Oyster. With a day date,' he added for effect. Exactly what this additional information conveyed was unclear to me, except that the watch told you the date. However, if I knew anything about Rolexes, which I don't, it probably would have told me a great deal more.

'I bought it in Miami,' he continued, 'and then I had the diamonds put all around the face in Las Vegas. They're real diamonds. The watch were eight thousand and the diamonds were three thousand. That's where I get my eleven thousand from.' Bernard was counting every penny in that careful Yorkshire fashion, making sure that it all added up.

I asked Bernard if I could feel it. I've held snide Rolexes so light that the wind in the corner of a bar in a nightclub could carry them away. Paper-thin, like the veneer of their owners. This one was heavy, like a lump of lead. I started apologizing about leaving sticky marks on the face of it. Bernard sat back and took a long hard puff on his cigarette. 'Don't worry, lad, examine it all you want.'

I began by asking Bernard to explain how he had made it in these hard times. But this was the kind of account that Bernard liked to avoid, not because there was anything dodgy or unseemly about it, rather it was because it was all about graft. In Dalton you take graft for granted. You can safely assume that making anything, let alone millions, takes graft; you can safely assume that moving out of Dalton to any other part of Rotherham takes graft. You don't talk about graft. They graft in the mines and in the steel works. It's a fact of life.

'I made my money in fire protection for factories, you see, cladding steel work. I was a millionaire by the time I was thirty-nine, that were three years ago. The business is really pretty obvious if you think about it. In the eighties everything was being built in a hurry, but you need to protect these structures against fire. I got in there at the right time and worked hard at it. Now I like to live like a millionaire. I spent a third of a million quid on a villa in Spain. It's in La Manga Country Club on the Costa Blanca. I'm also having a Victorian house in Sheffield done up with about twenty-eight acres attached. I've had it gutted and done it really nice. By the time it's done, there'll be a million quid's worth of house there. It's nice to have the money to buy the things you like. I bought my daughter Kerry a gold sequinned suit worn by Marilyn Monroe for her fourteenth birthday. It cost me two grand and came with a letter of authenticity and photos of Marilyn wearing it on her honeymoon with Joe Di Maggio. But my big hobby is boxing. I've seen all the big fights. Buster Douglas *v* Evander Holyfield at the Mirage, Bruno *v* Tyson at the Hilton Hotel, Las Vegas. It's more than a hobby. If I'd had the talent, it would have been my way out of Dalton. I've got a lot in common with the boxing boys.'

Bernard reached inside his orange jacket and pulled out a large wad of photographs. 'Just in case you think I'm all talk. Here's a photograph of Eddie Murphy, which I took myself.' He passed me a photograph of the back of the head of some black man in a blue blazer. It could indeed have been the back of Eddie Murphy's head, but it could also have been the back of anyone else's head. 'Here's a photo of Mr T from the 'A' team, with a gold knife, a fork and a spoon round his neck. Do you watch *The A Team*? It's on TV on a Saturday morning. When I bumped into Mr T he turned round to me and said, "From the ghetto to this." Here's a photo of Thomas Hearns and his henchmen, and here's one of Frank Bruno at the weigh-in for his fight with Mike Tyson. You can see that Frank is shitting himself there. Here's one of Frank where he seems to be hiding behind the curtains. In my view Frank lost it right then. My dad was a big boxing fan. He always wanted to see Muhammad Ali in action, but he could never have afforded anything like that. He was a miner all his days. He ended up

Mick Mills and Bernard, Mr Big from Rotherham. 'You wanna see his house,' says Mick. 'If he brings a bird back there, she'll be easing her knickers down as she goes up the drive.'

as a cripple walking on two sticks. He's dead now. So are the mines,' Bernard added after a moment's pause.

Bernard was making up for all that his father had missed. 'I'm a big fan of world championship boxing. It cost me five grand to take me and two of my boxing pals to one of these fights. I offered to take Mick Mills with me because of his involvement in his early days with boxing. He's a pal of mine from Dalton. One of the roughest little fuckers ever to come out of the place. He's broken six jaws – only one of them in the ring. Mind you, he's had his own jaw broken, but that was in a professional fight. The only trouble with Mick is that he had a raw deal. It's not the boxers that get the cash unless they're right at the top of the tree. I saw the trip as a reward for his efforts. I brought Gary as a travelling companion for Mick. I went first class, so Mick would have been on his own. I stayed in the Mirage, and Mick and Gary stayed in one of the smaller hotels. So Mick really needed a travelling companion. Gary is a bouncer, he's never really done any boxing, but he loves the sport and all the trimmings that go with it.'

So what was in it for Bernard? Was he as magnanimous as everyone was suggesting, or desperately needing to believe? Was he trying to do his bit for the boys who had not had his breaks? 'To be honest, it's a bit of a nobble to travel with two tough guys in tow. They look like my bodyguards. I've seen Arnold Schwarzenegger with his bodyguards, and Mike Tyson with his. When I walk into the Mirage with Gary and Mick beside me, I look like a VIP. I've spoken to Arnie and Iron Mike. I just walked up to Arnie and said to him, "Hi, Arnie, I've come all the way from Sheffield, England." Well, it's actually Rotherham, England, but I guess he wouldn't have heard of Rotherham, so that's why I said Sheffield. "Knives and forks, Arnie, knives and forks." He got my drift. "Do you mind if I get my photograph taken with you?" The Terminator and Bernard Atkinson from Rotherham, England. Something to show the lads back in Yorkshire. Iron Mike talked to me. I was sitting a few seats away from him. Only the best. Iron Mike came up to me and said "Shift!" At least I can say that I've spoken to one of the greatest scrappers this century.

'I like to be around boxers, I always have done. Do you know Big Clifton – the big black guy, the big heavyweight – I've bought him four or five hundred quid's worth of training tackle. It's because I like to be with them. I like the company. I like to talk to 'em. I just like to be around boxers. It's a tough sport. It's different to your ordinary everyday football matches. I definitely like the heavy-weights. I'll watch the other weights fighting, but I prefer the heavy boys.

'When I told Mick that he was going to Las Vegas with me he couldn't believe it. I told him a good three months before the trip actually happened. He told a lot of his friends who all live in the back of beyond. I wouldn't say that they live in the slums, but near enough. They all told him that I wouldn't take him, that I was just making it all up. Mick asked me two or three times: "Is it right, Bernard, are you really going to take me?" I said to him, "You just wait. You'll have the tickets in your pocket within a couple of weeks." He still couldn't believe it until I handed him his tickets. He was over the moon when he got them. He just couldn't thank me enough. I think

100

he thought it was the drink talking, and then it all became realism when he got the tickets in his fist.

'We flew from Manchester to Chicago and from Chicago to Las Vegas. It was lucky that Mick had flown before. He'd flown in his amateur days. He'd been out to New Zealand or wherever. I was in first class. Mick and Gary were in economy. I think that one of the things about Mick is that he's a very good talker. He had this oldish lady at the side of him, and I think that her earhole must have fell off by the time she got to Chicago. He talks like he's in the bloody launderette, like a bloody woman talking about what's gone off the day before. Mick is the type of person who can talk with almost anyone. We had a few drinks on the plane and talked to people mainly about the boxing. People were asking us why there were three chaps travelling together. I mean I don't think that they could weigh it up. They were asking us why we were going to America and we were telling them that we were going on to Las Vegas, to the Buster Douglas–Evander Holyfield fight. I think it excited them as well. I mean one or two people on board the plane were interested in boxing, so it was of interest to them.

'By the time we got to Las Vegas we were absolutely knackered. And I must admit that I went to bed, because I'd been to Las Vegas before, but I'm told that Mick and Gary just chucked their bags down and they were out. I don't think they went to bed for twenty-four hours, because they were that taken in by all the bright lights and the casinos and the slot machines and everything else. And also Mick and Gary like their food. In Las Vegas the food is really cheap. You can get a steak for a couple of quid. If you sit near the slots you can order a steak and they'll give it to you for nothing, and the drinks as well. I think that the size of the meals amazed them. And you could eat as much as you like in the casinos. Their revenue comes from the gambling. Mick and Gary had their own spending money. The only thing I paid for except for the flight was the hotel and the fight tickets.

'I stayed in the Mirage. I don't know what they were up to. They were out and about as soon as they arrived. I was very much the same on my first trip to Las Vegas. This was my third trip. I'd been previously to see the Bruno–Tyson fight, then the Tyson–Razor Ruddock match. I'd pretty much seen an awful lot of Las Vegas. The first time I stayed for four days, the second time for a week. I had time to adjust, to see the sights. I went into Johnny Tokos's gym, where Tyson trained. Johnny Tokos is a real old guy, about eighty, a typical trainer. We just shouted through the doors, "Can we come in, Johnny? We've come all the way from Rotherham, England." He invited us in and showed us around. Tyson wasn't in at that time. He had been training previously. We had a chat to old Johnny, and got to know a bit about him. Johnny were white, he was a white guy. He'd been in Las Vegas for many, many years. To be honest he didn't say a lot. He were quite an interesting guy, but when we asked him what shape Tyson was in, or how he thought Tyson'd fare against Bruno, he just told us that he would probably knock him out, and that he was training very hard. Tyson had gone through at least half a dozen sparring partners by the time I was there. I thought Johnny'd be a lot more forthcoming. At that time, Tyson was in the news a lot with Robin Givens and his divorce and all this business. The press were saying that he were in bad shape. I think Johnny Tokos had been told not to talk to anybody.

'On the trip with Mick and Gary I didn't see an awful lot of them. Where I stayed, in the Mirage, it's sort of out of bounds unless you're staying there. But as Mick generally does, he got in – by the pool. Mick has got the gift of the gab and the cheek of the devil. He got past the security guards no problem. I'm laying by the pool with a gin and tonic beside me. All of a sudden I get chucked in, and there's Mick and Gary stood there. Mick is in his Union Jack shorts, crew cut and dark glasses. He looked like one of the Blues Brothers. He says to me, "Bernard, I've met this coloured guy down the road and he's selling diamond rings." I said to him, "Mick, they'll not be genuine. These coloured guys are pretty fierce in what they do, and I don't think we should mess with them. The rings won't be genuine." But Mick says, "No, I've spoken to him, I've had a word with him. I've spent at least an hour talking to him. The rings have even got the tabs on. They're stamped. They're knocked off, like, but they're genuine." Mick had come to get me to go down there with him and to lend him some money. So we goes down to this car park, just down from the hotel in Las Vegas, and there's two black guys there stood waiting for us. Anyway, when we comes up to them Mick introduces me to them. So this black guy gets out a nice velvet cover that he had with all these diamonds with big chunks and I mean big chunks. They were as big as bottle tops. And we stood there in that car park bartering with them. The rings were marked up at ten thousand dollars, some were five thousand and one ring was twenty thousand dollars. I said to Mick, "Listen, these aren't real." But he says they are real, and he says, "Look, if you don't want to spend any money, lend me some." I ended up lending him a couple of hundred dollars. He had a few hundred himself, so he bought a few rings. I bought a couple as well, spending about a thousand dollars in all. Well, I had to. Mick kept telling me that they were real.

'I finished up buying the bloody things because of Mick. Mick had a bloody fistful of them. He had about three or four rings on his fingers. In fact, the rings looked that genuine that Mick was telling me how he was going to flog them when he got back to England for five or six thousand quid at a time and buy a big BMW. I must have been soft as a brush. Anyway, we're all walking back to the Mirage and we're all thinking that we've done a real good deal here. We kept looking at these rings, and they're shining in the sun. I mean they were really big carats, these diamonds. Two or three hours pass and I'd got these two gents' rings on my fingers. So I decide that I'm going upstairs for a shower. So I takes this ring off and it's green round my finger. So I gets on the phone to Mick, and I've got to admit this – I didn't know how I was going to handle it with Mick. I didn't want him to come round and spark me out. I'd better handle him a bit careful. But I was so annoyed. I rang Mick's room. There was an answering machine. I said, "Mick Mills. Phone Bernard immediately at the Mirage." I got in the shower. The next minute I hear Mick shouting, "Hello!" as he does. He says, "Your finger's green. Mine is an' all." I says to him, "You better get down to that car park and see if them black bastards are still there, and you'd better knock them out. In fact, I want them knocked out and I want you to get my money back." We'd spent nearly two thousand bucks on bloody rings. The black guys were never seen again. Me and Mick, two streetwise kids from the roughest part of Rotherham, had been ripped off in Las Vegas. I couldn't believe it. Mick tried for some compensation when he got home, by selling his ring. He sold his pair of rings to one of his mates for about three hundred quid. I gave him mine, and I told him I don't want to see the bloody rings ever again. I told him that if there's any money made on the sale he could keep it. I wanted nothing more to do with them. They just reminded me of the rip-off.'

In the course of this conversation Bernard had shifted from his usual laid-back style into a state of some tension, as he relived the great rip-off in Las Vegas. 'Green bloody fingers,' he was saying to himself. All this talk directed my gaze towards those digits from which all trace of that green metallic colouring had been scrupulously erased. But something on one of his fingers held my gaze. It was the biggest, chunkiest diamond ring I have ever seen. Even in the half-light of this dark bar at noon it sparkled. Surely not another Las Vegas special? Surely not another green genie?

'Er, Bernard. That's a beautiful ring there. Is it real?'

Bernard looked at me as if I had called his manhood into question. Here was a streetwise kid from Dalton who had become a millionaire, who had been to Las Vegas three times, who associated with boxers, who had taken this duffer for lunch only for this very same person to imply that despite having made one little mistake in his life in some dirty car park in Las Vegas he might be subject to other errors of judgement.

'Is this real? Of course it's bloody real. That were five thousand quid. I had that made up in Las Vegas.'

I had started to ask the next question before I could stop myself. 'Are you not worried about that not being genuine?'

Bernard nearly choked on his lump of steak. 'Not genuine! I got that in a proper shop. It was a jeweller's shop. It's a hell of a ring. I designed that. I told them what I wanted. It cost a lot less in the States than it would here, because the tax is a lot less over there. I haven't had it valued over here, but it cost me five grand to have it made.'

The diamond in this ring was the biggest I have ever seen. Improbably large in fact, impossibly chunky. Sometimes one has to be extremely delicate in interviews.

'That's a hell of a big stone.' I laughed nervously for at least five seconds as my comment terminated.

Bernard's affirmation came out low and deep, as if he was trying to work out what exactly I might be implying by this. Was it a compliment or a question, a statement or an interrogative, a shoulder pat or a kick down there in the nether regions from which the 'yeah' emanated.

104

'Did you buy that on the same trip as the one on which you were ripped off?'

'No. That were a different trip. I bought that in a shop where Mike Tyson was buying some jewellery. I can't remember the name of the shop but Tyson was there. If that shop was good enough for Mike Tyson then it was good enough for me. You see, I've been OK on every other trip. The first time I take Mick "The Bomb" Mills out with me is the first time I get bloody robbed. I thought I was taking Mick Mills out there for a bit of protection. That didn't happen – it was quite the reverse.

'On the trip with Millsie my luck just wasn't in. I also had a thousand bucks on Buster Douglas to beat Evander Holyfield. He didn't, of course, so I came back well unhappy. I'm not a gambler, I just like a little flutter, but my luck wasn't running with me on that trip. I just thought that Buster Douglas would be too big for Evander Holyfield, but Holyfield floored him in the third round.

'The fight itself was very disappointing on two counts. It didn't last long enough, and the undercard weren't very good. I think Buster Douglas just laid down in the third round. He got a clout on the chin, and he just laid down. He just took his money and run. I've learned that if you're going all that way you might as well go to a Don King promotion, because that way you see all the top boxers right down the card. This one wasn't a Don King promotion. I'd brought these lads all the way from Rotherham with me, and it were all a bit disappointing.

'But I'd still rather travel to Las Vegas than London to watch boxing, because you've got freedom of movement over there. You can move around without having burly bouncers telling you what to do. You can have a drink in your seat. You can have a cigarette. I can walk around shaking hands with Jack Nicolson, as I have done at the Razor Ruddock–Mike Tyson fight. Tyson brings all the stars in. I've shaken hands with Clint Eastwood. I've shaken hands with all these guys because they're all ringside, and I always sit ringside. It's about eight hundred pounds for a ringside ticket, but it's worth it. Eight hundred dollars, I mean, I get dollars and pounds mixed up. It was a bit of a nobble having Mick along with me, because Mick can do the business, if there's any trouble. There's no two ways about that. Mick would just knock them out. People like Jack Nicolson would have bodyguards with him, but the funny thing is that we didn't see them. Arnold Schwarzenegger were there. He probably had bodyguards as well. I shook hands with him as well, but his bodyguards didn't stop me. They kept out of sight as well. I arrived at the fight with Mick and Gary. Superstar. The secret in shaking hands with the stars is the approach. You have to let them know that you're going to approach them, rather than just rushing up to them. If you just rushed up to them, then that's when the bodyguards close in. You're far better off shouting, "Hi, Jack! Can I shake hands?" I think that if you just rushed up and put your hand there, then they might think you were going to shoot them or something. When Tyson fought Razor Ruddock the first time around, I was ringside but maybe six rows back. I went down to see Tyson when he got into the ring and I was standing just a foot away from him. I could have touched him. The supervisors asked me to move back. This guy from CBS heard my accent and started talking to me. He gave me a pass which enabled me to stand touching the ringside. It was a controversial decision in that fight because the referee stopped it in the seventh round. Everybody who was everybody got into the ring. This guy from CBS suggested that I should move away from the ring because he told me that "there'll be more pieces in that ring than in the average Western". When he said "pieces", he meant "guns". He told me that there was going to be some fireworks. It frightened me to death. I thought to myself, "Aye, aye, somebody's going to get shot here." I moved away from the ring, because everybody were throwing punches. The boxers, the promoters, the minders. That's not why I took Mick on my next trip, because I don't think that Mick Mills could do much with somebody with a gun anyway. It's just very nice to have somebody who's handy to the side of you. The funny thing is that they hadn't really heard of Mick "The Bomb" Mills over there. But the chap in London who organized the flight had heard of him. He knew Mick were an ex-boxer. But nobody else knew him out there. But that didn't bother me that much.

'You see, Millsie and me have a lot in common with these boxers and promoters, from the Bronx or wherever. People like Iron Mike and Don King have had it rough, but the fight game let them come through in the end. That's what I love about it. But my trips to the States have taught me something else about life over there. It's tough out there. I thought that I knew the score, coming from Dalton, but over there they're even meaner. But the next time Millsie and me go to the States we'll be ready for them. If I've learned anything coming from Dalton, it's that you only get burnt once. Just the once.'

Life on the Undercard

The Morning After

Steve Howden fought on the undercard of Prince Naseem Hamed's contest against Antonio Picardi in August 1994 at the Hillsborough Leisure Centre in Sheffield. Steve was another of Brendan's boys. A crowd-pleaser. He put up a terrific show, but the punters were wandering in and out during it. He was a warm-up man. From his appearance it was clear that Steve had a particular role to play. He was a skinhead covered in tattoos. I had been told that he had got his first tattoo at thirteen and his last one, the Geisha girl on his stomach, when he was fifteen. You wanted to boo as he entered the ring. It reminded me of wrestling, or the pantomime. But this wasn't acting. This was deadly serious. Steve's opponent, who didn't much like the look of him either, won on points. His opponent was clean-cut and good-looking.

Steve was twenty-five, and this was his eighth professional fight. He had won four of them. He seemed destined to a life on the undercard with a record like this, a fifty-fifty man. Steve had been out of the ring for nine months with a broken hand sustained in his last fight. He's a family man with two daughters – Chelsea, four, and Perry Louise, six months. He had booked three days holiday from Fletcher's Bakery where he works as a fork lift driver to recuperate after the fight. He told me that he was on a lot of overtime at work at the time so he was earning about two hundred and fifty a week. He usually gets a little more than a week's wages for a fight. It's hard graft, because of the amount of training required.

After the fight at Hillsborough he went to his in-laws to talk through the fight with his father-in-law, who's a keen fight fan and who was ringside that night to watch him. He had a couple of oranges to drink with his father-in-law. His eyes were puffed up and his wife asked him, for the first time, to pack in the boxing. This was the first time he'd ever been marked in a fight. His wife said she didn't want him to end up as the Elephant Man, with kids in the street running around after him calling him names.

We sat in the gym in Newman Road on the morning after the fight, Steve nursing his cuts and bruises from the night before. He was at the gym for his money. He reckoned it was going to be about six hundred quid for this one, but he wasn't sure. He began by talking me through his professional record. 'I won the first fight of my professional career, then I lost three on the trot. I got stopped in two, and then Brendan pulled me out with a shoulder injury in my third. The next one on my comeback I was boxing down in Great Yarmouth, against a lad called Edwards, who was recently an ABA champion. I knocked him out in nine seconds with my first punch. It felt brilliant. It was the first fight where I'd actually stopped somebody.'

I asked him to describe the feeling. 'It were a right good feeling. I went into the ring and I saw him stood there, a big black muscley guy, and he put fear up me. I was right scared when I first saw him. He came out with a right, I ducked it and caught him with a left hook, and he just stood there, and I thought, "What's happening here?" And then he just went over. He went straight over and fell on the floor and that were it. It were all over. I felt on top of 'world. It were brilliant. For a second or two I didn't realize what had happened. Then the referee just waved it all over.'

This may have been Steve's first knockout in the ring, but I asked if he had ever knocked anybody out outside the ring. I felt that I was responding to how he looked.

'I've had a few knockouts on the street. I used to be fighting all the time until I started with Brendan. I first met up with Brendan on an enterprise scheme, called Starting Point, about nine years ago. I'd had two amateur fights with another club before then. I've got a twin brother, Jamie, and me and him were always in street fights and gang fights up in Parson's Cross, which is a pretty rough area. We used to be fighting all the time. At first me and Jamie were fighting everybody on the enterprise scheme as well. And then I got teamed up with Brendan. He split me and my brother up because we were that bad, and Jamie got a painting and decorating course, and I went with Brendan on a gardening course. Then he took all the trainees over to the gym. He had fourteen of us all going into the ring. He used to put gloves on us so we could have a fight – all the lads, and sometimes the lasses as well. The lasses were right rough, so they enjoyed having a go. This was a scheme for lads and lasses who were in trouble constantly, but Brendan put us on the right road. He used to have an allotment at Rivelin, and we used to go out there and do a lot of gardening for him, and he used to take us into pubs for a game of snooker, and an orange. He got us all straightened out. None of us were getting into trouble at home any longer. We all straightened ourselves out, and most of us now have gone on and got married and calmed down.'

I asked him what had become of his twin brother.

'Jamie couldn't take up boxing. He fractured his skull when he was younger, fighting in the street. And he's broken his arms a few times fighting, and his hands are all bashed up. He's got right weak hands with smashed knuckles, so he never actually got into boxing, but sometimes he used to come down here with me and watch me train.'

I wanted to know which felt better – knocking somebody out on the street or in the ring?

'It's better in the ring. If you're fighting in the street you're not getting any money for it. It's a waste of time, really. There's no real satisfaction in just knowing that you've knocked somebody out. Only you and the other kid might know about it. In the ring it goes nation-wide. Everybody knows that you've done it. But me and my brother were always fighting in the street, when we were about thirteen or fourteen year old. We were fighting every other night. I was a good fighter. I was a bit dangerous with me head, which I can't use in the ring. I'd just go close up to them and then all of a sudden I'd turn and headbutt them, and then start punching them. I'd always go for the nose, because the eyes start watering and they can't see nowt then. Then you start punching them, and that's when you do all the damage. I've always liked to use the head. When me and my brother were really young – about eight years old – we got picked on a lot. Bigger lads were always picking on us because we were twins and we stood out a lot. Plus, we were always in trouble, pinching the footballs off the older lads or being cheeky with them. We were always a bit thin as well. So that's another reason why we were picked on. We had to fight back.'

I couldn't stop looking at the marks around Steve's eye. I asked him whether he was in any pain the morning after the fight.

'No, not really. I feel all right, but I'm very tired. It's only the second time that I've gone the distance. It takes a lot out of you, I feel right drained. The first fight I went the distance was in my first professional fight, I felt terrible for about three days afterwards. I won that, but I felt terrible afterwards. I couldn't lift my shoulders for days. But I feel all right today. I've just a couple of marks around my eye but that's all, and a mark on my neck, but that's where I got caught by the rope. My eyes were a bit puffed up last night. He caught me with his thumb in my eye and he blinded me for a round or two, and I couldn't see nowt out of it, that were really bad. But today I feel brilliant, and I felt good last night. Even after the six two-minute rounds I felt as though I could go on. When I lost those three fights on the trot I felt right disheartened. I thought that I was in the wrong game. But last night I showed that I could go six rounds non-stop, and it felt right good. I enjoyed it. I were right happy with it.'

What kind of preparation goes into a fight like the one the previous evening?

'I train every day, so that's not a problem. I didn't find out I was boxing until yesterday afternoon. The first time I had sight of my opponent was when we got into the ring. I wasn't frightened by him or anything like that, but I think my tattoos probably put him off. When I used to fight in the amateurs, I got really frightened of kids covered in tattoos. I think the only reason I lost last night was because I hurt my hand in the first round. I caught him on the bridge of the nose, or on the top of the head, which is really hard, with my left jab, and this really hurt my hand. I thought I'd broken my hand again, so I was a bit hesitant for the rest of the fight. I was still jabbing with it, but I just didn't feel at ease to let it go as much as what I would. I think I boxed non-stop for the fight, but I would have won if I'd thrown more punches.'

I was wondering what advice Brendan gives to these young men who are destined to live on the undercard?

'Brendan likes you to keep your looks. He doesn't like you to get in there and have a war. He doesn't want you walking around in a couple of years' time with your nose flat to your face, and your eyes

Steve Howden: 'Brendan likes you to keep your looks. He doesn't like you to get in there and have a war.'

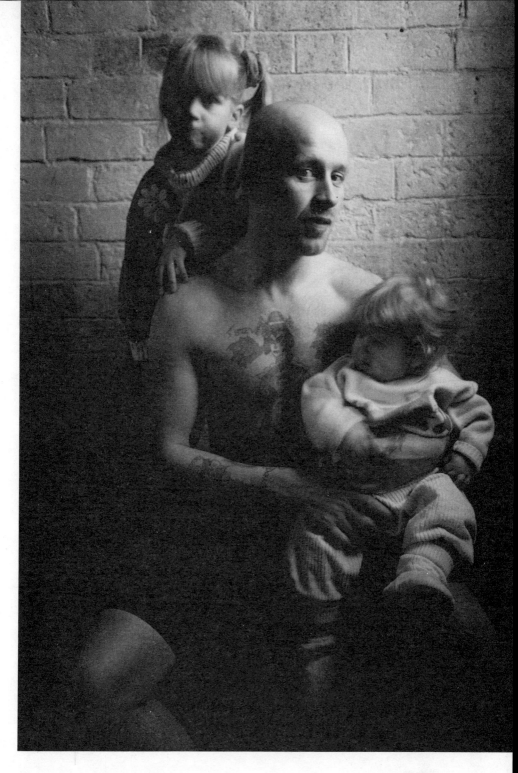

all puffed out. I've had eight professional fights, and this was the first time I've ever been marked. I haven't had me nose broken or 'owt like that, but I've still got a few marks. If I were getting marked all the time and a broken nose I think I'd get out of 'game, but I'm not getting hurt so I want to stick with it and try and get on to better things hopefully. Brendan teaches you to move about without getting hit. That's his motto – "Hit without getting hit." It usually works, but I got into a bit of a brawl at times last night, instead of moving off and using my jab more, but I just couldn't get it to work properly last night. Brendan's is a great gym, because it's the only gym I know of where all the sparring is done to the body. At other gyms they put you in with their best boxer and you just get beat up. A lot of gyms do that, but down here you don't get beat up, you don't get hurt. You're down here to learn. That's what I like about this gym – you get well looked after.'

What about his dreams and aspirations? Could he ever even in his wildest dreams be a Naz?

'Naz has some right talent. He really muddles his opponent 'cos you don't know what he's going to do next. Sometimes Naz stands straight on to you so you don't know whether he's going to lead with his left or his right. He's very awkward to suss out, especially when you're sparring with him. I spar with him twice a week, and I still haven't sussed him out. He's got a different movement every time he spars. He's got a great punch on him as well. I've been hit by heavy-weights and his punches hurt me more. And he can take a right punch on the chin, he never hits the deck. He's also one hundred per cent dedicated. He's not got a job. He's relying on boxing, because he's getting all his money from boxing. Plus, he's a single man, whereas I got married when I were young. I got married and got a job and I just couldn't pack my job in to do boxing fulltime, 'cos I have to support my family. I went into boxing professionally 'cos I'd done so many years in the amateurs. I thought it was just a waste if I didn't make something out of it. I'd done all these amateur fights, and I didn't get nowt for them. So I came back when I were nearly twenty-two and Brendan said, "Do you fancy having a go at turning pro?" So then I had the medical, the brain scan and the eye test, and passed all the tests. Then I had my first fight in May 1992 and I were right pleased with my performance. I got three and a half hundred for the first fight.

Hopefully, I'm going to be getting better and better opponents, so the money's going to get better.'

So how did Steve manage to fit training into his busy schedule of full-time work plus his young family?

'I work from six in the morning to six at night at Fletcher's. I get up at half four in the morning and go for about a three- or four-mile jog. Then I go to work until about six o'clock. I go to the gym straight from work until about half past seven. Then I go home, have me tea, and flake out on the settee. It's hard for the kids. When I get in from the gym they're usually both awake to see me, 'cos the kids like to see me before they go to bed. But I'm usually knackered. A lot of people say to me, "I don't know how you do it, working the hours you do and then finding time to train." But I've got to do it, I've no choice.'

He paused momentarily, and unconsciously his hand moved up towards his face and his fingers gently felt the puffy area around one of his eyes. It was time for the dreams. 'Unless I make it really big, of course, and make some decent money out of it, like Naz is going to do. Then I would devote myself one hundred per cent to boxing.' His hand stopped on his face, as his forefinger probed the long cut below the right eye. 'But I've got to make sure my family are secure. Even if I don't make it big I owe a lot to boxing. It helped me settle down. Even though I'm not winning all my fights, I know that there are customers out there who want to watch me fight. I'll be able to make a bit of money out of it for a few years to come. There are a lot of punters who want to watch a skinhead go to work up there in the ring, and put up a good show. But then hopefully get a good hiding.'

Half the Battle

He was one of Brendan's boxers from Birmingham. He had rung Brendan the night before, suggesting that it was about time he had another professional fight. Brendan rang him that morning to say that he'd managed to get one arranged. It was in Sunderland. But the boxer's car had broken down, somewhere between Birmingham and Wincobank. Brendan, his son John, the man from the garage and myself were packed into Brendan's car.

Brendan was in full flow. 'I got hold of this fella at work this morning. He's a lovely kid, but he's a right moaner. He could moan for England and Ireland and the whole lot put together. He just rang me up two minutes ago and said "B-r-e-n-d-a-n, I've got a right problem." I thought to myself, he's in Birmingham, he doesn't want to fight. He's changed his mind. He says, "The clutch has gone on my car." So I says to him, "Where are you?" And he says, "Savacen-tre." So I says, "Savacentre where? Savacentre Birmingham? Savacen-tre M1? Which Savacentre?" So yer man says, "The Savacentre just down the road from your house," which wasn't so bad. The first thing is that there are two of them travelling up here from Birmingham. He's got his pal travelling with him for company. Yer man should have had the intelligence to walk up to the house and leave his mate with the car. But at least he had the sense to ring me.'

We headed off towards the Savacentre, the one just down the road from Brendan's house. John spotted someone walking along the street, and pumped the horn. A small Arab boy waved back. 'That's Ali, Naz's brother,' explained Brendan. 'He's a brilliant footballer. As an amateur boxer he had nineteen fights and only lost one. That's better than Naz's record. At fourteen years of age he came up to me and says, "I want paying for boxing." I says to him, "Ali, you can't get paid just yet. Wait a few years and I'll make you a rich man." So he turns round and says to me, "I'm not fighting for nothing." I told him that he was doing his apprenticeship in the ring. For the time being he's playing football. With the boxing he would have made a fortune. The kids these days are all crazy. They want everything immediately. They don't want to wait. They can't wait for anything. The fight game isn't like that. You have to be patient.'

The man from the garage was going on about how difficult it was to replace the clutch in some cars. The mood was bleak and growing bleaker by the minute. 'I look after my boxers,' said Brendan, 'and they sometimes turn round and do the dirty on you. I had this black kid who was built like a tank. He could fight all right. He had a problem with his car about eighteen months ago. So I told him to nip round to my mate's and he'd repair the car for him. So what did he do? He fucked off without paying. So I got the bill off my mate and I captured this boxer in Sunderland to get the thirty quid off him, just after one of his fights. I had to go chasing the money. That's what it's like. One other fella left me with a bill for a thousand pounds. Then he wrote to me from the nick. "Sorry about that, Brendan. You know I'll be coming out soon and I want you to train me and look after me again. I want you to give me a second chance." What can you do with these lads? Sometimes it seems that the easy bit is when you get to the ringside.'

We drove into the Savacentre. 'Look at that fella there.' Brendan was clearly growing exasperated. 'That's a typical black stance. It says "I'm in trouble." There he is, just holding the lamp-post. The one inside who owns the car is the real moaner.' The man from the garage was shaking his head. He was not impressed by the car. 'He will be a moaner in a minute having a clutch fitted in that fucking thing. Ooooh, God. Now then, it would be cheaper to buy another fucking car than replace the clutch on that. He couldn't have picked a worse fucking car. Oh, God almighty.'

'Don't tell him,' said Brendan. 'That'll depress him before he goes up to fight.' The boxer and his pal got into Brendan's car. We left the man from the garage to it. Brendan started imitating their Birmingham accents. I think he was trying to cheer them up. 'B-r-e-n-d-a-n. I've broken down. What am I going to do?' But this was just the warm-up, the prelude to having a go at him. 'You see, I got hold of this guy here this morning at eight o'clock, and I told him that I'd got a fight for him tonight. So he says to me, "I don't think I'll be ready,

Brendan." So I says, "Why not?" And he tells me that he doesn't think he'll be able to get the time off work, so I tell him to get his gaffer for me to talk to him on the phone. So I sort it out for him. I sort everything out for him. He tells me that it's too short notice but I says to him, "You were on at me only last night about a fight. What's the matter with you?" You know that you have to be ready and willing in this game, if you want to get ahead. You don't think that Muhammad Ali would have said, "I'm sorry, I don't want to fight. It's too short notice." You have to be willing.'

It was a little moral tale for the boxer and his mate. A little public humiliation for expressing some reluctance to fight at less than a day's notice. But Brendan needed to start building him up again. 'Don't worry about the fight. He'll not get past your left hand. Take it from me. Tonight you'll not be moaning, there'll be a big smile all over your face.'

The boxer put on his best Lenny Henry Birmingham accent. 'I know I will because I'm going to knock him out.'

'*Knock him out! Knock him out?*' shouted Brendan. We all jumped. Brendan seemed more than a little agitated. 'Knock him out and we're out of business. I want you to beat him up, but nicely, over a few rounds. I want it to last a bit. He'll come in like this to you.' And Brendan took up a boxing stance. 'I want you to go bomp, bomp and then walk away – bang. He won't get near you. I had this fella here in with the Olympic Gold Champion in Germany in Berlin last year. Did you have a good time when you were there? Yeah. Right. If you hadn't had to lose the weight at the last minute what would you have done? You would have beaten him. Right? He would have beaten a fighter who was unbeaten in fifteen fights. I said to him, "Shuffle, walk away from him, fiddle him around." He stood him on his head. But he had five pounds to lose before the fight. If he had been a pound within his weight he would have done it. I rang him up the week before to check on his weight and he told me that his weight was all right. You can't keep your eyes on them twenty-four hours a day. The *British Boxing News* said that he was the best technical boxer they had ever seen in Berlin. Then I took him down to a fight a few months ago and I got him twelve hundred quid for the fight. I told him how he was going to outbox this fella. But the decision went the other way. The referee gave it to the local man. The local crowd got up and booed the decision out of the place. You do your best for these lads, but you have to keep your eyes on them.'

The man from the garage in the meantime had got his tow rope out. We started towing the car with the broken clutch slowly along the streets of Wincobank. None of it seemed to disturb Brendan, or interrupt his musings. 'So after me arranging this deal, me persuading the kid to fight, me persuading his gaffer to give him the time off work, me persuading this other kid, who I also happen to manage, who's a pal of his, to travel up with him for company, then this happens. The fucking car breaks down. It could have been worse, I suppose. It could have broken down outside the Savacentre in Birmingham. Once you take the job, you've got to turn up. You have to be reliable in this game. My job now is to get him up to Sunderland tonight, to box, to win and to get him back down here so that he can pick up his car in the morning. He'll probably stop at my house tonight, sleep on the floor, whatever the crack is. So when people come along and talk to me about being Irish or English or black or Pakistani, I don't want to know. We're all in the fight game together. There's piles of bodies on my floor some nights, and I don't care what colour or nationality they are. If we don't get up and get out to work, and hustle and do what we're doing, then at the finish we don't get nothing. We have to work together in this game.'

We ploughed slowly through the streets of Wincobank. This fighter had a big night ahead of him and I kept thinking that this was hardly the ideal preparation. Brendan, in the meantime, was distracting him from the here and now, the present imperfect with the broken clutch and the long trip to Sunderland still to look forward to. He was focusing the young boxer's attention on the job ahead, motivating him. Making himself busy, as he liked to put it. Getting him to go through his lines. 'Tell me again what you're going to do. That's right – bomp, bomp and bang. That's right. Walk away from him, fiddle him around. That way we might make a few bob.'

121

The Backstage Players

The Card Girls

In the early nineteen eighties the nineteen-year-old Shearer triplets were the girls to be seen out with in Sheffield. Joy had just won the Miss Lovely Legs competition and was doing part-time modelling and promotion work in nightclubs, Julie was also a part-time model and doing promotion work, and Joanne was a go-go dancer. 'Go-go dancing was quite enough at the time. That was the era of "Rock the Boat" and "The Birdie Song",' explained Joanne – 'fabulous days for the go-go dancer.' They showed me a photograph of the three of them, all long legs and blonde hair – 'although not our natural colour' – arranged around a bald, middle-aged man whose natural colour would have been hard to ascertain. 'He was a racing driver,' said Joy, by way of explanation. 'And we were in a top restaurant at the time.' But that was more than ten years ago. Now they were back in Sheffield, all living in little terraced houses in Hillsborough, within two hundred yards of each other. What had life been like for them in the meantime?

The girls gazed at their image from the past. It was powerful enough to evoke old memories. Joanne spoke first: 'Part of my job was to get the audience on to the dance floor doing the right dance, which wasn't always easy. We had to do this by going and mingling. We started them off and they'd follow us on. We used to sit on the floor for "Rock the Boat". We were getting good money – £20 for three nights' work. Jobs were scarce in Sheffield at that time. Both me and my sister Joy had started as hairdressers, earning £14 a week. Julie's hands couldn't stand the chemicals involved in hairdressing, so she worked in a boutique. Modelling and go-go dancing paid a lot more than hairdressing and boutique work for a quarter of the hours. You see, the problem was that our dad always said that an education wouldn't be that important for girls with our looks and personality. He always wanted us to be in a singing group – "The Three J's". That's why he gave us all first names beginning with "J".'

Their big moment came when the manager of a casino in Sheffield asked Joy if she'd like to do some promotion work at the impending title challenge by Herol Graham. 'He'd seen my photograph in the paper and obviously thought I could bring some glamour to the fight,' said Joy. 'I said that I'd do it if my two sisters could join in as well. Joanne had come third in the Miss Lovely Legs competition anyway, and Julie came second – or so the paper said, even though she hadn't entered it! She was touring around the world with her Greek boyfriend at the time.'

'It was really fantastic,' said Julie. 'I went round the whole world on a boat. I'd been married at seventeen and was now divorced. My boyfriend was the steward on this big ship, and everywhere I went people gave me things. I just couldn't believe it. In South America they gave me coffee; in Japan they gave me roses; in America they gave me a big compact of make-up. I could get an atlas out and tell the country by what they'd given me.'

The largesse of the whole world washed over us as Joy looked for an opportunity to continue her story. 'But it was still marvellous for three sisters to get first, second and third in a competition like this.'

And there they were in November 1981 posing with Herol Graham at the weigh-in, and at the after-match party. 'We were the card girls,' explained Joanne. 'We had to walk round the ring with the cards between rounds. It was super. Joy did round one, Julie did round two, I was last. But I got the biggest cheer. I think that the reason was that Joy and Julie had all-in-one catsuits on, whereas I wore a blue leotard – I've still got it, and it looks better on me now. It was a great job – we got forty pounds each plus expenses.'

The title fight between Herol Graham and the Commonwealth Champion Kenny Bristol went the distance, so the girls and their legs got quite a bit of exposure that night. 'I remember the after-match party well. Bomber Graham got to the party a bit late and they started without him. They had this big cake and everything with his name on it. But they'd cut it all up, and just left him a slice on a plate. I thought that was very mean.'

This was only the start of the good life for the Shearer sisters. But it was not without its hitches. Joanne got married the following year to an 'entrepreneur'. 'He wasn't very keen on me doing a lot of things, and particularly not go-go dancing, even though he met me through my go-go dancing. I used to dance at one club where I could wear little dresses. It was really stylish – you were up on this stage, and the men were lower than you, so they couldn't really leer at you when you were doing your routine. Then I started in a new club, where the other go-go dancer wore a basque. You had to wear something a bit more revealing. In this new club the men were at the same level as you, with pints of beer in their hands, and they could leer. I only did one night. My husband came along to watch. He weren't terribly keen on my work – even if it were showbiz. He wanted me in the home. We had a big house and a big garden. I was well set up, but it was boring. I felt that I was missing out on the good life. My sisters had gone to Skegness as cocktail waitresses in a holiday camp. Joy eventually made it to entertainment assistant, which basically meant that she didn't have to wear a little cocktail dress, then she started doing promotion work down in London. I remember her telling me that she was doing a promotion for Camp Coffee at the Ideal Homes Exhibition, and how they used to swap coffee for wine. It sounded great. I knew that I was missing out. I always said that I wished I could have put my husband on ice at the time. I hadn't really had my time with the girls. I knew that we had still got a bit to do. I wanted to put my husband in a fridge for three years so that I could live a bit. He weren't really keen on that idea. I was really envious when Joy got her job with Playboy.'

The word 'Playboy' had them all looking misty-eyed. Later that year Joy, who had some previous experience as a croupier in Sheffield, went to join the Playboy organization. 'That's our Joy,' said Joanne. 'If she fell in s . . ., you know sh . . ., she'd come out smelling of roses.' Joy took up the story with some pride: 'I went down to London with this girl who was a couple of years older than me. But even though she was older, she was very protected because she was Italian. But after a couple of weeks, halfway through one shift, in fact, she took off and went home to Mummy. That left me on my own in London. I had to find a girl to move into my flat – all on my own. But it were magic working for Playboy. You were treated really well down there – you had your own beauty outfit, your own hairdresser, your own chiropodist, your clothes were all washed and cleaned for you. You used to get half an hour on and half an hour off, and you used to have someone running around after you getting you drinks

The Shearer triplets and Herol Graham in 1981. 'When you've got the looks and the personality what more do you need?'

and things. It were magic. When I was working there, this bloke stopped me and said, "You're her, aren't you? You've just won Miss World." So I said, "Give over. I've been working here all night." But the next day I saw the paper, and the hair of the new Miss World was exactly the same as mine, the jaw line was the same, everything. It could have been me. I was on top of the world. I looked like a celebrity.'

Julie couldn't resist joining in the telling of the story of Joy's time at the Playboy Club – the story was obviously part of the cultural history of the family. 'They used to line all the girls up, and they used to pull Joy out and say, "If you looked like Joy, you'd be all right." We were right proud of our sister.' Joanne chipped in: 'I've seen her in uniform – it looked really cute.' 'In my opinion Playboy really was the height of glamour,' added Julie thoughtfully.

'What were the men like?' I asked. 'Rich,' said Joy. 'Very rich, in fact. Let's get real.' The answer was a little more cut and dried than I expected. 'But is wealth really that important?' I enquired. 'Yes, as long as they spend it on me.' Then, after a very long gap, 'It's not the most important thing. That's, er, um, living and breathing,' she added, somewhat enigmatically. 'But money was very important down there. When the Arabs won a lot of money they'd try and tip the girls, not knowing that you weren't allowed to do that in this country. They'd try to give you thousands of pounds in tips. The girls couldn't take it – they used to burst into tears. But you had to work for the money – you had to look your best all the time, and keep your weight right down. You got told off if you put a few pounds on. We used to be told that you can either drink or eat, but not both. I was thin anyway. I'd had the slimmers' disease a few years earlier.'

Playboy was the pinnacle of these girls' dreams. 'Playboy always fascinated me. I would have loved to work there,' said Julie. 'It would have been fantastic for triplets like us all to work for the same club. We could have been world famous. I still dream about the club today. I had a dream the other night that they reopened Playboy and they had all these men working there with little dickey bows, and trousers but nothing else. When I woke up I was convinced that this had happened. I wanted to tell my sisters the news, but it was only a dream.'

After Playboy, anything was possible – especially for Joy, the beautiful one, although beauty does have its drawbacks. 'You know what they say about beautiful women, after all,' explained Joanne. 'Beautiful women are like cats – they're lazy, they look gorgeous, but they're damned useless. Joy will ring you up at ten o'clock in the morning and ask you to come round and make a coffee, especially if she's got a hangover.'

But the cat eventually found the cream. 'I started to meet these really rich men after I left Playboy. People always say that I must be a real gold digger, but I'm not. I don't go out to meet rich men. I always say that I'm not that attracted to them, they're attracted to me.' She laughed. 'Even when I was looking for a toyboy a little while back I found money instead. I do prefer men of a certain age, though – either a bit younger than myself or quite a bit older. The reason is that I like men when they're a bit daft and not totally serious. Young ones are daft and they just want a good time, so are older ones – the same as me, basically. Guys the same age as myself always want to get serious and marry me, and I can't be doing with that. I don't want any commitment.'

Joy lived with one of these older men for five years. He was another entrepreneur. He gave her a seven series BMW for a birthday present. Together they saw the world. 'It was like a dream,' she said. 'We stayed in the Fontainebleau Hotel in Miami – you sometimes used to see that hotel in *Miami Vice*. Then we went to Barbados, St Lucia, Cyprus. Only the best, really, it was better than being Miss World.' Now Joy was with another entrepreneur, who was also treating her well. 'He takes me to all the top shows: "Abstracts of Love".' '"Aspects of Love",' corrected Joanne. '"Phantom of the Opera",' continued Joy without any perceptible gap. 'Him and his friend even took me and Julie to the States. They took us to a show and when they came back we were being chatted up by Lionel Richie. It wasn't really Lionel Richie, but we called him that because it looked like him. My boyfriend was still mad. He always says that he's my last boyfriend.

'The funny thing about all of my boyfriends is that they've all been in steel – scrap metal, aeroplanes, steel containers – all sorts, really. I once went out with this tic-tac man, but the uncanny thing was that he gave it up and moved into steel. Mine are all into steel, Julie's all work in occupations beginning with the letter "A" – aeroplanes, accountants, architects. Joanne seems to like scientists. At the moment she's seeing someone who works with toxic waste. They all want to get us settled down, but we really value our independence.'

But now all three sisters were waitresses, and back in Sheffield. They were all single, and in their thirties. So what do the next ten years hold? 'It's funny,' said Joanne, 'all the men who want to marry us ask the same question. It's a way of putting pressure on us. But as our dad used to say, "When you've got the looks and personality, what more do you need?"'

On a Short Fuse

He was sitting hunched over his beer in the dark, dreary club on a Sunday afternoon, with his mates. He was wearing a sweatshirt and Wranglers. A broad, muscular back which was just a bit too muscular, the proportions evidently shaped and moulded by hard work in the gym, and steroids. The barman in the club looked a little wary. 'I saw that lot in a restaurant one Sunday night. Three men came in with shotguns to shoot them. I couldn't believe it.' He pulled the beer slowly. 'I wouldn't fancy getting on the wrong side of them, would you?'

It was the kind of inoffensive communication meant to bind the barman and me together in some mutual bond of disapproving togetherness. But I didn't really want to hear it. I was two hours late for my interview with John, an ex-Paratrooper, a Falklands vet, and a man, in his own words, on a very short fuse. I had come to talk to him, because I knew that he did security at some very big fights. I had seen him on the television, hustling the fighters into the ring, glowering at the punters stretching out their hands for a touch. Simmering. As I approached their table I could see John staring at his watch in disbelief. To break the ice I mentioned his reputation and recounted the tale from the restaurant, without identifying the source. Anyway, the barman seemed to have nipped out for a minute.

'I couldn't believe they only got eighteen months for it,' said John. 'A pal of mine pinched a calendar and he got twelve months.'

I was busy midstream, mid-stammer, expressing my horror at the vagaries of the judicial system at the present time, in this particular country.

John cut right through my waffle. 'Wise up, Geoffrey, for fuck's sake. That's a joke.' All of the men with the distended backs burst out laughing, leaving me in this deep hole in the middle of the table. A more foolish man would have taken offence. I laughed it off.

I asked John to tell me about his background. 'I joined the army at nineteen, back in the early seventies. I left school at fifteen and was an apprentice butcher for a while. Then I went into the iron foundry, but it frightened me to death. I thought that there had to be a bit more to life than this. Whenever they tapped the kilns out, you were always getting burned. The fumes were terrible. It was like Dante's Inferno. I didn't have any qualifications, so I joined the army.'

But why the Parachute Regiment? 'I joined the Paras because I went down to the Careers Office and there was a guy there from the Paras who had just completed his training. I saw the beret and the belt, and I thought, "Yeah, I'm having this." I forget his name, but he really did look the part. It all seemed very glamorous. This was in the late seventies. I turned up at the depot in Aldershot wearing a Second World War flying jacket, a pair of loon pants I'd bought from Virgin and a pair of platform soles. When I was walking through the gates this man said to me, "Where the fucking hell have you parked the Spitfire?" Then he gave me a bit of useful advice: if you want to get anywhere in this life, lad, you'll buy yourself a pair of Wranglers, a pair of desert boots and a sweatshirt. I did this immediately. I thought that if I was going to get through this I'd have to conform. I paid about seven pounds for a haircut before I went to Aldershot, and they still shaved my head. That cost me a further two pounds fifty. They deducted it from my wages.

'I found the training hard. It were very hard in those days, but I managed to get through it. Nowadays the training staff can't be brutal to men. But in my day they could do what they liked to you. And I'm not talking about a little tap on the head, either, I'm talking about a proper punch – on the back of the head, anywhere, to get you motivated. Nowadays it's the soft shoe shuffle. That's why I think the soldiers today aren't as good as they were. But we all suffered the same together. That was important. The section corporals beasted us. That's what they call it – "beasting". But you need that to motivate you. There was one corporal in particular – if I saw him today I'd kill him.'

I wanted to point out that this seemed a little incongruous. After all, he had just praised the training methods of the Paras. But I kept quiet.

'I was small in them days,' continued John. 'I was built for running, carrying my pack on my back. Just like a snail, really, carrying all that I needed to live. Only faster. They teach you everything in the Paras – even how to shower properly, because a lot of the guys didn't really know how to wash. They were from the slums without bathrooms. They started with the basics, and then tried to weld you into a little team.

'My first posting in Northern Ireland was Crossmaglen. A right place – plenty of action. In those days the IRA were pretty keen, so if you weren't keen you were going to get yourself dead. In 1976 a pal of mine from Sheffield took cover beside a bike and the frame of the bike was packed with plastic explosives. There wasn't a lot left of the man. All he got from the army was a sanger, a fortified position, in Crossmaglen named after him. They send you out in a fire position after an explosion like that, but that's stupid. The man who did it is already gone. He's sitting somewhere on the other side of the border, drinking a cup of tea and having a sandwich. All you're left with are bits of body to pick up. This was my initiation into the dirty war. I was a bit shell-shocked. They got us straight out again on patrol. Just like if you fall off a bike, you get straight back on again. That's what they did.'

He leaned back in his chair. 'Over the years I lost quite a lot of friends in South Armagh. The IRA were dead keen.'

It was a curious word, 'keen'. I kept thinking of keen ornithologists or keen stamp collectors rather than keen killers. Were the Argentinians as keen? John's eyes narrowed, until he was looking at me through two watery slits. 'The Falklands was the coldest, most inhospitable place on this earth. In any month of the year it can snow, rain and be sunny – one after the other. And there's always a wind. It's basically the asshole of the world. In my opinion it was not worth saving. Put that down – not worth saving. We only went there so that someone could win an election. We did our main action on a place called Mount Longden. We went in for a silent attack. But that all fucked up, big style. A pal of mine stood on a mine that blew his foot off. The next thing we knew this mountain was just ringed with fire by these Argentinian conscripts and the 501 Bouzo Tactico [sic], their equivalent of our SAS. The whole mountain lit up. We were frightened to death. Well, not frightened to death – but really frightened. We were tramping up this hillside thinking there's nobody fucking here, then all of a sudden "bang!". It's when you grow up real quick. People were crying, people were screaming. That's what it was like. People say to me, "War is all about Queen and Country", but that's a load of shite. You're fighting for yourself and your mates. The Paras drill this into you. You skirmish forward in pairs. You do things until it becomes second nature.'

He took a long hard swig of his lager. 'But do you know something? In proper war it all goes out the window. In proper war you end up on your own. You've lost the rest of your section, and you meet other people who've lost their section. You go forward with them for a bit, then you have a cup of tea, with these mortars screaming past you. You keep moving forward, because you know that the only way home is through the top of this mountain. The Argentinians were well armed and well fed, contrary to what people have said in the past. They had brilliant clothing. We ended up wearing their boots, because ours was that crap. We ended up using their rifles, because ours fucked up. We used their grenades. Ours were good but we couldn't get enough on the mountain, so we used theirs. Their special forces were very good. They were taking out people from eight hundred metres with one-shot kills. They were well-trained men and brave, but they died like all the rest. Some of the conscripts weren't very brave. We found some conscripts cowering in a hole, but we killed them anyway. We killed whatever we could.'

When people mentally relive events, you can sometimes see their eyes with a faraway look, with the pupils darting this way and that. 'It went silent on the mountain, and you could hear somebody shouting in English "Fix bayonets!" and all you could hear was bayonets being fitted to rifles. We did the last bayonet charge the British army has ever done.' John's eyes were miles away; his pupils had a life of their own.

'The thing about war is that all the things that you can't do in this life you can do in war. I had nightmares about it for years. My mum came in and disturbed me in bed and I nearly killed her. It was like in *Magnum*, when they have flashbacks to 'Nam. It's a right old cliché, but it's true. Every night I was under artillery bombardment. I can't tell you how frightening that sound is – when it's whistling in and you know that it's coming for you. You can make yourself so small, when you try. You can get into any tiny little gap.

134

'We came back from the Falklands and after two days were sent home on leave. We were all totally fucked up in the head. After the Gulf War they gave people counselling, but not after the Falklands. It would have been too expensive. They sent six hundred madmen back to this country from my battalion. A lot of guys got locked up because of excess aggression. The public thought that we were rowdies, but we weren't, we were just fucked up. I got into a lot of trouble. I'll fight at a moment's notice. The fuse was about a quarter of an inch or less. I once punched a guy in for putting "Don't Cry For Me, Argentina" on the jukebox. It was just the name that did it. My head came off quite a few times. It was only when they introduced the words "post-traumatic stress disorder" that I realized what was wrong with me.'

John bought himself out of the Paras a year after the Falklands. 'I got a job as a hod carrier in 1983. It was then that I took up weight training. I saw really big men walking around town and working on doors and I thought they looked really good. They were all on steroids, of course. People who rave on about not taking steroids don't live in the real world. There's no way eating chicken breasts can make you that big. Get real. The people who call steroid-users cheats are basically assholes. They haven't the balls to do it. But you have to know what you're doing. I eventually found a doctor who gave me good advice. Although I'm only five foot eight I went from eleven stone to fifteen stone seven pounds through taking steroids. I have been seventeen stone, but that was too big. I got nosebleeds. I worked on doors, but I was never a thug. I never had really bad "roid" rage, unlike some of the big men I know.'

The security work for boxers came through personal contacts. 'You meet a lot of entrepreneurs in my line of work, and they recommended me to some boxing promoters they knew. I've done some really big shows in Sheffield, even down in London. I really enjoyed it, though. I liked the atmosphere, the buzz. I was sometimes more hyped up than the boxers.'

John told me that he felt that he was calming down. He hadn't been in a fight for nearly two weeks. 'My wife has helped me enormously. She wants to listen to what I've been through. The last time I kicked off was in a club. A man started to chat me up. He asked me to guess how old he was. I said to him, "Give me some space. Fuck off." I didn't want to kick off, because I thought that I might have misinterpreted what he was saying. The following week he came up to the club again and said, "Oh, it's cold. Does anybody want warming up?" My head came off then. So I walked him down the street and then I punched him. I told him never to look at me again.

'You see, the thing is that I'd much rather not fight. I like a peaceful life. But I won't be fucked about and I won't suffer fools. I don't throw myself about to get people to have a pop at me, but if they want to I'll accommodate them. There are certain people who have positive presence and people who have negative presence. There are some people who get mugged and people who are left alone. Some people have "victim" stamped all over them. You think, "Look at this dork here, he's just asking to be rolled." I've got positive presence. I've never been mugged. I never will be.'

He looked me straight in the eyes. 'Would you tackle me?'

I have to admit that I had answered his question before he had managed to enunciate the last syllable.

Rolls-Royce Gerry

Gerry is the man behind the wheels of the Roller who might pick the new champ up from the hall to take him to the reception afterwards. Gerry, like the card girls, is the sort of man we take for granted at big fights and the receptions afterwards – an accessory, a prop, part of the scene rather than part of the action. This is his story.

'There is something about a Roller,' said Gerry as he pulled out into the Hillsborough traffic. 'It seems to command respect. Even bus drivers let you out. Now that doesn't happen very often in your average car.' And at that very moment a driver waved Gerry into the road. 'The thing about a Rolls is that it just seems to roll along the road because of its wider body. I think that might be why it's called a Rolls-Royce.' We rolled out past Hillsborough on a warm summer afternoon. On the pavement you could see the ordinary punters craning their necks to see who was in the car. A smart lady in a seventy-five-grand Merc turning the corner smiled straight at Gerry. 'You see, the funny thing is that everybody assumes that because you're in a Roller you must be somebody. You can see them looking at the car and saying, "Who have we missed here?" This car only cost nine grand, it's a 1977 Silver Shadow. That lady's Merc would be worth, well, rather a lot more, but she still wanted to have a look at me. But she was rather nice looking, so I didn't mind.' Gerry may now be sixty, but he still has an eye for the ladies. 'When I was young everybody told me that I looked like Tony Curtis, although once I was mistaken for Billy Graham by an autograph hunter, when Billy Graham made his first visit to England. I was at the Ideal Home Exhibition when I was asked for my autograph. So I suppose I must have looked like a cross between the two of them. My friend Peter, who's now my boss, used to look like Gregory Peck. He was always debonair. While we were going off to Skegness and Blackpool looking for work he went off to Miami and Freeport in the Bahamas, pampering these rich people on

the lovely beaches. Unfortunately, he looks a bit like Mr Bean now.'
Gerry pulled up at the first petrol station and put ten pounds and fifty
pence worth of petrol into the car. 'This will get us out to Derbyshire
and back. Hopefully.

'The car isn't mine,' said Gerry. 'It belongs to Peter. He owns
Pinegrove Country Club. We go back nearly forty years, Peter and
myself. I do weddings in the car, and big nights after the boxing when
I'll drive them round. Most of the boxers are lovely lads. Success
hasn't had the chance to spoil them yet. Most of the times I'm in the
car I'm working, but Peter lets me borrow it on special occasions, so
a lot of people see me driving about in it. I take the ribbons off the
front and the flowers out of the back window and I'm away. Superstar
playboy. Sometimes I've forgotten to take the flowers out of the back
and then you've got a bit of explaining to do if you're trying to impress
some lovely young lady and she notices the flowers. I get other jobs
in the car as well. I've driven Peter and his friends to the British Open.
We all sat together. I wasn't the employee, the chauffeur, I was with
friends. Champagne and strawberries, the works. I'm part of the crew
when we go down to Ascot. We need a coach for that and a forklift
truck to shift the booze on to the coach. We fly in for the last three
races. I loaned one of our crew a tenner and she was walking around
two hundred quid up. She got a tip from one of the celebrities on the
coach. I'm sitting with one woman with big money pissed up on
champagne trying to focus her opera glasses on the race card. She
picks "Property Owner", so I bet it as well, on 12–1. But I was late
back to the coach because I had to queue to pick up my winnings.
The first two years I didn't get any wages because I was pissed up.
One of the big celebrities on the coach asked for some gin, but I'd
done the lot in. They helped me off the coach when I got back to
Sheffield, whereas I should have been helping them off.

'One of my best jobs was picking up a Queen Victoria and a Prince
Albert lookalike from Sheffield station. It was for the Lord Mayor's
show. They had the red carpet out for them, and the station master
was there in all his best regalia, with the gold braid on the front and
this, that and the other. The TV cameras were there as well. The game
had gone so far that I thought that I was picking real royalty up,
obviously not the real Queen Victoria and Prince Albert but real
royalty none the less. They came out of the station and shook hands

Rolls-Royce Gerry. 'When I was young everybody told me that I looked like Tony Curtis, although once I was mistaken for Billy Graham.'

with me. I didn't know whether to nod, to bow or what. Prince Albert had all the feathers in his hat, all the gear on. They had travelled first class up from London as well, like real royalty. They were opening a shop in Orchard Square and I just drove up the pedestrian precinct in the car, because of the age of Queen Victoria and Prince Albert. I didn't want them to have to walk. The police didn't bother. It was the Rolls, you see. Any other car would have been moved on. That and the fact that Prince Albert and Queen Victoria were in the back.'

We pulled into a pub in Dore Village. The posh end of Sheffield. 'The landlady will like this parked outside her pub,' said Gerry. Gerry knew the landlord and the barmaid and assorted lunchtime customers ringing the bar. Many assorted customers. Everybody, in fact. Gerry has a tight weekly schedule: tennis club, posh bars all over Sheffield, the Polish club dance on a Sunday. 'I drink a hundred per cent proof Polish whisky. It's called Crutnik, but I call it Sputnik. I'm that pissed when I'm on it that it's like being on a Sputnik. There's a good Polish crowd, all ex-comrades, a cross-section of us the general public, but not too many. I keep telling the barmaid in the Polish club that I'm going to go to that Poland one day – I'm going to the Zachapony mountains. She says, "I have a sister there, Gerry, four-bedroom house." "Tell her to light the candle," I says, "I'm coming. Put the candle in the window so that I know where I am when I get there." My friend Peter wanted an accordion player for a Beaujolais evening at the club, so he says to me, "Where can I lay my hands on a good French accordion player, Gerry?" So I got him one from the Polish club. He wasn't French, in fact, he wasn't even Polish. So Peter says, "What kind of wages will he want?" and I tell him six bottles of Gold Label for starters and as much beer as he can get down him. By the time he's due to play he's just about done it, he's pissed up. So I tell him to take it steady. The music came out like an Irish gig, but it was a marvellous evening. Marvellous.'

Ten years ago life was very different for Gerry. He had been a market trader in Barnsley market for years. 'I didn't so much have a stall as a table. I used to sell blades, which were a copy of the Wilkinson sword. Then Bic biros, which were a great invention, three for a shilling. I used to sell Christmas paper, but that was seasonal, and Sellotape when it first came on the scene. My other big lines were ironing-board covers and ladies' umbrellas. You see, a man needs a razor blade and a woman needs an ironing board cover and an umbrella. I was catering for the basic needs up in Barnsley. But then the miners' strike came along and it went on and on. I only had £150 tied up in stock laid out on the table, the bedding people had six grand's worth tied up. The traders who survived the strike were the food people and the small fancy goods people. Then I got divorced. I was drinking heavily and got very depressed. I was thinking to myself, "What do I have to get up at half past six in the morning and drive out there for?" The customers had gone. I disappeared from the scene for two or three years. It was Peter who pulled me back out of it, by giving me this job. I thought he was going to put me on a little stage, a little orange box. I didn't realize at the time that he was putting me on the Palladium. He used me as a kind of a rep for the club,

140

Gerry my pal. He put me on the right platform to project the little bit that I had, which was a bit of personality and the ability to talk to people. This comeback of mine is due to him. They say that fighters can't return, and I believe that, but I think that genuine people can return if someone has a bit of faith in you. I can't write down in money what I owe Peter but he gave me a lovely new zest for life.

'And this car,' he added as a beautiful woman in a black BMW threw him a gorgeous smile.

Manning the Toilets

This is the North's ultimate nitespot. The very acme of sophistication. Women aren't allowed to bring their drinks or cigarettes on to the dance floor let alone their handbags. There may be a recession on, with gloom descending from Sheffield's seven hills, but tonight it's party night. And tomorrow night and the night after that. I saw a statistic in the free paper they push under the doors in Sheffield that suicide is the third biggest killer of the under-25s in the area. But you can forget all that doom and gloom tonight. Tonight we're going out, we're going to let ourselves go, we're going to have a ball. This is where the boxers come to celebrate. When they make it to Josephine's they know they've arrived.

'Welcome to Josephine's party night.' A huge culture of contrasting sound. Lisa Stansfield in the background, a girl with short dark hair in the foreground, gabbing to her friends. 'Has anybody ever told you that you look just like Lisa Stansfield?' said a lad with gelled-back hair. He interrupted her mid-flow. She spun round looking slightly peeved. 'What?' 'Has anybody ever told you that you look just like Lisa Stansfield when she had the kiss curl?' 'Ooooh, really.' 'Yeah, really.' 'My mum does say I look a bit like her, but she says I'm prettier.' 'What?' 'I'm prettier.' 'Oh. You'll have to shout into my ear,' said the man with the gelled hair, offering up his ear as a suitable conduit for all further messages. 'I'm not doing anything in your ear. Not without my rubber johnny.' And Lisa stood tweaking a rubber johnny pinned to the side of her dress like a brooch. It was set off with two condom packets and an 'L' plate, curiously sitting side by side with the word 'EASY' cut out of a newspaper. Lisa was a bride-to-be. This was her last fling whilst she was single. 'I'm going on *Take Your Pick* on stage later. We can have a dance after that, if you want. Ooooh, here comes my mum. See you later.' Madonna sang about her holiday in the background. The man with the gel was now telling a different girl that she looked like Lisa Stansfield with her new hairstyle.

Paul gazed out into the smog of sound from behind the toilet door. He had seen it all before. The hopes, the dreams, the disappointments. 'I've had lads in here who've picked up two birds in the one night and they've had to come in here to hide. Sometimes when they decide it's safe to go back out both birds have gone off with other fellas. You can never be certain about anything in nightclubs.'

Paul stood in front of a large mirror lined with styling gel, styling mousse, Starkie Spray Gel, Nova hairspray, deodorant, toothbrushes, antiseptic mouthwash, Polo mints. 'It's all thirty pence a go, except the toothbrushes – they're fifty pence each, but you get a squirt of toothpaste thrown in.' Sitting at the far side of the mirror was some Pond's Cocoa Butter. 'That's for lads who come in with a bit of sunburn. The lads are very vain about their appearance these days. They put a lot of effort into it. I'll stock anything they might need on a night out.' He stood with his back to the condom machine. 'Unfortunately I don't get any profit from that.' He turned to the products that were on offer. 'The aftershave is also thirty pence a go. I stock Paco Rabanne, Armani, Kouros, Aramis – only the best.' I noticed one curiously downmarket product called Gossip, which I'd never heard of. 'Some of the lads want to be a bit adventurous on their big night out. They'll try anything when they've had a few drinks.'

Paul talked with a slight East European accent heavily overlaid with a strong Sheffield dialect. 'I've had all the stars in here. Some right famous stars.' He read off a large, invisible scroll. 'I've had all the famous boxers – Herol Graham, Michael Watson, Johnny Nelson, Prince Naseem – and all the big stars – Emlyn Hughes, Ron Atkinson, Carlton Palmer, Jimmy White, Stephen Hendry, Dean O'Kane, Alex Higgins, Norman Collier, even Des from *Coronation Street*. I don't know Des's full name, but he's been in my toilet with the rest of them. The stars remember me from one visit to the next. They'll all say, "How's it going?" We have the snooker players in once a year, when the Embassy World Championship is on at the Crucible. They all say hello. That Jimmy White is a kid and a half. He's very generous. The stars wouldn't dream of just forking out thirty pence for a squirt of gel or a slosh of antiseptic mouthwash, they always give a good tip. Especially Jimmy. Some of the stars are a bit pissed when they get

143

here, but I wouldn't want to mention any names. It's a professional position I hold. The boxers come and talk to me after their fights, and sometimes before, as well – even though they shouldn't be out in a club a week before they have to go out and do the business. I psyche them up. I tell them when they step out in the ring just to imagine that their opponent has raped their daughter. If they've got one, that is.'

Paul came to England in 1956 from his native Hungary, when he was seventeen. He worked as a fitter in the steelworks for thirty years before being made redundant in 1986. He saw the advert for the job as Wash and Powder Room Attendant in the *Sheffield Star*. 'It was necessary at the time. For me it was a must to continue to work. I get on well with people. After a few months this toilet became a home from home. I wasn't embarrassed to tell people where I work, and I'm not ashamed to tell my relatives back in Hungary. I don't call myself a Wash and Powder Room Attendant, I just say that I'm a toilet attendant and leave it at that. But I tell my relatives back in Hungary that they have never seen a nightclub like this one. We call it the ultimate nitespot – Josies. In Hungary there are places where you can drink all night, but you have to be able to stand up. They serve you in these little cubicles but you have to stand in them. They'll continue to serve you as long as you're steady on your feet. There isn't a club like this in Hungary. I get £2.95 an hour, working from half past nine at night to half two in the morning, but I also take the profit from the sales of the toiletries. I select the toiletries myself. I've become a bit of an entrepreneur, and I can say that I make a reasonable living from this.'

Just then two girls tried to run into the men's toilet. They were shrieking and screaming as they approached the backs of a long line of men. 'Shield your eyes, Michelle, if you don't want to see any willies.' Paul jumped in front of them to block their way. The girls were still shrieking. 'We're desperate, Paul. Have you seen the queue for the ladies?' 'I'm sorry, girls. You can't come in.' The lads with their backs to the girls had all managed to twist around. 'Go on, Paul, let them in. They only want to have a look,' said one tall blond lad waggling something in his hand. Paul ushered the girls back out. 'I'm also an expert at removing blood stains from garments. We do have the odd fight in here. I've found that chewing gum remover is the best thing for cleaning clothes covered in blood. We've had the odd guy

144

knocked spark out in the toilet. The last time it happened this guy came in and this fella walked in behind him. He waited for him to do his business, then he cracked him as he was turning round. He didn't give him the chance to turn right round. The guy was half blind anyway, he didn't have his contact lenses in. He needed a lot of chewing gum remover that night.'

Two more girls appeared at the door. 'It's sometimes quite a job keeping the lasses out of here when they've had a drink and the queue for the ladies' gets long. It's always worse on a Thursday. That's because it's hen night, when all the girls get together. Sometimes we have to have an amnesty and keep the lads out of the gents' for ten minutes while the girls go, just to get the queue down.'

But tonight there was to be no amnesty. Paul guarded the door. At the stroke of midnight it was the brides-to-be show on stage, and the girls rushed off in a different direction. Paul explained that there is usually a rush to the toilet by men at this stage. 'This is when they get the drinks and go to the toilet. They're not really interested in the stage show unless it's a friend of theirs making a fool of themselves on stage.' The stage show was Take Your Pick. But first the yes/no round. 'The beautiful Kathy will bang the gong if you say "yes", "no", or "don't know",' announced the DJ. 'You have to try to avoid saying any of these things for thirty seconds.' The first contestant was Helen, to be married on Saturday. 'Are you pissed, Helen?' 'Yes.' Gong! Nicola was festooned with condoms. She didn't fare much better. 'Are you getting married this week?' 'Yes.' Gong! But at least the question was longer. 'That's nearly three seconds,' said the DJ to Nicola who was now trying to blow up a condom on stage. The next contestant, Susannah, wasn't a bride-to-be, she was just about to be divorced. 'No doubt we'll see you again when you meet your next fella.' John was a bridegroom-to-be. 'You've got time yet if you want to get out of it.' 'No way,' slurred John, but you could see that he was seriously thinking about it in a slow, ponderous and highly intoxicated sort of way. 'Right, John. Is that your real name?' 'Could be.' John clearly had his strategy well worked out in advance. He said 'could be' to everything. He made it through to the next round. But not before trying to touch the beautiful Kathy, trying to look demure in a tight lurex dress. 'Don't touch the goods, John, or we'll disqualify you,' warned the DJ.

Even Nicola, with her three seconds on the clock, had made it through to the second round. Her friends helped her on to the stage. Several of the condoms had fallen off, leaving her in a large pink shift. Her outfit looked strange without the condoms, like a soldier's uniform without the patches and badges. Vulnerable, almost. Her mother stood at the base of the stage. 'What should she do? Should she take the money or should she open the box?' The DJ held two fivers up to her face. 'You can have all that, or you can open the box.' 'Open the box!' shouted her mother. The DJ waved the two fivers in her face once again. 'All that, Nicola. Just think what you could buy with all that.' Nicola moved her large heavy head from side to side. 'No way, Jose.'

Kathy went to open the box. The card inside told her that Nicola had won a bottle of Moët. Nicola looked stunned and somewhat confused. 'A bottle of Moët champagne is worth more than a tenner,' explained the DJ. Nicola gave a very delayed whoop of joy. 'Well done,' said her mother. 'I hope you're just as lucky in your marriage.'

The man with the gel who compared everybody and anybody to Lisa Stansfield had made it as far as Paul's toilet. He was slumped in the chair below the condom machine, pouring his heart out to Paul. This was the refuge, away from all the excitement. The music still pumped in. 'Forget about the bad times,' Madonna wailed. He thought that Madonna was talking directly to him. 'Forget about the bad times? She's one to talk. I'm fucking unemployed.'

'Look on the bright side,' said Paul. 'At least you don't have to get up in the morning.'

And on that note, Paul reached up and turned the speaker off, leaving the toilet in perfect silence. Or almost.

Hard Men with Time on Their Hands

Dead Game

The setting was a barn just outside Scunthorpe. I had been taken there by an ex-boxer from the gym to see how he spent his leisure time. The venue had been kept secret until the very last minute. And even then you had to be in the know to get sensible directions to this barn in the middle of nowhere. The entrance fee was a fiver. It was one o'clock in the morning and it was wet and miserable, but they didn't seem to feel it. There were about fifty of them all gathered around the twenty-foot-square ring. This was the one they had all been looking forward to. The big one. This was Sledge, the local hero, and his big chance against a champion called Peace. You could tell that Peace was a champion just by looking at him – he had one eye and one ear. Most American pit bull champions are missing an important part of their anatomy. Peace's missing parts were plain to see. The stitches looked very crude indeed. 'Well, you can hardly take them to a vet,' explained one of the ringside buffs.

The two American pit bull terriers were being displayed, not so much like race horses – more like gladiators. Or boxers. This was going to be a real display of guts, in every sense, and the crowd knew it and loved it. Peace was being carefully scrutinized. 'Awesome,' said one regular. 'Awesome,' said another. It was already obvious that the specialized vocabulary of the American pit bull terrier fraternity was somewhat limited.

Peace was led our way. 'Peace has been through the wars, you know,' said one of the regulars, pointing at the awesome creature in front of us. A dog with the most incongruous name imaginable, as well as the most incongruous teeth. The teeth, which were really fangs, dwarfed its stocky little head. 'Peace isn't technically a champion, which would mean that he's a three-time winner,' said my informant, seeking to clarify things. 'Peace is what you call a "two-time winner", but that's still pretty good.'

I could see already that if three victories made a dog a 'champion', its fighting life was really rather short. I was already thinking that they must retire rather early.

My companion interrupted my musings. 'But old Peace has got a lot of fight left in him yet. He may be half blind but he's still as game as hell. That dog likes fighting more than fucking. All good pit bulls do, you know. I owned one pit bull who was up this bitch, and just after he'd finished the business he was trying to bite the bitch's head off. But that's pit bulls for you. They're great dogs, and great companions, they're all very game. See Rottweilers, they're useless. As soon as you injure them that's it – they're off with their tails between their legs, if they could get them between their legs, that is. It's exactly the same with Alsatians and Dobermanns. They're good guard dogs, don't get me wrong, they're good at biting people, but they can't fight. My pit bull killed an Alsatian in the street a few weeks ago, and the Alsatian was a right big brute as well. I kept my pit bull in a pen at the bottom of the garden, and it got out somehow. A friend of mine saw it run across the road after this Alsatian. But the Alsatian had no chance against my dog. My dog topped it in a few minutes. My dog's a big 'un, mind you. It stands twenty-three inches and weighs sixty pounds. It has a twenty-one-inch neck as well. It's right solid, really awesome. It'd tackle anything.'

The ex-boxer leaned back, relishing every minute of the tale, basking in the pride that emanated from this great breed. 'Pit bulls never give up, they're one of the few breeds that'll fight to the death. They're bred for gameness. But even some pit bulls quit after they've given everything they've got. But I've heard that Peace never quits. He just keeps going and going. I've got great respect for that dog, and I've spent all my life with dogs so I should know. Pit bull fighting does come in for some criticism, but the way I look at it is that the dogs love it. These dogs have been bred for it. And when you watch them fighting, the first thing that you'll notice is that their little tails are going all the time. They love it.'

This ringside aficionado was getting into his stride. 'Pit bull fighting is just like boxing. It's like two trained, fit men fighting. It's all run in a very professional way with a referee, a time-keeper and judges. There are some idiots who own pit bulls, but there are idiots in all walks of life. I know of one guy who had a pair of dogs and he set

150

them at each other when he came in from the pub one night. He had them fighting right in his front room. They wrecked the place, the ornaments were all over the place. There was such a hell of a commotion with all the breaking glass and yelping that his neighbours actually rang the police. He panicked when they told him. He couldn't get the pit bulls separated so he ended up having to drag the dogs outside and stab one of them to get them apart. Idiots like that shouldn't be allowed to own any dogs, let alone pit bulls. They're also the guys who get away with fighting pit bulls. Those that organize proper fights get prosecuted. You see, the way I look at it is that it's like the difference between a scrap in the street and a professional boxing match. There's rules here. The main rule is that when one dog turns away from its opponent it's taken to its own corner. The other dog is held in its corner. The dog that has turned is then given ten seconds to go after the other dog and cross that line there, or it's lost. It's a way of seeing that the dog is still game, that it wants to get stuck in there one more time. Of course, if the owner of the dog touches it during a contest, then that dog has lost. That's really like throwing in the towel, you see.'

At this point in the proceedings I noticed that the dogs were being scrubbed. My companion noticed my perplexed expression. 'That's to make sure that their owners haven't put any stuff on the dogs to stop the other dog biting it. Before big contests the owners always swap dogs and wash them to make sure they haven't been coated in anything. Just look at the shape that Peace is in – it's awesome. Greyhounds are bred for running, pit bulls like Peace are bred for fighting. Just look at the neck on Peace. It's a bit like Mike Tyson. Of course, like boxers, pit bulls fight in different weight divisions. This particular pair of dogs have been matched at fifty-five pounds. Peace has come in overweight tonight so its owner has had to pay a £200 forfeit. It's not his night, let's just hope that it'll be Peace's.'

It was time for the fight to begin. 'Face your dogs!' shouted the referee. 'How long is a round?' I asked, naïvely as it turned out. 'There's no rounds, they just fight to the end,' said the ex-boxer. But the end was a long time coming. One hour forty-five minutes, to be exact. At that point Peace was picked up by his owner. Not before time: his bottom jaw was hanging right off. But the contest was not stopped on humanitarian grounds or whatever the equivalent is for canines, as my informant pointed out. 'He's gone,' he explained. 'With a jaw like that he can't bite properly. There's no point in letting the fight go on, he's useless now.' Sledge's owner picked up the £600 prize money.

But the entertainment wasn't over for the evening. The consensus around the ring was that Peace was still dead game, so it was decided to give him a courtesy scratch. His owner held him in the ring to see if he was still game to fight. He stood there motionless, half blind and half deaf, with his lip hanging off like some freshly cut liver on a butcher's slab, and with his lower jaw resting at a very odd angle. He stood there trembling with anger and determination. And presumably pain. There were all these people hanging over the ring egging him on. His owner's eyes seemed momentarily to fill with tears – of pride rather than sorrow. Peace bolted forward – blindly, obediently, instinctively – beyond sensation, indeed beyond sense. Sledge, still held firmly by his owner, seemed to brace himself for round two. The seconds should have been out, as Peace tried to bare his heroic fangs which could not grip or bite or even meet any longer. Sledge rolled his muscular shoulders, bracing himself for the impact, which never came. Peace was dragged up and out of the ring. 'Game to the last, what a dog. What a scrapper. They'll be talking about this fight for years. Your dog is a hero, mate.'

The hero, which couldn't even eat after going the distance that night, was kept for one week after the event, and then shot. I remembered what I had been told about not being able to take such dogs in that condition to the vets. 'It was good for nowt,' said his owner afterwards. 'Perhaps I should have dragged him out of the ring sooner, but there was Peace's pride to consider.'

That was a wet windy night outside Scunthorpe. Now it was a bright winter's afternoon in Dalton, outside Rotherham. I was sitting in the front room of another ex-boxer – Mick Mills. The man who had given me my introduction to life in the ring. The man who had paralysed my arms. His lurcher sat on his knee, licking Mick's face affectionately. Drawings of his favourite pit bull Eli occupied pride of place in his living room. Mick saw me looking at the drawings. 'I had to get rid of it, because of all the bad publicity that pit bulls were getting. If you've got a pit bull everyone expects you to fight it. I got fed up with all the hassle. A lot of people were asking me when they were going to see it in action. It would make a change, they said, from watching all the druggies around here topping themselves.'

Despite all the hassle he'd had, Mick agreed to try to explain to me not so much the thrill of pit bull fighting – because he considered me too soft – as the inevitability of the sport. 'Pit bulls need to fight. It's like some people. They're bred for it. It's best to put them in against something that can fight back. It's just like professional boxing, and, like boxing, the sport is well regulated.' I felt I had heard all this before, but from Mick it sounded different – not necessarily more convincing, just different. Mick continued: 'In America it's an even bigger sport, but the Yanks always do everything in a big way. I went up to Newcastle a while ago to see one of the all-time greats from America. This put bull was valued at ten grand, the stud fee alone for that dog was a grand. This dog was truly incredible. It had the biggest teeth I've ever seen on a pit bull – they were two and a half inches long. This dog was a real champion, a three-times winner. In its first two fights it had killed both its opponents in half an hour each. In its third fight it was put up against another champion. Now that, believe me, is a real test of the character of a dog. But this particular animal managed to break the other dog's pelvis in forty-two minutes.'

I flinched. I didn't like to think about broken pelvises, I didn't even like to hear about them. I mentioned Peace's broken jaw from my night in Scunthorpe. Mick knew all about this classic fight. He reached for the video-recorder in the corner of the room. I assumed that he was going to re-run the fight in Scunthorpe from a pirated video – all one hour forty-five minutes of it, in all its glory, but, no, this ring was different. This ring was out of doors, and I could make out Mick's stocky form laying punch after punch into another boxer called John Ridgman. Mick was fighting on the undercard of Herol Graham's open-air contest against Lindell Holmes at Bramall Lane in the summer of 1984. Mick was tearing at Ridgman, wearing him down, snarling around the heels of the taller boxer. In the second round Mick floored him. Whilst the viewers watched the re-run of Mick's bomb landing, Mick explained that something happened at that point in the fight. 'That's when he broke my jaw,' explained Mick. 'He broke my jaw and dislocated it and split it right down the middle.' And sure enough when the camera eventually returned to the action you could see that Mick's jaw was now resting at that improbable angle. I had only seen a jaw at that angle once before, and that was on a dog.

'I had to retire at that point in the fight,' explained Mick, 'in front of my home crowd at Bramall Lane, but I'm not finished yet. I've had two fights since. They say that I've made more comebacks than Frank Sinatra. And don't worry, I've broken a few jaws myself – six, to be exact, and only one of them in the ring. I broke my first jaw when I was sixteen in the car park of the pub at the bottom of the hill, and that's the only one I've ever been prosecuted for. I'm getting on a bit now in boxing terms, but I still keep on training. Did you know that the referee Harry Gibbs described me as having the hardest punch since Randolph Turpin? When you've got a punch like mine there's always a place for you in boxing. Perhaps one day I'll be back. I'm still very game, you know – very game indeed.'

'As game as old Peace,' I added, 'and used probably just as much.' But my half-hearted comment was drowned out by the noise of the video-recorder and the crowd at Bramall Lane baying for blood.

Postscript

After I had researched pit bull fighting, I was approached by the RSPCA, who wanted to put me straight on a few things about this particular sport. I met up with a chief inspector in the Special Investigation and Operations Department of the RSPCA. He had been out in the field and working undercover in the Doncaster area for ten days. He was extremely critical of the view that American pit bull terrier fighting is a fair sport between equal, game opponents. 'They call it a sport. They say that it's just like professional boxing, and that it's well regulated, just like boxing. They actually say that the dogs love it, and that their little tails are going all the time they're at it. This is all rubbish. Who are these characters who set themselves up as referees at these contests? They're just the men who breed the dogs. How can they say that the dog is still game when it's literally being torn apart? The fights are all about self-preservation. The dogs realize that they have to go after the other dog or die. I've never seen any pit bull wagging its tail after more than a few minutes of fighting. And anyway, these dogs aren't in a natural state when they're brought to fight in the pit. For six weeks they're fed on a false diet. They're given steroids, they're trained on treadmills – all sorts are used on them, anything to get them going, basically.'

He continued. 'There's also something that the aficionados of this particular "sport" don't like to talk about, and that's how they test the dog to see if it's game in the first place. You see, if you're a big macho type, and you've just got hold of this pit bull, you might fancy its chances in a scrap. But you don't want to take it along to one, just to watch it bottling out. It would look bad on you. So you have to make sure it's game before you set anything up. So the way that they'll test the pit bull is by putting it in against a badger. But, of course, they don't want to lose their prize pit bull, which may have set them back a few quid, against some old badger. Especially because some badgers can put up a bit of a fight. So they make sure that the odds are well and truly stacked against the badger. That's what always makes me laugh when they use words like "sport".

'So the first problem for this macho crowd, wanting to see if their pit bull is game, is to get hold of a badger. It's illegal, by the way, to take a badger away from its set. It's also illegal to have a badger in your possession, or any part of a badger. People we call "badger diggers" use border terriers or Lakeland terriers to frighten the badger out of its set; they then use padded gloves or coal tongs to pick the badger up. In my experience I've never found badger diggers particularly brave at actually handling the creatures. They know that badgers can be dangerous. When badgers are cornered they can bite, and if they do bite they'll hold on. This is the time to test the pit bull against the badger they've captured. But just in case the badger puts up a bit of a fight against their pit bull, they'll either break the badger's bottom jaw or else they'll break its hind legs. Then they'll tether it to a pole so that it can only come forward just so far. This is how they test the pit bulls to see if they're game. This is how they work out if they've got an awesome little creature on their hands. They call it all a sport, but it's really all rigged. These people think that it increases their macho image if they've got a dog that kills things.

'The whole thing's a fix, and in my view it's not natural, either. Pit bull terrier fighting is a manufactured activity. American pit bulls are a mongrel, they're a cross between an American Staffordshire and a Staffordshire Bull Terrier. They're not recognized by the Kennel Club and you can't show them at Crufts. Of course, there are other manufactured dogs as well – dogs that have been bred so that they can hardly see, or Jack Russells that are bred for killing badgers and foxes. In Victorian times they would test Jack Russells by seeing how many rats they could kill. I think this is all very cruel as well. They breed these dogs for their entertainment value. It's really just entertainment for immature minds.'

The chief inspector didn't have a dog; he had a cat instead. But he said that if he were to have a dog, it would be a pit bull rather than a poodle. 'As a companion, a pit bull would earn its crust, I'm sure about that. They may be a mongrel, but they have some outstanding qualities, which you have to admire. There are other ways, however, of testing this dog's outstanding qualities, without giving it the ultimate test.'

And on that note he tossed me a photograph of a dog that had been given the ultimate test, but had failed gamely and horrifyingly. 'And very, very slowly,' he added. 'And to think that some moron actually enjoyed watching this, and now swaggers around the place believing that his involvement in the whole sordid business has somehow made him more of a man. It's all beyond me.'

The Hunt

The air was crisp and clean. The sun was just starting to rise. Dawn over the English countryside, the flattened earth of Lincolnshire. You could see for miles. There were eight of them spread out across the field. They had left their Land Rover (S-reg, admittedly) and their Escort Estate at the end of the narrow lane. A hare began its jagged run, some forty yards in front of them. Pat released his two lurchers, Blue and Pip. 'These are great dogs,' explained Pat. 'Not classic dogs. I've had dogs that were living legends, these ones aren't living legends, they're just great.' The dogs set off after the hare. They disappeared from sight even on this flat landscape. They were gone for maybe three or four minutes. The six other dogs had started to get restless. Suddenly, Pip appeared with the hare in its jaws. The hare was still alive, but not kicking. 'Training,' said Pat. 'Some dogs would have tried to tear the hare to pieces. Pip is very gentle with them.' Pat removed the hare from Pip's jaws, held it up by its hind legs and punched it in the back of the neck. 'It's gone,' he said without even looking at it. 'One punch breaks its neck, you see.' He held the hare's lifeless body up for us all to admire. Pat always was a good puncher; even in his retirement from boxing, he was still good.

The hunting party walked on. They hunt every day. None are in full-time employment. All but one have been miners, in some distant past. The majority now sign on, Pat and some of the others do part-time work – on doors, a bit of labouring, a little bit of this and that. But they've all given up looking for full-time paid employment. 'There's nowt round our way,' said Pat. 'And if there is anything the wages they're offering are an insult to your intelligence.' Pat retired from professional boxing when he was thirty. Hunting was now his main pastime. 'To be honest, it's the highlight of the day. We left Rotherham this morning at 4.30 a.m. We'll be back about eleven. When I get home I'll go to bed for a bit, but then there's nowt to do for the rest of the day. Drugs is the main pastime where I live for the rest of them. But for me it's the dogs. I'll feed them, take them for a walk, get them ready for the next morning. Some of my mates go to bed at ten o'clock to be rested for the morning. I work on the door of a club four nights a week. Some nights I go home, have a cup of tea and then I'm ready for the off with the dogs.' We walked on through the crisp, bright morning. 'It's better than down 'pit, this. This is the best air in the world,' said Pat. We all filled our lungs greedily. We were trespassing on farm land, but because there was such a large number in the hunting party we all felt secure. 'If a copper comes along he'll just tell us to fuck off. He'll not try to tackle a group like this. If they catch you on your own, though, you're in trouble. I've had a couple of fines for trespassing in pursuit of game without a licence, but a couple of my mates have had dozens of fines,' said Pat. 'The other problem is gamekeepers. I had to flatten one a while back. He wanted to impress this bird he had in the Land Rover beside him. He pulls up in front of me and says, "You've just been on my land." So I just stands there and denies it, so he says, "D'you think I'm fucking stupid? Next time I'll bury that fucking dog of yours." So I says to him, "I'll bury thee." So he gets this big stick out and tries to hit me with it. Just one punch put him down. I left him there, with his girlfriend screaming away in the Land Rover.'

Pat does not think highly of gamekeepers or the police, but he thinks the world of his dogs. 'Magnificent animals, they'll run until they drop. My best lurcher ever were called Gip. She only cost fifteen quid, but she were a hare's nightmare. She killed her first hare at seven months and didn't stop until she were eight years old. I ran her to death. It were my fault, really. It was on this particular morning that there were just a lot of hares. I were like a kid. Gip had already killed three, she were tired. It took her about twenty minutes just to come back. She were absolutely knackered. Then this other hare jumped up in front of her and she were away again. When she got back she were dragging her feet. I knew she were dying. She had a massive heart attack in the back of the car. She were as stiff as a board in seconds. I picked her out of the car and she was like a stick. I could have stood her on the side of the road. She would have stood up on her own. I were heartbroken.'

Occasionally one of Pat's friends will sell a hare for a few quid back in Rotherham, but most feed the dogs with them. The hunting is for sport rather than profit. He doesn't feel that it's cruel. 'What is cruel is those shooting parties with those upper-class types on their shooting sticks. My lurcher has caught hares with only three legs, where these toffs have shot one off. My dogs have killed hares with shotgun pellets up their backside. They can run around for months full of pellets. You know it takes a lot to kill a hare.'

I wanted to say at least one of your punches, but it didn't seem appropriate. Or that's what I told myself afterwards. Pat hadn't finished with the hunting habits of the gentry. 'Those upper-class types will think nothing of shooting three hundred pheasants at a time. If we kill ten animals we think we've done well. We're not greedy like them.' And then he added after a brief pause, 'They don't need to do it.' The implication was clear and inescapable. I had been to Pat's estate in the middle of the afternoon and seen the glow from the tellies through the curtains. I could see what he meant.

Pat said that he didn't miss full-time work. 'I've got used to my new life of leisure. It would be nice to have a bit more money, but some of the best things in life are free. When,' he added after a moment's pause, 'you're prepared to grab them.'

One-On-One

Steve was a face in Sheffield. I heard it said that he had had as many as two thousand bare-knuckle fights. This I found a little improbable. Where would he get two thousand opponents from? There aren't that many mugs in the North of England, surely? But it shows how his reputation went before him. He had made it: a nice house, a club of his own, several cars including a Merc, a big bike, the works.

To be accurate, there were two Steves in Sheffield whom everyone knew: Big Steve and Little Steve – father and son. Big Steve owned the gym for a while in which Little Steve, an amateur boxer, trained. He was setting up in opposition to Brendan Ingle. He even employed Herol Graham as a trainer. Big Steve also promoted a couple of fights. Indeed, he promoted the amateur night where Little Steve first fought in public. Little Steve was cut in the third round and the referee stopped the contest. Little Steve may have been trying to make a name for himself in amateur boxing; Big Steve already had one. Wheeling and dealing, bare-knuckle fist fights, sorting out trouble. Tonight it was arm wrestling. 'And we're not talking about muppets, either,' said one of Big Steve's many friends, 'we're talking about the real thing, professionals. They're coming here tonight to do the business all right.'

For some reason, which I find hard to recollect, I had got myself into the position of organizing this arm wrestling competition. It was being held at the Pinegrove Country Club, which was built on the site of a rubbish tip in Sheffield and catered for the 'common man', with a monthly instalment plan to help the unemployed pay their membership fees. The TV cameras were going to be there, and all the faces were arriving, including Herol Graham, plus all the local hard men.

Rod Johnson, who at that time was part-owner of Josephine's night-club, was there with me. 'I've barred most of this lot at one time or another from my club. I know all sorts about these characters. I feel sorry for Wee Steve tonight.'

I thought I was hearing things – 'Wee Steve'? Who in the name of God was Wee Steve? Surely not Big Steve? My perplexed expression did not stop the flow. 'I've read about these weightlifters taking steroids and all the rest. Steve doesn't bother with any of that muck. He trains on steak and chips, and good old Yorkshire pudding. His is real muscle, not this artificial business pumped up with drugs.'

Wee Steve, all six foot one and fifteen stone of him, arrived in his pink XR3. He had warned me repeatedly to get the colour of his car right. 'It's metallic amethyst, not pink, just remember that.' Steve's tone always had an aura of extreme confidence and menace, all mixed together. One year he was runner-up in the British arm wrestling championship, just losing in the final to Beefy Trevor Lloyd. Beefy Trevor Lloyd wasn't in Sheffield that night, so Steve wasn't expecting too much trouble. Anyway, the audience didn't want to watch a real contest, they wanted a ritual sacrifice. They wanted to see Big Steve in action.

It was the kind of evening for false crises and phoney wars, and only these. 'Look at that big brute, there. Go on, Steve my son. Wham! That's our boy.' That, at least, was the plan. This contest was providing the golden opportunity for Steve to show off exactly what he could do. Peter Hayman, one of the owners of Pinegrove, had wanted to stage an arm wrestling competition for some time. Or perhaps it is more accurate to say that he had wanted to stage an arm wrestling competition in between a Yorkshire-pudding-eating competition and some obscure competition that involved contestants placing bottles at different distances from their feet and then retrieving them. But with which part of their anatomy I wasn't entirely sure. So he was delighted with what was unfolding on the premises. Steve was the star attraction. 'We'll bung him a few quid,' explained Peter. 'It'll be a bit of a nobble.' He hoped.

The contest was to be held in the public bar of Pinegrove, and it was now starting to overflow with a whole host of characters who looked as if they were auditioning for a bit part in *Pumping Iron*. The word had somehow got out about the contest, and here were all the bouncers, weightlifters and boxers from Sheffield, all gathered in one small place. The room didn't look big enough to hold them. It was a night for reminiscence, as bouncers who hadn't seen each other for years discussed old times. 'He was just like that guy in *Raging Bull* in those days. He always trapped people's heads in the door when he was throwing them out. Just for a nobble.'

Rod bumped into a very small, stocky man called Becksy, whom he hadn't seen for perhaps twenty years. For some reason they did not display the customary delight that you would expect from old friends meeting each other after that length of time. 'It's Becksy. Remember me?' 'Of course I remember you.' All I could think of was that it seemed strange for a man in his forties to retain a nickname like Becksy. Twenty years ago Becksy was a bouncer; twenty years on he was still a bouncer. 'But now I'm a driver and bodyguard as well,' he explained proudly. 'Still a gofer,' said a voice in the background. Rod spotted an opportunity to impress me. 'Becksy remembers me from the days when I was really fit. I used to work out a lot, and run in weighted boots. Press-ups on my knuckles, the whole works. I was always testing myself in those days. I used to hit myself with a hammer during my lunch breaks at work to see where it hurt most. I was game then.'

I recognized my cue. 'What was Rod best at in those days?' I enquired enthusiastically. 'Bench presses? Shoulder presses? Squats?'

Becksy thought long and hard about this one. He answered in a deadpan way: 'Sacking people. That were always Rod's forte. That's what he were really good at. That's how he got to be where he is today.'

I then noticed that Becksy had the curious habit of using Cockney rhyming slang of his own invention, which seemed all the more curious in a pronounced Yorkshire accent. Some of it was rather hard to interpret, and I was clearly not alone in having problems here. He explained to Rod that he had been working recently as a plumber, and that he had plumbed in a new cistern for a friend of his. 'I told her to pull the chain once for a hit-and-miss, and twice for an Eartha Kitt. She had no idea what I was talking about. So I had to explain it to her. She dropped this tray of tea she was carrying when she realized what I was saying to her.'

The conversation was suddenly interrupted because Big Steve, the star attraction, had arrived, decked out in a tracksuit and obviously ready for action. Nobody else seemed to have prepared for the contest

162

in any way. But his arrival was eclipsed by the arrival of two others. A hushed silence, emanating from the entrance to the bar, told you that someone – or something – of considerable significance was trying to come through the door. You could just make out two huge figures clearly visible above the heads of the very large punters already crowding the bar. It was Jamie Reeves from Sheffield, who was then officially the World's Strongest Man, and John Paul Sigmundsson, the Icelander whose title Jamie had recently taken. These men competed for this title by dragging buses around with them. A little arm wrestling, even with Big Steve, was certainly not going to intimidate them.

The arrival of these two men coincided with a sudden downturn of interest on the part of the other prospective competitors. None of the hulks wanted to know any longer, even though both Jamie and John Paul explained that they were only there as spectators. Peter Hayman called out a list of competitors who had previously put their name down for the event, only to find that there had been a very sudden outbreak of tendon trouble among all the weightlifters in Pinegrove that night. Reputation is, after all, a fragile thing. Eventually, Kevin Fletcher volunteered to have a go. The fact that he could not back down in front of his ten-year-old son, Brett, may have had something to do with it. The fact that he was not a face and therefore had nothing to lose may have also played some role in this. All competitors had to sit at the side of the bar, where the TV crew were already positioned. Becksy joined Kevin Fletcher, Steve and a nondescript youth with a mop of curly hair in the hot seat, growing hotter by the minute because of the television lights. None of the big men dared move, in case their slightest twitch was interpreted as a sign that they were willing to take part in the contest.

Kevin put up a brave and sustained effort, but he was no match for his opponent who, though he looked incredibly ordinary, turned out to be ranked number three in Britain in arm wrestling. I had learned already that looks could be deceptive when it comes to this particular sport. Even Becksy managed to get through several rounds. I say 'several', rather than specifying the exact number, because the organization of the contest was fast breaking down. Becksy did not seem to mind. 'Not bad for a Selwyn,' he said proudly and somewhat enigmatically. I think that I alone in that bar realized that 'Selwyn' could be expanded to 'Selwyn Gummer', and that this rhymed with 'plumber', which was at least one of Becksy's many occupations. *Selwyn* was invited by name to take part in several other bits of the competition.

Steve was keeping out of the early rounds. He was saving himself for the final. And despite the disintegration of the contest, everyone knew who would be in the final. John Paul had agreed to arm wrestle Steve for a £500 side-bet. Steve put up £250 of his own money. One local businessman, Dave, was asked to put up the remaining £250. 'Just a moment,' said Dave as he hastily went into conference with a number of his friends from Pinegrove. Every so often you could see them scrutinize the sheer volume of John Paul Sigmundsson. You could hear these worried questions seeping out of this little huddle in the middle of the floor. 'How did Steve do in the British Championship again?' 'Do they arm wrestle in Iceland?' 'Is size really not that important?' Their eyes told them one thing, their hearts something else. Steve's six-foot-one-inch, fifteen-stone frame, it must be said, seemed puny in comparison with that of John Paul. The cartel eventually came up with the £250. John Paul took his position. All the hulks in the bar crushed forward for a better look. Steve gave a quiet smile. I remembered what I had heard about the tendons of weightlifters snapping during arm wrestling contests. When you looked at John Paul's tendons you realized that there was going to be fireworks, of one sort or another, here tonight. Mick Walker, who was a bin man but was also ranked in the top ten of British arm wrestlers, refereed the contest.

Steve had told me earlier that evening that you cannot tell how strong someone is until you take hold of them. It may have been my imagination, but Steve's smile started to fade the moment he gripped John Paul's hand. There was no turning back now. The contest began. Steve's hand shook with the sheer physical effort for just a split second and then it fell crashing to the bench. They clasped hands once more, and then, bang! It was all over. The whole contest, from start to finish, couldn't have taken more than ten seconds.

'A quick way to make five hundred quid,' said one of the hard men on the way out. 'Or to lose it,' I added. Among the losers Big Steve was the only one who didn't look crestfallen. 'Sheer power,' he said. 'Sheer power, just like the sea. It was worth every penny to feel that power.'

164

Bare Knuckles

I heard the word the night before in a nightclub. It was to be a fight, the like of which I hadn't seen before. Bare knuckles, anything goes, a fight to the bitter end. It was Big Steve who gave me the word. 'Bring your camera if you like. You'll get a few good shots.' It was his older brother who was fighting. He wasn't with Steve in the club. 'He's in bed, resting,' explained Steve. 'What's it all about?' I asked. I was told not to worry about that. It was a grudge match. The nature of the grudge was never explained. 'But he's fighting a blackie,' added one of Steve's entourage, trying to give it a bit of extra sparkle. 'Just remember to bring your camera,' said Big Steve again. 'We want you there to record it for posterity. One of my pals is going to video-record it for me. We'll have something to look at when we're old men, something to look back at when we're past it.' The venue and the time were whispered in my ear. I was a little surprised by both. I thought that he might be setting me up.

It was a bright, sunny spring afternoon and the park in the posh west side of the city was full of children, ducks and lovers. The sunshine had drawn them all out. A circus tent had been erected in one corner of the park, and the children were congregating down that end. At the opposite end by the duck pond stood three men in their late twenties or early thirties. One wore shades and a bright yellow Levi jacket. He had the build of a bouncer. He and his friends were obviously waiting for something. It just wasn't clear what. They didn't look like the type to waste a few hours in a park, even on a sunny afternoon. They looked like the type who should be bobbing and weaving in some dark corner somewhere. The sort who don't get up until lunchtime.

They sounded lost. 'Are you sure this is the right spot? It's the only needle thingamajig in the park. It must be here. I bet your other man

165

doesn't show, anyway.' The man in the yellow jacket with the 52-inch chest seemed to be thinking aloud: 'This is going to be a right waste of time.' 'A right waste of bloody time,' echoed his friend, as another young couple with their nice, neat middle-class children in tow walked past in search of the ducks. 'I've better things to do on a Saturday afternoon than this, you know,' said the man with the huge chest and shades. Suddenly a cavalcade of cars approached along the road at the side of the park. 'Ey up, something's happening,' said the man in the shades. But you couldn't see his eyes to determine whether he thought that what was happening was positive or negative. A series of cars pulled in and from each one poured groups of men of the most unlikely shapes. One was at least six foot six and twenty-two stone. None of the men looked far behind in terms of build. I could only guess at their occupations. They were clearly not men to mess with. Out of the last car emerged two females, with unlikely shapes of a different sort, and tight-fitting clothes accentuating their shape. The men poured into the park, the females hung back gingerly.

Two men seemed to be leading the group. One was smaller and older than the other. 'He's ready,' said the large one. It was Big Steve. He winked across at me. 'Fit and ready for the fight,' he said again reassuringly. His older brother wore what looked like an old casual shirt, khaki-coloured combat trousers and trainers. 'I came down this morning and swept the concrete slab where they'll fight,' said Big Steve. 'I bet it'll be as slippy as fuck,' said his brother. 'I'll be slipping all over the fucking place.' And at this point he performed a few mock slips, before going into a hand spring. 'He may be forty-five and he may not have had a proper fight for fifteen years but he's as game as fuck,' said the man in the yellow Levi jacket. And the bare-knuckle fighter stood in front of the assembled throng demonstrating his kick-boxing technique. 'Whamo,' he said as he kicked the air. 'Whamo. I may not have had a proper fight for all those years, but you never lose your ability. Isn't that right, brother?' Big Steve just nodded. 'My whole family have natural fighting talent, natural talent. None of this steroid crap,' Big Steve added after a slight pause. 'I fucking hate steroids. You see all these bastards walking around full of them.' The man with the very large chest, indeed the unnaturally large chest, dressed in the yellow Levi jacket, winced.

Steve's brother did another hand spring on the grass. I wasn't sure whether he was warming up or giving us all a demonstration. But a demonstration of what? A demonstration of the fact that although he was forty-five years old he could still do hand springs on the grass? Or were these moves he was going to make in the fight, the fight where anything goes? Even hand springs.

We all waited patiently. Mick Mills had been one of the first to arrive. I just hadn't noticed him. He had been sitting on a memorial to Queen Victoria. He looked pleased to see me. 'I hope you've not come to fight in those clothes, Geoffrey. They might get a little bit dirty.' They were all laughing, including Big Steve's brother. I suppose that it was a way of relieving the tension. I just happened to be a convenient target, the fall guy. 'Things may get a little bit out of hand, and you're poncing about as if you're going out for the night. I mean black trousers and an orange bomber jacket. What the fuck do you think you're here to do?' It hadn't occurred to me that I might be involved in any of the fighting. My imagination did not stretch that far. They were all roaring with laughter, but they got bored quickly. It must have been the tension. I asked Mick what he knew about it all. 'All I know is that it's a bare-knuckle fist fight between our man and this black kid, who's twenty-four. It's a bit of a grudge fight, really. The dispute's been going on for months. It flared up again in a casino in the middle of the week. There was no way it was going to be settled amicably so they agreed to settle it here today at two o'clock. Big Steve asked us down here to show a bit of presence, to back him and his brother up. Big Steve's well respected in this town, in fact he's got the hardest reputation in the whole place. But it's his older brother who's involved today. The rest of the family will have to stay out of it, if the blacks do, that is. If they get involved it could be really dangerous, because some of them could be carrying knives and that sort of gear. It could be a war down here today.'

It was now five minutes past two, and the seriousness of the occasion seemed to be lifting. The birds were singing, for goodness' sake. Big Steve's brother continued to loosen up with a series of kicks and hand springs. I thought he might wear himself out. The hard men with the fifty-inch chests continued to greet each other and remake old acquaintanceships. 'What time did he ring you at?' There was a certain pride in who had been contacted first. It was a measure of each individual's personal worth. Then it was time for other chit-chat – 'Did

167

Bare knuckles in the park. Anything goes.

you have a lot of trouble on the door last night?' I overheard one boxer talking to his friend – 'I know somebody who's put two hundred quid on the black kid not showing. My pal says he hasn't got the bottle for it, and look at all us mugs standing about here on a Saturday afternoon. I bet we look like a right circus.'

There was almost a party atmosphere, growing as every second passed. The other kid was late. 'No bottle.' You would have had to be deaf not to have heard the whispers. 'No bottle.' But suddenly the whispers stopped. 'Just look down there. It's like something out of *Zulu*.' And there across the park walked this large group, nearly all black. Just one white guy with a shaved head and an Alsatian dog and girlfriend in tow. There were over thirty of them, nearly all big just like the other group. 'This is war,' said one. 'Jesus, they've even brought their families for a day out,' said another. The bare-knuckle fighter momentarily stopped his kick-boxing and stripped off his shirt. He wore a black singlet under the top. 'There's the black kid down

168

there in what look like brightly coloured pyjamas.' And sure enough one well-built black guy with a shaved head walked up to the concrete slab. 'Right, brother, you're on,' said Big Steve. One of Big Steve's pals with a camcorder made his way down to the slab to record the whole thing for good measure.

The two fighters faced each other from opposite ends of the slab. This was a fight from a different era. They circled each other slowly. The white fighter appeared to be smiling ever so slightly. The other one looked extremely serious. This was, after all, a fight with no rules. This was a fight that nobody would stop. The large contingent of spectators would see to that. I noticed that some kids from the park had crowded in for a better view. One little girl with long blonde hair was playing with the toggle on her hooded sweatshirt. It seemed an age before any punch was thrown. The black fighter missed spectacularly with one. The white fighter smiled again. The crowd grew impatient. 'Go on, get stuck in, stop fannying about.' 'Go on, get stuck in.' '*Go on, finish it.*' '*Go on.*' '*Go on.*' The first punches landed with dull thuds. A boot made the same kind of dull noise on a groin. Blood was already appearing on the white fighter's face. The two bodies locked together and tumbled on to the ground. The brightly coloured pyjamas pushed and heaved and toiled their way to the top of the dusty heap. The crowd swarmed in. 'Don't touch them.' 'Leave them to it!' '*DON'T FUCKING TOUCH THEM!*' A black fist was still free to work inside the hold. It smashed into the white guy's face. His teeth sank into his ear. 'He's going to bite his fucking ear right off.' The group of blacks opposite were going wild, sensing that their man was winning. 'Finish him off. Fucking do him proper. *Do him!*' shouted one in dreadlocks. The blood poured out of the older guy's face. The black guy standing over the pair of them took the initiative. 'He's had enough.' 'Do you want to call it over?' he asked of the battered and bloodied white fighter. No words were spoken, but then again perhaps none needed to be. It was obvious who had won. The black guy in the bright pyjamas got up slowly. Big Steve was trying to smile. The large contingent of blacks walked back through the park. The whole thing had only taken seconds from start to finish. The large gang supporting the white fighter looked crestfallen. 'He got too excited before it started,' said Big Steve. 'He'd got nothing left when the fight itself started.'

Big Steve's brother slowly got up off the ground. His face was covered in blood. There was a deep bite wound by the base of his ear. It looked like the ear might have come off if the fight had been allowed to continue. 'How bad is my ear?' he asked his brother. 'Not too bad,' his brother replied. 'It'll look better once it's been washed.' 'That was a load of bollocks,' said the fighter. 'I never really got going.' 'Never mind,' said Big Steve. 'These things happen. Don't worry about it.'

The group made its way back slowly out of the park. Mick was disappointed. 'That was fucking crap. I've seen better fights than that in my local boozer.' The large gang seemed very disappointed with their man's performance. 'If I'd fought like that last night I'd be in hospital today,' said one with some teeth missing.

Suddenly a number of police cars screeched along the road. Police wagons and other vans with dogs hurtled across the park. 'Don't run,' said Big Steve. 'Just make your way out. Don't look up, for fuck's sake. Just try and walk right past them. If they ask about his ear, just say that he was climbing a tree and fell off.'

We shuffled out of the park. 'Stop right there!' shouted the senior officer on the scene. 'What's been going on? What's happened to his ear?' We were like the deaf and dumb. We just walked in a straight line. The police did not try physically to stop this group of large, dangerous-looking men. I kept my gaze focused on the ground in front of me. Without glancing up, I turned instinctively to the right of the gate. Unfortunately my car was parked somewhere along the road on the left. I seemed to be out on my own. I had stuffed my camera up inside my bright-orange bomber jacket. I walked quickly, trying not to run. I got to the end of the road and turned right, trying to double-back on myself to get to the car. A large van of police screamed to a halt beside me. My bright jacket must have stood out a mile. They asked me what I had been doing in the park and what I had inside my coat. 'You've been photographing the fight, haven't you?' they asked. I said that I had been photographing the ducks. They asked for my name. When I said, 'Dr Beattie,' they said, 'Go on, Doctor, sorry for bothering you.'

I saw Big Steve that night in the same nightclub as the night before. He was in a foul mood. His brother had been beaten and his friend who had been given the video-camera to operate had forgotten to turn it on. He told me that there was going to be a rematch, but this time

'If they ask about his ear, just say that he was climbing a tree and fell off.'

it was going to be in a barn somewhere, with no possibility of any interference from outside. He said that his brother had taken some tablets for a bad back and that these tablets had weakened him. 'That's why he lost. It was just because of these tablets, you see.' I thought it would be unwise to dispute this. 'The next time, though, he'll be ready for it. I'll make sure he is. The next time he'll win and win well.'

Before I left he asked me if I knew how to operate a video-camera.

Butcher

They call him 'Butcher'. He had classic boxing features, from the old days when boxers took a beating. He was sitting in an ex-servicemen's club near Manor Top at midday. There were huddles of men in the dark, dreary club, and men on their own. Solitary drinkers, sitting pretending that they didn't need company. Ignored by the men in company. Butcher was not one of these. Some of the club members were clearly past retirement age, many were not. It was a working day, or it would have been if there was any work. So here they sat for hours. Young and old, some with their memories, some without. They all knew Butcher, they shared his memories, they would talk for hours about his fighting in Madison Square Garden in the thirties. One man brought some greens into the club in a carrier bag. He gave Butcher a cauliflower. Butcher sat over the one bottle of stout. 'I'm not a big drinker,' he said.

The nickname did not come from his merciless style of boxing. It came from his father who was a butcher who was killed while slaughtering a goat; the goat moved and he cut the artery at the top of his thigh. His mother, he told me, knocked around with a lot of men so he ran away from home when he was twelve. He started working in the market where he would sleep rough. He worked as a porter and built up his strength that way. He started training in a Sunday gym until he was spotted by Jack Greaves, who started coaching him properly at Rotherham Boys' Club. 'It was the biggest mistake I made in my life, that.' Butcher was laughing, but in a sad, quiet way. I was watching those men on their own in the club, the men ignored by the man with the vegetables in his bag, and it was obvious why Butcher had never regretted it. 'I was professional for thirty-one years. A middleweight for most of those. I've been round the world at it. I had three hundred and forty fights, including three world championship fights against Freddie Mills, John McAvoy and him from France. I forget his name. It'll come to me. I boxed in Madison Square Garden in 1937 against this fella from the Argentine, and also against this fella from France.'

Butcher turned professional at fourteen. 'I was the youngest professional boxer in the country. I fought Freddie Flue in my first professional fight on a Sunday afternoon at Sammy Mons boxing show.' Memory is a remarkable thing. He had forgotten the name of one of his world championship opponents, but he remembered that his first fight in 1931 was on a Sunday. If I had asked him about the weather that day in Rotherham I am sure that he would have been able to tell me. 'I won in just over twelve seconds. My opponent was sixteen or seventeen. You got a pound a round in those days.'

I suggested that he should have made it last a little longer in that case.

'Oh, you still got your pound for the round, even if it was all over in twelve seconds. You still got your money. For my first world championship fight I got two hundred and seventy-five pounds. It was nothing like the money the boxers get today. Boxing isn't a sport today, it's a racket. That's my professional opinion. I don't go to the boxing these days. I don't want to watch anything that's all pre-arranged. I think it's all fixed. It's all a fiddle. In my day you could box six days a week and you could pick and choose where you wanted to fight. When you made a name for yourself you could demand the money. All the fights were hard, and there was a lot of good opposition. In my day I did roadwork seven days a week. You never see the boxers doing the roadwork today. You had to be fit. In my day you could sit down and mention twenty or thirty good boxers in each weight division. How many can you mention now? There's that many bent people in the game today. At my peak in the thirties I was earning one hundred and forty pounds a week, which was good money then. But you earned it with fights every week. These days they just need one big fight to give them all the money they need to buy themselves a business. They're set up for life. In my day you had to work at boxing, week in, week out.'

So what had Butcher to show for all this work, except a few memories, crystal clear here, blurred there, worked over by him and his friends in the club? Butcher laughed again. This time it didn't have that sad tinge to it. 'Oh, I did all right. I banked my money. I was always very careful with it. You'd be a mug not to be. I've still got my money to this day, and I'm still careful with it. I have to be. I've got six thousand pounds left in the bank. I draw thirty-nine pounds a week to supplement my pension, and that's just enough to make me comfortable at my age.'

But boxing wasn't just about earning a good wage, it was about giving a young man from Sheffield experiences that he could only have dreamed about. It was about giving an old man from Sheffield tales to tell. 'Madison Square Garden was incredible. Oooooh, it were right grand. You could have put two Hillsborough football stadiums in it. I saw the man who created it. I saw him just sitting there. I asked this guy who was showing me round, "What do they call him?" but I was told that nobody knows his name, and he was the man who created Madison Square Garden. I've boxed in Japan, but there's no clapping there, no nothing. They just put their hand up. If they appreciated the fight, they put both hands up. I fought in France, Germany, Holland, Jamaica, Ireland. The time I was over there was when all the trouble was on. In 1934.'

After a long, illustrious boxing career, Butcher got a job working the boxing booths. 'I used to work for a circus. We used to go to the Nottingham Goose Fair, Ilkeston, Belfast. The challenger got a fiver if he managed to go three rounds. I was on forty pounds a week, but you earned it. There were some tough men wanting to fight, especially when we went over to Ireland. But I had experience on my side. Even tough men have a weak spot, and I knew how to find it. That's what I was paid for. I can't remember ever losing a fight in the boxing booths. You didn't get paid for being beaten. You only got paid for winning. I was very fit. The challengers may have been good tough men, but they didn't have my level of fitness. It was very rare for the challengers to go the three rounds. You see, I was at it all day, every day. I was having about twelve fights a week. I never retired from boxing as such, it just died out in the end. The government closed the boxing booths down, and they got rarer and rarer. I knew that it would die out one day, so I used to study. I went to night school and then I put in for exams. Now this really was hard work. I qualified as an engineer and got a job in a power station, when I was finished with the boxing.'

The slot machines were clicking away in the background. Butcher

Butcher. 'I got two hundred and seventy-five pounds for my first world championship fight. Not like this lot today.'

took another sip of his stout. 'But the funny thing is that nobody in the club ever wants to talk about the time I was studying for my exams and the struggles I had there, they just want to talk about the big fight with Freddie Mills or John McAvoy. To them I'm not Ernest the engineer. I'm just Butcher Gasgoigne, the man from Sheffield who climbed into the ring in Madison Square Garden on a wet Monday in March.'

Serious Distractions

The Club Trip

Darren and Gary were both seventeen. They were amateur boxers, with their childhood years behind them and their eyes now on the future. Both were unemployed. Their future lay in their own hands, or rather in their fists. They had made a pact, every day they had been in the gym. Darren always said that it was 'now or never'. They had egged each other on. This was their one day off. Their mums were going on the club trip, and they thought that it would be a right laugh to go with them. 'It's nothing posh, like,' they explained to me, 'but it's usually a right good laugh. If,' they warned, 'you're prepared to join in and let yourself go for a change.' I promised that I would try, that I would commit myself fully to what was going on, to see less and do more. To be a part of the whole. Darren pulled up his vest to expose a white, skinny knobbly chest. 'I'll get a bit of a tan. It'll look better when I'm in the ring.'

It was half past seven on a Sunday morning in the middle of summer. The British weather was living up to its reputation and being rather unpredictable, to say the least. There may have been one or two good days quite recently, but now the rain was lashing down. A queue on the pavement stretched all the way from outside the Working Men's Club to the roundabout at the bottom of the road. It was three deep. Most of the women wore thin anoraks, and had brightly coloured umbrellas with spokes broken by the wind. Some of the men wore nylon ski jackets, usually in grey, many of the others just wore t-shirts. They had their arms folded tightly across their chests to try to keep themselves warm. They were wet already, with the long day of pleasure still stretching out ahead of them. The children were dressed in tracksuits in this year's colours – crimson, sea blue, shocking pink. The wind tore right through them. Darren and Gary had come in their t-shirts, 'to show off our muscles'. They were wet through.

A member of the committee supervised the goings-on. 'The coaches will be here in a moment, lads. Don't worry. Then we'll be off to Skegness.' He tickled some little girl under the chin. 'Cheer up, Lisa. You'll be in Skeggie in a few hours' time.' Little Lisa scanned the wet, bleak streets and the cold, iron-grey skies in order to imagine what it would be like when she finally reached that Eldorado of the east coast. 'And don't worry,' continued the committee man, 'it'll be lovely there. The sun will be shining. It's just raining in Sheffield today. Take my word for it. It won't be like this in Skeggie.'

He turned away. 'This trip has been planned for a whole year, you realize. It's the only holiday that some of these kids will be getting. Trust the weather to change today. We collect all year for this trip. All the kids today get seven pounds spending money in their hand, donated by the club, and, don't worry, they'll manage to get through that all right. They travel free, of course. Adults pay four quid for the trip. Not bad for a flipping day out to Skegness.'

Only one of the coaches had so far arrived. The Queens Road Social Club sat next door to a used car lot selling a whole load of exclusive and customized cars. The committee man's gaze had left the iron-grey skies and fixed instead on a bright red Porsche. 'Marvellous, that. Absolutely bloody marvellous.' There was no envy in his voice, or not much. 'But my mate drove into a Merc on his way home from the club last week. You should have seen the damage. That's the problem with cars like that. You'd be frightened to go out in them. Too much to lose.'

We turned away from these millstones to look for the coaches. A female in her mid-twenties in a tight black dress with a thin, white cotton jacket over the top tottered past in high white stilettos. She was accompanied by a much smaller man, who was balding and look-ing very depressed. 'She doesn't wear any knickers, you know,' the committee man whispered. 'Or a bra,' he added thoughtfully. 'They say in the club that she's got three kids from three different fathers. I don't know about that, but I do agree that she's one of the best lookers who go down 'club. She'll be back at 'club later on tonight for the bingo. There'll be one flyer tonight – that's a line or a full house at the bingo, with a right good turn to follow.'

It was now five minutes to eight, and the remainder of the seven coaches slowly drew up in front of the expectant crowds. Over four hundred people were standing in the rain waiting to board the coaches for their trip to Skegness. The committee man explained that he would not be going on the trip. 'Don't forget to mention the lads who have to stay behind to mind the fort while you lot are away having a great time,' he said. 'It's all right for some,' he shouted as he hurried back to the comparative comfort of the club. The rest of us shuffled wet and dripping on to the coaches. Darren and Gary sat at the back.

All of the seats on all seven coaches were taken. A smell of damp clothing pervaded the bus. There were 'no smoking' signs prominent on every window. An old man wearing a Tam o' Shanter and a hearing aid was the last on to the bus. 'Hurry up, or we'll miss the show,' somebody shouted from the back. I didn't think that the man in the Tam o' Shanter heard anything. I didn't know what show they were talking about. I wondered if the man in the Tam o' Shanter did. The buses pulled away. The committee men waved from the windows of the club.

Immediately in front of me sat Dave, a telephone engineer, and Ann, a cleaner at the Queens Road Club. She normally starts work at half seven on a Sunday, but that morning she had had to be in at half six. She looked worn out. Ann was thirty-six and a grandmother. Her daughter, who was 'seventeen and a bit', sat with her baby, who was one and a half, and her husband on the back seat. Ann was immediately concerned about the no smoking sign. 'If you want a fag, you have to go to the back of the bus,' she said helpfully. 'There's no stickers down there. It's like being back at school.' Her daughter, meanwhile, had already lit up on the back seat. Audrey, one of the committee responsible for organizing the trip, was called down. She looked worn out as well. 'I didn't sleep a wink last night, worrying that everything would go well today. It's a big responsibility to organize the club trip.' She was delegated to go and speak to the driver. The negotiations were successful. 'He says he doesn't mind if you smoke even at the front,' said Audrey. 'Well, a day like that, what could he say?' Ann immediately lit up. The sound system of the bus played 'Hi, Ho, Silver Lining' as the coaches snaked their way out of Sheffield. The whole bus now seemed to be smoking. Ann was already coughing. She said that she wasn't too dismayed by the weather, because there was a Working Men's Club in Skegness, near the bus station, where there would be bingo on.

The coach was now creeping up some hill or other, heading towards Lincoln. Crisps and a cheap cola-flavoured drink were distributed free to all the children on the coach. It was ten minutes to nine. Several of the youngsters were wearing peaked caps made out of paper, stating that Pepsi was 'The choice for a new generation', but it was not the real thing, or even the other real thing, that was being handed out.

The first stop for the toilet came soon after that. Two huge queues – one for the toilet and one for the tea – snaked out of the little roadside café. Some braved the elements, stood for a few minutes in the pelting rain, and then hurried back, having failed either to relieve themselves or get any tea. Some had the sense to stay where they were. On the seat behind me sat William, a self-employed electrician, and his wife, with their two young children, Natalie and Jemma. William's father-in-law and mother-in-law sat opposite. The mother-in-law was eating a cheese and tomato sandwich. It was now half past nine. William explained that he couldn't afford a holiday this year because he and his wife had been involved in a hit-and-run accident a few months earlier and he had been off work for six weeks. His foot had been broken. Last year they'd had a week in Bridlington, but that was beyond them financially this year. They had, however, managed to get half of the number of the Sierra that had hit them. His daughter Jemma had her arm bandaged as well, but this was not connected with the accident. She'd got her arm trapped in a door. Luck was not running for the family this particular year. 'The kids have been looking forward to the trip for months,' said William. 'They've been asking "When are we going on our holidays to Skegness, Dad?" It's only a day trip, really, but it's a holiday to them.'

It was now 10 a.m. A woman of indeterminate age in white cotton trousers and top moved carefully from seat to seat with a card with numbers on it. You had to guess the number where the prize was located. 'We call it spot the ball,' she explained, even though it had nothing to do with football or any other game involving balls. 'It's twenty pence for one square, and the winner gets four pounds.' Puddles of condensation were forming at the base of the windows. As the bus jolted this way and that, tiny rivulets started forming and making their way on to the seats. Darren and Gary had written their names on the window. Gary had snaked the condensation down across the window down the back of the seat. He looked at me almost despairingly. 'My dad's unemployed, my two brothers are unemployed. They all make jokes about me and say that they'll be all right when I'm the champion of the world. But when my dad takes me down the club he always says, "Here's my son Gary, the boxer." That always gives me a bit of a thrill. My amateur record is I've had seven fights, won five, lost two. But I wasn't ready for the two I lost. I wasn't fit. I was smoking a lot. But now I've stopped all that. Darren and I are pushing each other all the way.'

We pulled into the coach park in Skegness at 10.55. A child at the back of the coach was immediately sick. It could have been the excitement of finally arriving in Skegness after three hours on the road, or it could have been all that cheap cola and crisps. The boy showed a sense of responsibility and ended up carrying the bag to the front of the coach, having first sprayed the bag and its contents with air freshener. Someone at the back of the bus, perhaps a veteran of club trips, had had the canister of air freshener handy in her bag.

The bus finally ground to a halt. This sudden final movement unfortunately caused a grey ski jacket from the overhead locker to fall on to the head of the man immediately in front – Dave, the telephone engineer. There was a muffled moan as Dave tried to dislodge it by shaking his head. After what seemed like an eternity his head finally emerged. His wife, Ann, was much amused. 'I bet you thought you'd just had a blackout,' she said. Dave looked slightly shaken by the experience, as if that might be exactly what he had thought. I overheard another woman with grey hair explaining to her neighbour that she had already had three funny turns on the trip so far. The ski jackets were buttoned up for imminent disembarkation. One child, already sucking a large bright blue teat, had some matching blue sunglasses placed on him. 'He looks a picture,' said his mother. 'A right picture,' as she carried him down the steps on to the tarmac of the coach park in the torrential rain. Only little Lisa spoke: 'I thought it was always sunny in Skeg, Mum.' Her mum didn't answer, as she had already stepped into a large black oily puddle.

The coach park at Skegness was full of hundreds of coaches from all over the North of England. We had six hours to kill. Thousands were heading for the exit in the lashing rain. Some only made it as far as the bus shelter. Others headed immediately for Skegness Working Men's Club. The remainder, including Darren, Gary and myself,

'Surfin' USA' in Skegness.

headed down a street where every other shop was a chip shop. We sheltered in the doorway of what looked like a shop called 'His Place', just opposite the Salvation Army hostel. It sold funny mirrors in something that looked a little like a windowframe, with images of Jesus on them – Jesus with some sheep, Jesus knocking on a door, Jesus preaching – for £2.75 each. These were called 'mirrows', an obvious blend of 'mirror' and 'window'. Some of the day-trippers were looking covetously at the 'Praying Hands', a snip at 79 pence. I looked at these praying hands and then at the dark, grey sky and headed for the sea front. Miraculously, the rain stopped. I passed a man with a broken foot with his foot in a plastic bag that had filled with water. He kept stopping on his crutches to try to shake the water out. I wanted to introduce him to the praying hands. We headed for the beach. Two girls of about twelve decided to go into the dark brown sea in their t-shirts and jeans. They emerged soaked through, singing 'Surfin' USA'. A family group sat next to them, paying them not a blind bit of notice. Despite the singing and dancing of these two very loud and very chubby pre-pubescent girls, a man in a grey ski jacket, grey socks and grey hearing aid did not look their way once. 'Everybody go surfin',' they continued to sing. Their message finally got through. One mother with her young child set off for the brown waves. They returned a few minutes later with a dark brown sludge right up to the knee of the woman, and right up to the nappy of the child. 'Who's idea was that?' she shouted. 'It was horrible down there. I've never been anywhere where the water is so dirty.' Gary was laughing for the first time that day. The two young boxers went for a run on the beach. I could see them shadow-boxing in the distance, on the damp sand. Going through the motions. Demonstrating that they didn't really belong here.

We headed back to the town. Three loud youths passed, weaving their way unsteadily along and tossing their chip paper in my direction for good effect. Darren and Gary looked at me to see what I would do. I did nothing. One of the youths wore a hat that said 'Pie Tester'. I wanted to appreciate the full semiotic significance of this message. I asked him what it meant. 'How the fucking hell do I know? I just bought the fucking hat. I didn't fucking well write it.' I thanked him for his trouble. Gary threw him a look that had him scuttling off.

The afternoon stretched out endlessly.

Finally, it was time to go home. I met Dave and Ann boarding the coach. They had spent their time in the amusement arcade with their grandchild, and visiting the shops. Ann had bought herself a new handbag for £13.99. They had also managed to spend a few hours playing bingo and 'supping a few' in the Working Men's Club. 'But,' said Ann, 'I didn't win anything today.

'In fact, come to think of it, I haven't won anything for ages,' she added after a long pause, which was just long enough to allow both her daughter and herself to light up, before the coach had even left the coach park. Her daughter asked Darren what Naz was really like. And then as an afterthought asked, 'Is he courting?' We were all evidently dreaming of escaping. My friends fell asleep on the back seat. Tomorrow they would be back in the gym, perhaps punching that bit harder. I watched Skegness slowly fade into the distance.

Going to the Dogs

Even in boxing you have a night off. Mick Mills and I went dog racing. Mick said our luck was in.

'Go on, Special Lover! Go for it! Come on, Lover! Go on now, baby! *Baby! Do him! Do him!*'

It went on for about thirty seconds, no more. Then silence. The air was still, but the smell of chips and peas still wafted my way. Then the sound rang out again. '*Bastard!*'

He stood just behind my left shoulder. He was a skinhead with a large earring and a bright-green sweater bulging over his shoulders. He was still swearing, lower this time, almost inaudible, almost to himself. 'It's only a bit of fun,' chided his mate. 'Only a laugh.' The large skinhead was not laughing.

Upstairs in the Panorama Suite and Restaurant, they had almost missed all the excitement. Sure enough, they had a panoramic view of the greyhound stadium from up there, with a large glass front on the restaurant and the bar. They could even watch the race from the numerous video screens, but they wouldn't have been able to hear the man with the green sweater or smell the chips and peas in the air. Or hear the dogs, barking and yelping in the background. Up in the new exclusive surroundings the punters were a lot more subdued. 'Marvellous race, marvellous.' A bottle of Lanson champagne peeped out of the ice bucket sitting in front of the couple beside me. Their faces may have contorted as the dogs raced, but their lips were silent. Or almost. One five-year-old didn't know the name of his favourite. 'Come on, number three,' he shouted into my left ear. This five-year-old could certainly spot form. Number three was steadily closing in on the hare, who I couldn't help but think looked more like Sooty, as in Sooty and Sweep, than a real-life four-legged animal noted for its speed over rough terrain.

Owlerton Stadium had seen its Diamond Jubilee the previous year.

Over sixty years of dog racing, with a regular Speedway session thrown in. But change was in the air. The stadium was leased from Sheffield City Council by A&S Leisure Limited, a company that has made a great success out of nightclubs and casinos. They rapidly brought the greyhound stadium upmarket with a million-pound-plus facelift. Ruffled curtains, red speckled carpets, plastic pot plants, and mirrors everywhere. Plus a floor that could be used for dancing. All on a dog track. I was joined by John Hackett, General Manager. 'I'm still very much a discotheque person. I've been in that game for twenty-seven years,' he explained. Before joining A&S, John worked as a director in Peter Stringfellow's company. Part of his job involved greeting the celebrities in Stringfellow's and the Hippodrome, with the occasional flying visit to Stringfellow's, New York, to keep an eye on things. So how come he had found himself on a dog track?

'I've moved back to my roots. I was born in Parkwood Springs. It's not there any more. They've built an artificial ski slope where my old street used to be. I used to live just where the slope ends. I came to this stadium as a baby to watch the Speedway. I wasn't that interested in dog racing. I didn't come to my first dog race until I was thirty. I'm starting to learn a little about dogs in the process. Slowly, very slowly. They tell me it takes years.'

I laid the official programme out in front of him and pointed at the next race. Nothing needed to be said. If you can't pick a winner in this game, you know nowt, lad. Nowt. You might as well go back to your flaming discotheque. It was the ninth race of the evening – the Stones Handicap Trophy. The programme gave you all the dogs' form; it told you which dog had stayed and which had stopped, which had been hampered and which had stumbled, which was British bred and which had simply been knocked over. It told you everything and nothing. 'It's all nods and winks in this game,' one informant had told me. 'They have all sorts of ways of interfering with the dogs. I've heard stories where they've thrown a cat on to the tracks to muck up a race. They've even pulled a wire up buried in the sand to stop the leader when their dog is behind. I've heard that they'll even wank a dog off before a race to stop it winning. They'll go to any lengths, them boys.'

John read the form book carefully. Out of a field of six runners he picked two, then added a third for good measure. This was no commitment at all. I pushed him a little and he settled for number three: Nook View Champ. It romped home. 'Even though it was bumped on the bend.' John's slightly world-weary face looked relieved.

'But what about the fiddles in this game?' I wanted to hear it from the top. 'What (gulp) are some people prepared to do to stop a dog winning?'

'Some things do go on at unlicensed tracks – so-called flapping tracks, or flappers – but here it's licensed. Everything is scrupulously fair and above board.'

Down below the tension was building. The dogs were being led out for the next race and paraded in front of the stand; the other dogs, sensing what was happening, were yelping in the background. Mr Birch, the Paddock Steward, showed me where the dogs are kennelled prior to their race. Every dog is locked into its kennel. Only he, and the racing manager, knows which dog is in which kennel. 'You couldn't interfere with a dog if you wanted to. You wouldn't know where to find it.' Mr Birch is not a betting man. 'There are men who can read dogs like books. I don't see anything in the dogs. Like most people at the track I love the animals, but my interest in the dogs is seeing that they're properly kennelled up and that the correct dog is in the kennel at the right time, and that's it.'

It is a strange, old-fashioned world, where everything is done methodically, by the book, where correctness is the order of the day. Where the book is an old well-thumbed exercise book rather than a microcomputer. Where the stewards are referred to formally, never by Christian names. Mr Kenny, another steward, took me from the kennels to the weighing-in area. Every dog is weighed before it races and checked over by a vet. Mr Kenny has to check the earmarkings on the dogs, to compare the tattoos on the inside of their ears against the register. He's been doing this job since 1946. 'You get a lot of pleasure out of doing a job correctly,' he said. 'Most of us here go back a long way.'

Arnie Dennis has been at the track too since 1946. 'I've been standing here and losing money every week since then.' Arnie is a bookmaker. 'The minimum bet is one pound, but we have one or two very big punters who'll put a grand on a dog. What kind of man would do this? A very clever man, if you ask me. A man who knows what he's doing. He would need to. Funnily enough, the punter I have in mind used to be a bookmaker himself.' Arnie returned to writing up the odds on the next race.

'This used to be a profitable business, but no more. We have to pay £168 a night to bet here – that's £14 a race, but this new company is great – they haven't put the rent up.' One of his sons was his tic-tac man, informing him of the other four bookies' odds. Our conversation was punctuated with this more distant, silent language. This silent language was remarkably simple, at least when it was translated for me: a touch of the head meant 'runner 1', the nose 'runner 2', the chin 'runner 3', the left shoulder '4', the hands down '5'. A waggle of the hands meant 'evens', a touch of the wrist meant '5–4', a touch of the shoulder '7–4'. A roll of the hands meant 'odds on'. At least the lexicon of gesture was simple. It was the speed and fluency that made it difficult to follow. Arnie talked over it, but took it all in. 'We take about eight grand in a night, but there's no profit in that. It all goes on expenses. It's marvellous what this new company has done to this place. The stadium is attracting a whole new class of punter – a lot of young people for whom a night at the dogs is very fashionable. But they're not big betters – yet! They'll grow into it. But most of those who like a bet are regulars. But there's no money in this game, none at all.' And he almost gave me a fully formed wink in that strange silent fleeting language of the bookie at the greyhound track.

Cyril has his regular position just by the side of Arnie's stall. 'If you ever wanted to buy a dog,' he began, as if I had given him some inkling that I was thinking of it, 'don't go by the breeding. Your people – the Irish – swear by breeding. They'll spin you a wee yarn that this here dog is the half-brother or half-sister of such and such a dog. Take no notice. When you're out to buy a dog, just go by its speed. Breeding is not a science, it's the luck of the draw as far as I can see.'

He went back to surveying the dogs. Cyril is the connoisseur, the expert, the man who could read the dogs like the proverbial book. The man who knows that genetics tells us little about speed, but a good deal about everything else. 'Dogs have personalities, you know, just like people. Some dogs just want to fight. Other dogs don't want to win. It's not chasing the hare. It's just chasing the other dogs that they're interested in. This is just a trait of the dog. It runs in blood

189

lines. Some dogs are just like that. We call them "dodgy". Dodgy dogs run in families. It's the worst thing that you can say in this sport – to tell a man his dog is dodgy. You can tell a man that his wife has gone with another fella, but tell him that his dog is dodgy and you're asking for trouble. They're not just dogs, you know, to the people in this game. Have you never heard of "Mick the Miller"? He was one of the greatest dogs of all time – he won the Greyhound Derby. He's been stuffed and put on display. That dog was not just a four-legged beast – he was a symbol of greatness.'

'But did he have the personality to go with it?' I asked. I didn't mean the question to sound facetious. Winners surely must have the right temperament. And punters too. Cyril was off.

Mick Mills said that perhaps he'd end up stuffed one day and on display. I suggested that it would be more interesting if they pickled his brain. We were still laughing when our dog romped home in first place.

The Making of a World Champion

Motormouth

'The greatest thing since sliced bread,' said Brendan Ingle. 'They used to call Muhammad Ali the greatest. Wait until they see what Naz is going to be doing over the next few months.' The tabloids had their own name for Naz, or Prince Naseem Hamed, as he was known in the ring. They were calling him 'Megamouth' or 'Motormouth'. They called him the man with the mouth the size of the Channel Tunnel. They said that Chris Eubank looked like a shrinking violet next to him, and that he even made the promoter Don King seem introverted. They were saying that he had a level of ambition and plans for world domination only seen before in James Bond villains.

But Prince Naseem Hamed had arrived in a big way. In his last fight, at the age of twenty, he had taken the European Bantamweight title off Italian Vincenzo Belcastro. People were still talking about the fight, not just because of the exceptional skill of this young southpaw but because of his taunting of his opponent in the final round. *Boxing Monthly* reported that it has never before received such a postbag of complaints about a boxer or his performance. He was the TV company executive's dream.

This was Brendan Ingle's gym in Wincobank in Sheffield, in August 1994, in the wake of the media storm, with all eyes here, at least, on the Prince's first defence of the title against Italy's Antonio Picardi. The next hurdle on the way to the world championship. This was real life for the young Muslim boy, with the paint coming off the walls, and 'National Front' scrawled on a wall outside. Naz grew up in this gym, training and sparring with professionals from the very beginning. Officially he fought as an amateur with the Unity Club, but that was only because St Thomas' got into trouble with the Amateur Boxing Association in 1979 for allowing amateurs and professionals to spar together, and Brendan was banned from coaching amateurs. Brendan brought the young boy to all of the Herol Graham and Johnny Nelson

'If he doesn't go mad, he'll go all the way.' Brenden Ingle on Naz.

fights. Naz's development took place in boxing halls up and down the country. Brendan wanted him to see it all – the dedication that has to go into boxing, the glory to be had from it, and the pitfalls. Especially the pitfalls. Naz won sixty-one out of his sixty-seven amateur fights, and Brendan persuaded him to turn professional on his eighteenth birthday.

By the time Naz was nineteen he was already a national hero back in the Yemen, with the government's education department issuing exercise books with his picture on the front and back covers. His name was appearing on boxes of tissues. In November 1993 Naz and

Brendan and a party from the gym toured the Yemen, giving five exhibition bouts across the country to crowds of ten thousand or more. The president of the Yemen, Ali Abdul Saleh, presented Naz with a £15,000 gold Rolex. The chunky gold watch still looks enormous, and mildly incongruous, on his small, five-foot-four-inch frame.

But Brendan knew he had found a winner, and not just on the TV screen and in the ring. He pulled me close for a confidential word in my ear. 'What do you think the biggest motivator in life is?' I looked around at this gym with its fading posters of past heroes. There was a cardboard cut-out of Herol Graham with a seventies hairstyle. I suggested ambition, and the need to prove that you're number one. '*Wrong!* It's *sex!*' He sounded for all the world like an Irish priest warning you off mortal sin. '*Sex!* People are dying of Aids, but it hasn't stopped the population having sex. I've had boxers before with great talent but they never had the discipline. I've seen boxers throw their careers away. I've witnessed terrible performances and when you ask them what they've been up to they tell you that they've gone round the back of a pub for sex in the freezing cold the night before a fight. I've seen fighters come into the gym wanting to tear somebody's head off because some girl has given them a dose. Naz, by contrast, is clean living. He doesn't smoke, he doesn't drink and he doesn't gamble. The hardest person to beat in the world is yourself, but to beat yourself you need self-discipline. Naz has got that singular determination to win. OK, he went over the top a bit in the last round of his fight, but that's because he was so psyched up.'

We watched Naz shadow-box in the centre of the gym. 'And he's got the talent. His balance is unique. His time/distance co-ordination is exceptional. His movement is so graceful. You hear commentators say that he's very awkward, but they can't appreciate what he does, they don't realize that it's all choreographed. He has the talent of a Ray Leonard, a Ray Robinson or a Muhammad Ali. If he doesn't go mad he'll go all the way.'

I watched Naz closely. He looked as if he was dancing in front of a mirror to very loud music. There was a certain swagger in every movement, but a lot of joking with the two other young boxers in the gym, Ryan and Kevin. Brendan covered his ears. 'This music drives me mad. What do you call it? Rap. Crap rap more like. Herol Graham used to train to Glenn Miller. That was more my style. But everything changes, everything has to move on. Boxing ability isn't enough these days. Just ask Herol Graham. You need a bit more – call it flair, call it showbusiness. Just look at Chris Eubank. But unlike Eubank, Naz has a unique talent. The funny thing is that some of these commentators can't see it. Not a bit of wonder the lad is full of himself. He can throw thirty-eight combination punches in eight seconds, with eight different foot movements, and ten different hand movements. In the last week he's got up to fifty-four combination punches in twelve seconds. Here, you time them.' He was practically shouting in my ear over the music.

I didn't dare tell him that my watch didn't have a second hand. I stared dutifully at my timepiece anyway, whilst at the same time trying to follow the intricacies of Naz's foot and hand movements. There was a flurry of activity that was too fast for the likes of me to decode. But what I could see was the strut in his stride, the cockiness, the naked ambition stripped and laid bare in every jab and punch. The determination. Ryan and Kevin finished for the day, Brendan went off to his house to make himself a sandwich. The Prince was finally on his own, and so we sat down to talk.

I was immediately surprised that Motormouth spoke in such a quiet voice, with his arms locked across his chest almost defensively. He tried to compensate for this vulnerable bodily posture by putting his foot on my chair. The result looked incongruous, to say the least, and I spent the first few minutes of the interview trying to make sense of these conflicting channels of communication. I asked him whether he was pleased with all the publicity that his last fight generated.

'The publicity is what it's all about. It's all about getting bums on seats. It's best to cause a big . . .'

There was a long pause as he tried to come up with a word that would summarize exactly what he had caused over the past weeks, in his mind at least. Eventually he settled for 'fuss'.

'. . . fuss about you or whatever, so people come and watch you. I was very surprised at the criticism of my last fight. I was surprised at how the people went against it. I think they went over the top. I wasn't trying to humiliate Belcastro. I respect anyone who is prepared to step into a ring. Belcastro, in addition, was a good champion, a crafty old fox.'

196

I asked him if he wasn't trying to humiliate Belcastro, what he was trying to do. 'You have to remember that I was very psyched up for that fight because it was a big fight for me at the age of twenty. It was only my twelfth professional fight and it was a very big step. I got a lot of criticism before the fight with people telling me that I was too young, that I would get knocked out, that I wasn't experienced enough. Everybody was reminding me that I had never gone past six rounds. So basically I was thinking I've got all this to prove now to the media, so that's what I did. It was my big chance. I made a different entrance to my usual one. Normally I flip over the ropes. This time I decided to fool the public. I stood on the ring and it looked as if I was going to do a flip over the top, and I turned round and just went "psyche", I'm not going to do that and just climbed in, in a real suave, cool way. Everybody was waiting for me to flip over the top rope, so I outpsyched them. I like to do the unexpected. I just climbed in. They all laughed, as if to say "Ah, he's a character." That's what I wanted. From the first round onwards all I thought was that this is the European Title and I'm going to take it straight off the champion. I got my opportunity and I took it with two hands. I won every round. From the start of the fight I just wanted to show him that I was going to take his title and that's what I did. All the marks I had on my face was from his head, he hardly hit me properly with any good shots. He was crafty and he was tricky with his head. He had a good old head on him what could get him out of trouble. It was a good fight and I wanted to prove that I could do twelve round easy with a world-class fighter who was number six in the world. I wanted to prove that I could overcome the champion.

'By the last round I had won every round. I dropped him in the eleventh. Brendan told me just to enjoy myself in the twelfth. I came out jumping all over the place. I wanted to show everybody that I had as much energy in the twelfth round as I had in the first. I wanted people to ask where I got all my energy from. When I came out in the twelfth I thought "I've done my work. I've dropped him a couple of times. It's a convincing win, so what I'm going to do now is to put on a show, just to prove to my critics who said that I couldn't go twelve rounds that I could do twelve rounds easy." I wanted to show that I could stand in the middle of the ring with my hands on my hips and show the champion that he couldn't hit me. I didn't want to ridicule him at all. I didn't want to take anything away from the champion. I just wanted to show the people that I could do twelve rounds easy and that I was fit and ready. People should give me the credit for standing square on to a champion with my hands down. I waved my hands a few times as if to say "I've won this" as well in the twelfth round and did a little bit more dancing and foot movement as well. I was excited. I knew I'd done it. I didn't get the credit I deserved, but at the end of the day I came out as the champion. I couldn't believe it when I read the papers in the days after the fight.'

Naz was still living in Wincobank with his parents. He was born the fourth of nine children. Wincobank, he said, was very down to earth, and very good for keeping his feet firmly on the ground. His father, Sal Hamed, came from the Yemen in 1967 to work in Sheffield's steel works, and later bought a corner shop, which is now owned by the Prince's sister. 'My parents are proud of me. They're proud to see their son up there. Their advice to me is to live my life cleanly and not to give in to the temptations of life. When people meet me they say that I'm totally different to how I appear on the telly. When people see me on the telly, they see a cocky, arrogant, brash, bombastic fighter who just wants to win, but then when they meet me they think I'm just normal.'

I enquired therefore whether it was all just an act, an act to get bums on seats, a big commercial front. He looked almost a little hurt, as if I was accusing him of something untoward. 'It's not an act when I'm in the ring. I can't put it on. It just comes out. It's just me when I'm in the ring. I really am two different people. It's the way I have to perform. It's the way I've been brought up. It's not under my control. I can't think about it. It just happens naturally. When something clicks on naturally, you can't stop it. Outside the ring I'm totally different. I'm more relaxed. It takes me a little bit of time to change from one character into the other. After the fight I'm still hyped up. I come down usually the day after the fight.'

I had watched the Prince that morning practising a new entrance. Jumping the ropes, or flipping over them, has always been a big part of the training routine in Ingle's gym. That morning Naz had his legs spread wide, his hands on the middle rope; he then jumped through the ropes, going into two flips. I asked him about this new Barnum-like aspect of his boxing training. 'If I have to fight in an open-air ring as my career develops then I might get a chance to do this. It's all good training for co-ordination and balance. Boxing nowadays has got to be different. It's got to be an entertainment, and I'm an entertainer at the end of the day. Brendan, Frank Warren who is my promoter and myself all sit down to work out how we can make it more entertaining. For the world title I might even make an entrance on a prayer mat.'

Brendan Ingle had already told me about his big ideas about the Arab Prince making an entrance on a flying carpet, with Paul Eyres, the carpet people, sponsoring the carpet. A prayer mat made it all sound a little different somehow.

As Prince Naseem developed, the comparisons with Eubank became rife. I asked him what he thought of them. 'I'm not flattered, because the only credit I can give to Chris is that he has made his money, but the way he's been boxing lately has been disgraceful. He hasn't even been winning and the judges have been giving it to him. In my view he's gone downhill, and I'm planning to take over the whole British scene in terms of boxing. He's boring the people nowadays. I rated him when he first came out. I used to like his arrogance, but now he's gone way over the top, not even going back to his corner. I can't learn anything off Chris Eubank. If anything, Chris Eubank can learn things off me. That's how I feel. I'm sure he watches me fight on video. He's even asked me about a few moves. My advice to him is that if he keeps on watching me he may learn something. For example, hitting an opponent while he's looking at the floor. This is something I do in my fights. I look at the floor, and I snap the punch out and I hit their face. My opponents think "How does he do that? He's not even looking at my face." It does their heads in.'

You could hear the arrogance again, the strut had reappeared, but it was all delivered in this low, quiet voice, with the defensive bodily posture. But I did notice that the foot on my chair was tapping more forcefully.

He was in full flow now. Megamouth at work, but with the volume turned so low I struggled to hear. 'It's a definite that I'll be a world champion. I'll be a world champion at three different weights. I'm so confident. I definitely will be a multi-millionaire. I'm planning to be a millionaire at the age of twenty-one and a multi-millionaire at the age of twenty-five. I'm not in this business for nothing. I'm in this business to secure my needs and my family's needs. I want my family to live like royalty. I plan to have a house in Sheffield, one in London, one in the Yemen and one in Europe, so I can go on holiday or whatever. With Frank Warren as my promoter I'm confident that it'll happen. He's right on the ball. After two fights he got me a European title fight. He's guaranteed me a world title before I'm twenty-one. Don King is going to promote me in the States. You get all the talk about Don King being a bit of a crook, but I think he's a great guy. He's never robbed me, he's never tried to con me. I think he's all right. He's great for the sport. He's something different. He'll promote me in the States, and I think he'll do a great job, just as he's done for Mike Tyson. There are even plans for me to be on the same bill as Mike Tyson when he gets out of prison. But Brendan is my trainer and manager. I've been with him since I was seven years old. He's been like a second father to me since the start. I'll always stick with Brendan. He's good for me. He's done the job. I've just signed up with him for another two years. If in the future Brendan did ever sell my contract, I would keep him as my trainer, and Brendan would be a millionaire, which he deserves to be.'

The Prince was training three times a day, seven days a week. The morning and evening session were two hours each in the gym, with a run in the evening for the three weeks leading up to his defence of the European title. He said that he would stop his opponent in the third. He sparred with all different weights in the gym from lightweight up to heavyweight. 'Guys three or four stone heavier than me. I spar with Johnny Nelson, the WBF heavyweight champ. That's when he wants to spar with me. He doesn't like sparring with me. He says I've got a bit too good now. He says he should have beaten me up when I was younger. He says I'm just too fast and I do his head in. I've always looked up to Johnny Nelson, he's been a great inspiration in my life. He's been a good fighter. He's still got plenty of time to mature as a heavyweight.'

I asked him about the pressures of fame. Was it hard to cope with the temptations that fame throws up? 'I've never tasted alcohol in my life, because of my religious beliefs, and it's helped with my boxing. It's kept me out of trouble. There are a lot of temptations if you've been drinking and getting up to whatever, like other guys do at a certain age. But it won't happen to me. I just thank God for putting me in that position. I can't commit myself to any girl at the moment.

200

Boxing comes first. You have to keep your feet on the ground. Fame is just a twinkle in the eye. I don't want the public to believe all the hype. I do know that I'm talented, but that's because I've got a gift from Allah. Allah is always on my mind. He's always been there for me. I always carry a small Koran with me in my sports bag. When I fight I take it with me. I don't think to myself "Who needs God? I can do it myself." I think that I'll always need God on my side. I'll always be religious and I'll be more religious when I finish boxing because I'll dedicate myself to the Muslim faith. I do need Allah, because he's helped me up to now to be very successful. If it wasn't for Allah I wouldn't be where I am today with the gift that I've got. I've been blessed.'

The Weigh-in

The hotel receptionist looked bored. 'Just follow the two gentlemen in front.' One wore a thick red lumberjack shirt and boots. It was the middle of August. He was tall, broad as well. But it was not his breadth you noticed. It was his height. Like one of those tall boys at school who got pushed into all sorts of things simply because of those extra inches. Now that he was grown up he had filled out. You imagined him as a minor heavy, looking the part because he stood above everyone else. Just out accompanying the middle-aged man next to him. Probably along for the perks, the free coffee and biscuits, and a few quid slipped into his back pocket. Brendan was there already. 'Let me have a word in your ear,' he said to the man. Conspiratorial. The real business of boxing, his arm around the shoulder of some middle-aged man, hushed voices. Talking to the wall. The television cameras were busy, periodically flooding the hotel room in white light. The Prince was prime time. A few young men with shaved heads sat by the wall, hollow-cheeked. They looked half starved. In fact they were young men at the peak of fighting fitness. The middle-aged men having all the conspiratorial conversations looked positively obese by comparison.

A dapper, grey-haired man stood in the middle of the room by the scales. Nat Basso, matchmaker and manager, a big wheel in the boxing establishment. There to supervise the proceedings. It was my turn to have my ear whispered in. 'Nat and myself go back thirty years,' whispered Brendan. 'Now *he* was poor. His family came over here from Russia. Why, it reminds me of my own childhood in Dublin. He fought his way out of that poverty.' It was the same old tired metaphor. Everybody fighting their way out and up. Everybody bobbing and weaving, ducking and diving, going the full distance. Nat Basso was, after all, in his seventies. But still he looked extremely smart and co-ordinated. 'He did it all through boxing?' I enquired.

'Oh, no,' replied Brendan. 'Through gents' tailoring. Boxing was always a bit on the side.'

It was time to try the scales. One of the boxers stripped off his tracksuit. He was wearing a G-string rather than more conventional underpants. He forgot to remove his cap. His manager walked behind him and flicked his cap off at the very last minute. They all agreed that the scales were about right. The first boxer was called. A heavyweight. It was the man in the lumberjack shirt, Carl Gaffney. The man next to me leaned in my ear and whispered, 'He's just a body brought in. Just a body.' Gaffney had a slightly funny face, with a hint of sadness overlaid on it. He reminded me of Russ Abbot. There was a certain challenge in how he undid the belt of his jeans. A tease. Everyone was craning forward to check that he was a plausible opponent. Everyone wanting to see his muscle tone. He pulled down his jeans and ripped off his shirt as if he was auditioning for a deodorant ad. 'A bit disappointing,' murmured the voice. 'He's a bit flabby. You would have thought they'd have trained him up a bit.' He weighed in at seventeen stone seven pounds.

Glyn Rhodes was shaking his head, watching the man on the scales. 'He's a bit heavy round the waist, if you ask me,' he said to his friend, a bouncer in a local nightclub with a baseball cap on back to front. 'Aren't you fighting tonight, then, Glyn?' asked a man in a green casual jacket. 'Aren't you going to make a comeback?' 'I've had more comebacks than Frank Sinatra,' said Glyn, 'but not this time.' 'You're still a young man.' 'You should have seen me when I woke up this morning. You wouldn't be saying that then. I've got grey hairs.'

I heard the man in the green jacket point Glyn out to his companion. 'There's old Glyn Rhodes. He's had more comebacks than Frank Sinatra.' 'And more grey hairs than Frank Sinatra by the looks of things,' answered his friend. They each belched a short sharp laugh, which stopped as abruptly as it had started.

Gaffney was to fight Clifton Mitchell, who stood amusing the other fighters at the far end of the room. 'Who's the big lad fighting? Is it old Paddy Reilly over there?' asked one of the old-timers in the room, pointing over at Clifton. 'He's not Paddy Reilly any more,' said his friend. 'He hasn't been Paddy Reilly since he left Brendan. He's with Frank Warren now. Ernie Fossey's training him these days. They've changed his image. I always thought that Brendan was pushing his luck when he tried to promote him as Paddy Reilly, the big, black Irishman just like Slugger O'Toole, who'd never set foot anywhere near Ireland. Well, Brendan says it's always worth a few extra bums on seats. Now, Paddy Reilly is Clifton "Dready" Mitchell.'

But the old-timer, a regular at these weigh-ins, wasn't convinced. 'I preferred the name Paddy Reilly myself. To me he'll always be Paddy Reilly. You can't mess around with people's names like that. You should never be ashamed of where you come from. If they'd wanted to change his name they should have changed it to Patrick Reilly.'

Mitchell weighed in at sixteen stone five pounds. 'Trim,' said Glyn Rhodes. 'As fit as a butcher's dog.'

Naz came in quietly, dressed in a grey tracksuit. Then he saw the cameras. The bright light filled the room. Suddenly he was in a jaunty mood, spinning, smiling, jeering. I noticed that he and Brendan were wearing identical running shoes, but in slightly different colours. Who knows, last year's and this year's model: this year's for the boxer, the man in the limelight, the man of the moment, last year's for the trainer and manager! Probably some sponsorship deal, all carefully worked out, with the manager only qualifying for remaindered stock. Everybody wants their returns on their investment. Everybody wants their pound of flesh. Naz sat down. The lights went down. He looked reflective.

There was a bustle of activity by the door. A small man with a broken nose came in, followed by another, then another. The trickle became a stream. All small and dark, their noses not just broken but pummelled into wide arches by fist on bone. Concave, like large spatulas. Disproportionately wide. It was as if their noses had been stuck on to their faces by an apprentice sculptor not yet sure of the perfect scales and symmetries of the human visage. The challenger, Antonio Picardi, and his entourage had arrived. The voice in my ear was whispering again. 'I wonder who'll be paying their wages. Yer man will need to borrow money after the fight to pay for the trip back to Italy for all of these.' One, whose nose had not been pummelled into this eccentric shape, wore shades. He knew many of the people in the room. He greeted the man who would be commentating on the fight that evening. 'Hello, Mr Gary Newbon. How are you, Mr British Television?'

204

I noticed that Naz for many minutes did not even look towards his opponent. It was not that he was avoiding eye contact, he just looked uninterested. Then I saw him watching as Picardi stripped off his tracksuit. It was a look of curiosity, with no discernible emotion. Not fear, not sadness, certainly not happiness. Just a look that said, 'So this is the man standing between me and my first million.' Naz knew that he had got to keep on winning. His whole boxing persona, the arrogant Prince who would taunt his opponents, the man they could not touch, the maestro, depended upon an unbeaten record. Every opponent therefore stood in the way of the million pounds he had been promised since he was a child, when Brendan would bring him ringside and whisper in his ear about the future.

'Does anyone speak Italian?' Picardi's entourage, all eight of them, were crowded around the scales. There was obviously some dispute over the weight. Alma Ingle, Brendan's wife and co-promoter with Frank Warren of Naz's first defence of his European title, was trying to find somebody in the room who could explain the exact weight to them and find out what they were jabbering about. Nat Basso just shook his head. 'I've never known a weigh-in not generate some little argument about something. Mind you, it doesn't help that the scales are on thick carpet. Move these scales to the other side of the room and you'll get a very slight difference.'

It was Naz's turn to face the scales. He had snapped out of his reflective mood. He was on again, on camera, in character, ready for the action. 'He's going down. Believe me, folks, he's going down tonight. I'm going to win in three.' The accent more American than Sheffield. The Italians smiled amicably. You got the impression that they couldn't tell what he was saying. He weighed in at eight stone five and a half pounds. Brendan looked relieved.

Naz pulled on his tracksuit. Nat Basso announced that all the boxers would have to stay in the hotel for the next two hours because the doctor couldn't turn up to examine them until then. 'He's got a day job, you know,' I heard Alma explain to one of the men in the mauve jackets. 'He's just like the rest of us. He's got to work for a living.'

Down to Business

The Flintstones were big at the time. Brendan was wearing leopardskin for the fight. In the bright white light of the television arcs, I had never seen him look so thin or so old. The lights gave him a hollowed look, they emphasized his greyness. He looked solemn. He had starved with Naz in the two weeks leading up to the fight. They had sat in Sheffield's leading hotel, going through it all together, 'watching each other like frigging hawks'. Brendan's weight had dropped from 12 stone 2 pounds to 11 stone 2 pounds, but it had been worth it. Naz had made the weight. Just. But Brendan looked gaunt. The leopardskin did not suit the colour of his skin. I was sitting ringside with the reporter from the *Sunday Sport* ('Wash your hands after you shake hands with him,' said the presenter from Sky Sport), the card girls, and the trainers of the fighters on the undercard who pushed in for the main attraction.

'Freddie Flintstone,' shouted one of the trainers. 'Freddie Flintstone's da, more like,' said his friend. 'It's just a bit of fun. We go back a long way. My last fight was against Brendan in 1979. I kept putting him down, and he kept getting up. I said to him, "For fuck's sake, stay down." And he just said to me, "Fuck off." He never knew when he had had enough.' Naz had come into the ring dancing to rap music, wearing a little gold turban. 'This is the new trend. It's not just an entrance in the old dressing gown, it's the full business,' said the commentator on ITV. Naz's best friend Ryan was carrying the Union Jack, Naz's brother was carrying the Yemeni flag. Ryan was trying to sway to the music as well, but he looked wooden. Naz was still dancing, across the ring right up to Antonio Picardi. Naz stood inches from him, pumping his very slight pectorals in his face. Picardi's

'If you were to tell me I'm a great fighter I'd say, "Tell me something I don't know." '

206

half-smile of amusement was tinged with slight embarrassment. The circus had come to town. 'You may love him or you may hate him,' said the commentator, 'but he provokes a reaction. And he *believes* all this. He really does think he's the bee's knees. If he was chocolate he would eat himself. He really is going steady with himself.'

Naz just kept dancing. No somersaults over the ropes, no hand-springs across the canvas, just slightly embarrassing dancing. The television commentator was getting desperate. 'I'm sure he'll do a somersault in a moment, he works on these routines in the gym.'

Picardi, at thirty-one, had been around, but he had never seen anything quite like this before. The Sheffield crowd were confident that their man could do it. They all pointed to Picardi's professional record. But there are always two ways of interpreting a set of statistics, so that even though a record of thirty-four professional fights with ten defeats might seem to indicate that Naz's opponent for his first defence of his European title had been carefully vetted, the fact that all the boxing commentators were, in addition, stating categorically that Picardi was not a puncher might seem to indicate that Naz's opponent had been very carefully vetted.

But every set of statistics has its downside. Picardi had made his professional debut in 1982 when Naz was just eight years old. He had thirty-four professional fights to Naz's twelve. He had once defeated Vincenzo Belcastro, Naz's last opponent, to take the Italian bantam-weight championship. He liked to fight in close with his head down low. Three out of five of his wins inside the distance had resulted from cuts to his opponents. Belcastro had cut Naz with his head, so what might this seasoned campaigner manage to do? Someone had pointed out to Brendan earlier that this was Naz's thirteenth professional fight. You can't be superstitious in this game, but sometimes the omens are there. Brendan seemed to be as white as a ghost.

Picardi was still smiling, slightly amused by the antics of this show-man from Sheffield. This was his fourth crack at the European title. He knew that he would have to take his chances. Since his win over Belcastro back in 1987 he had lost three times to him, twice in 1993, both times fighting for the European title. Here was the young man who had outclassed his victor, and who had gone on to taunt him in the final round. The show-off who had ridiculed his fellow countryman. Picardi's smile became a tight grimace.

208

Naz had some very vocal support from the local Yemeni population in Sheffield. A small cohort had come right up to the ringside enclosure. The security men were asking them to sit down. Naz was a hero back in the Yemen, and a hero to the sons of the former steel men who had come over to this country from the Yemen when it was still Aden. He had been invited back to the country of his parents the year before as a guest of the government. A gym was especially done out for him. He had performed several demonstration bouts there with Ryan, in front of vast crowds. The crowds had gone wild. He had been presented to the President and was given the fifteen-thousand-pound gold Rolex and a jewel-encrusted dagger. The watch never came off, the dagger stayed at home. Here was a cultural hero. Arabic television (MBC) were here to record the bout. 'N-A-Z'. The chant went up from the small cohort beside the ringside barrier. 'S-H-E-F-F-I-E-L-D,' came the chant from the back of the hall, from his non-Yemeni supporters. 'YABBA DABBA DO,' shouted the boxing trainer who had once tried to persuade Brendan to stay on the floor where he belonged.

Over the weeks before the fight I had been trained up to record Naz's speed of combination punches. A flurry had become a pattern. There was some order in that entropy of movement. Not predictable order; the transitional probability from one movement to the next was still impossibly low. But order none the less. You knew how many would land, and how long they would take. You knew that the man holding the pads would have sore joints at the end of the barrage. Brendan has trouble with his elbows, and would often ask his son John to take over with the pads. John would try to persuade Naz to take it a bit easier to ease the pressure on his joints. 'We're interested in speed, Naz, not hitting power, just take it easy.' Fifty-four combination punches in twelve seconds in training, with an almost infinite combinatorial pattern. In other words, you could never tell what was coming next. And neither could Picardi. Scores of combination punches in practice. I watched Picardi smile for the first twelve seconds of the fight. After that he was concentrating too hard to worry about the outer vestiges of social performance. Naz was managing to hit him while he was looking at the floor. He had boasted about this, and how it did in the heads of his opponents. Naz was a switch hitter, switching from southpaw to orthodox and back. Sometimes square on. Picardi looked traumatized by the whole event.

In the second round Picardi managed to hit Naz. A cheer went up from somewhere in the leisure centre. Perhaps it was an expression of relief from us mortals in the audience that up there in the ring was one of us able to read this fast furious flurry of behaviour, decode it, predict it and respond in kind. Perhaps it was relief that up there we had a fight on. Temporarily. Naz feigned a little wobble and went straight back to business. In the third Naz came out in an orthodox stance, quickly switching to southpaw. Punching hard with both left and right hands. Picardi was down in both the first and second rounds, but these were a result of pushes as much as actual clean punches ('We don't want two falls and a submission,' said Reg Gutteridge, the commentator on ITV). In the third he went down cleanly and the fight was stopped soon after that, exactly as Naz had predicted. Many of Naz's fans who had listened to his prediction made a fortune from the bookies at 10–1, a fortune by Wincobank standards.

At the end of the fight Picardi looked confused, as confused as he had looked when he had watched Naz enter the hall, as confused as he had looked whilst Naz danced across the ring, as he had looked whilst Naz had flexed his little pectorals in time to the music right in front of him.

Naz was back in the limelight, where he feels he belongs, giving his version of the proceedings. The bright lights of the TV cameras that had made Brendan look so old and grey lit up Naz's skin. It made him shine. It was time to pay the customary respects to the gallant opponent. 'I thought he was a good fighter, but I produced the goods. I boxed up to my standards and I did the business in style. No funny stuff, no showboating, as they say. I just went down to business tonight. I predicted the round in the third, and, boom, took him out. He caught me in the second. He was a pretty strong fighter. I could see the way he was trying to cover up and counter with the shots, but I didn't really give him the chance. I done the business, I done it in style. That's what I'm proud of.'

The finish had been almost clinical – straight, powerful shots to the head. 'It was a straight left, straight through the middle. Boom, oh yeah. I knew from then onwards a couple of shots more that the title would still be mine. I'm never letting it go and the world title is coming. Baby, good shot. He's gone, I could see it in his eyes. A couple following a right hand, a left hook. He didn't want to know after that.'

210

The funny stuff of the Belcastro fight was being quickly forgotten after this new businesslike approach. But that's not to say that it might never be dusted down and pulled out in the future. 'It can do a fighter's head in when you mess around, but tonight I wanted to get straight down to business, to show the crowd my punching power, to show the style. It worked out.'

And what will he be remembered for after the switches in stance and the speed of the combinations are long forgotten? Just one sentence to ITV interviewer Gary Newbon: 'If you were to tell me I'm a great fighter, I'd say "Tell me something that I don't know," and that's not being arrogant. I'm just a born winner, just born to be king.' The words on the back of his Fred Flintstone shorts said 'To be King'. Every fighter needs his advertising slogan: 'Simply the best', 'The Dark Destroyer'. All three-part catchy titles, like the writing on cereal packets.

Frank Warren was on one side, Brendan on the other, Naz's father Sal, making a rare appearance in front of the TV cameras, clutching the European belt, squatting slightly behind him. It was Warren Naz turned to first, to have his dreams confirmed. 'You know that, don't you, Frank?'

Gary Newbon turned to Naz's father. 'Mr Hamed, has he always been like this?'

'To be honest, yes,' came the reply.

Coming of Age

It was a mistake at the weigh-in for the Freddy Cruz camp to call Naseem a boy. It rankled. Cruz had even given him a peck on the cheek at the press conference, just like he was kissing some bambino. The bambino had been spitting fire all afternoon.

The Cruz fight was recognized as a step-up in class for Naz. They were fighting in October 1994 for the vacant WBC International Super-Bantamweight Championship at the Ponds Forge Sports Leisure Centre in Sheffield. A bit of a Mickey Mouse title, as Reg Gutteridge at ringside was keen to point out, for those not rated in the top ten of the super-bantamweight division. But another crucial stepping stone, and a slippery one at that. Naz had come up a weight for this fight. It was part of the grand plan to demonstrate that the Prince really could be world champion at four different weights.

Cruz was going to be a tough opponent. He had never been put down in fifty-six fights, and he had lost on only six occasions – four times at the start of his professional career in 1985 but since then only twice – on both occasions fighting for world titles, once for the WBA world super-bantamweight against Wilfredo Vasquez in Italy and once for the WBO world featherweight title against Steve Robinson in Cardiff the previous June. Both fights had gone the distance. This was no mug. No dead meat being dragged into the ring. Cruz was to be a stiff test. The television commentators were keen to market this fight as the one to really test the prince of hype. As Jim Rosenthal said in the pre-match warm-up: 'Prince Naseem Hamed is starting to make a very significant impact. Some of his antics can be annoying. He has been called "big-headed" and "arrogant", but can he fight at the highest level? We'll find out a lot more tonight . . .' Barry McGuigan was predicting 'a difficult struggle for Hamed'.

The Prince meanwhile was telling anyone who was prepared to listen that it would be all over by the fourth or fifth round. Rafael

Guerrero, Cruz's trainer, was not convinced. 'I think Freddy can win by points, but if Naseem is lazy when Freddy hits him several times, I think he is going to be down.' But lazy is never an adjective I would apply to Naseem, either in the gym or in the ring.

I sat ringside surrounded by Naz's immediate family, watching Brendan coach through all sorts of intermediaries. Ryan, Naz's best friend and the lad who carries the Union Jack into the ring, was working overtime. Brendan was whispering the instructions and Ryan was bawling them out. 'Keep the pressure on . . . Work off the jab . . . Everything off the jab . . . Work your way in, Naz.'

'Wicked, Naz.' The pitch was getting higher and higher as Ryan got more and more excited. 'Naz, the man!' shouted one of Naz's brothers sitting behind me. 'Naz, the main man,' shouted another brother. Cruz was in trouble in the first round, his normally sound defence in tatters. His face was already puffed up. 'Naz, the man!' shouted his brother again right into my ear. His family were going wild. 'Naz, the man . . . Naz, the man . . .'

Brendan was still using Ryan as his mouthpiece at the start of Round Two. 'Back on your jab. Work off the jab.' Brendan was continuing to whisper, and Ryan was bawling it out across the ring. In fact Ryan was adding advice all of his own: 'Bust his face up, Naz.' The MC was now asking one of Naz's brothers what he had done with the Yemeni flag. I thought his mind had skipped ahead a bit and that he was already anticipating the end of the contest. 'Where did you put that flag?' 'It's rubbish anyway,' replied Naz's brother. 'They need a new one, a bigger one. That one is way too small.' Cruz was afraid to lead with anything, because of the power and ferocity of Naz's counters. Naz's family continued to discuss the proportions of the Yemeni flag that would be needed in subsequent fights.

By Round Three Brendan had doubled his number of mouthpieces. His son John was acting as one conduit, Ryan was an alternative channel of communication. 'Dummy that jab!' shouted John. 'Keep him thinking!' screamed Ryan. Naz's family were still focused on one thing, however: 'Show him who's the man.' One wag from the audience wanted to see something different: 'Bring his breakfast up, Naz!' Who can say if any of this good advice from the audience ever gets through to the man in the ring pumped sky high with adrenaline? All I do know is that at that moment Cruz, almost by way of response, landed a good shot on Naz, probably his only effective punch of the whole fight. Naz slipped the rest. The advice from the front row got more frantic: 'Back on him, Naz.' 'Punish him . . . Punish him.' Punishment is the only word for Naz's reply to Cruz's single good shot. As Jim Watt said in his commentary on the fight: 'Nobody believed that Hamed would be treating him quite like this. This must be breaking Cruz's heart.'

Round Four: the coaching continued – 'Stick it out, Naz.' From the row behind me came more of the same. They were still concerned with that crack at the press conference, no matter how seriously it had been originally intended. 'Show him who's the man, Naz.' 'Naz, the man.' Both boxers somehow managed to fall over each other in this round, but as usual Naz managed to turn this into something spectacular by doing two full somersaults to get up off the floor. Reg Gutteridge commented that Naz had 'more front than Blackpool'. Jim Watt added thoughtfully that it was the 'worst thing Cruz and his manager could have done to play games with him at the press conference'. I knew what Brendan was thinking, because I could hear what Ryan was shouting: 'He's tired, he's blowing. Keep him on the jab.' Even I was starting to worry about what had become of the Yemeni flag.

'Nice, nice, nice.' 'Nice, nice, nice.' Brendan was evidently pleased with his boy's performance in Round Five. 'Nice and classy. Just pick him off.' Ryan was now using stronger language all of his own. 'Snap that jab in his face. Body shot. Body shot. Back on your jab. Downstairs, Naz.' The wag in the crowd was at it again: 'Not bad for a lad, eh?' Jim Watt was being convinced: 'A style nobody has ever seen before.' He was admiring how Naz could change the direction of a punch after he had thrown it. Punches were coming out as a jab and ending up as an upper-cut.

In Round Six Brendan was telling him to 'keep in the middle'. But there was no need for caution. Naz had destroyed the old pro who had never been stopped. It was all over. The referee stopped the contest. Naz's younger brother Ali was sitting next to me. 'Have you

'I would pretend that I was Barry McGuigan and Naz would pretend . . . well . . . that he was Prince Naseem Hamed. It was funny, he always wanted to play himself.' John Ingle.

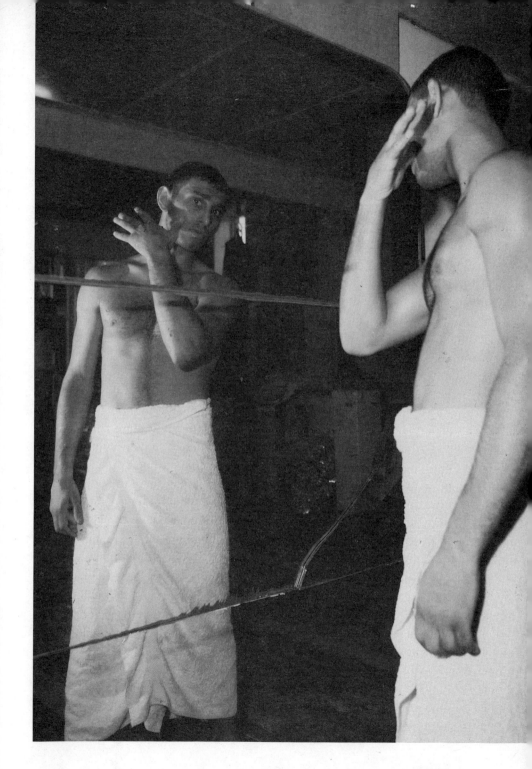

seen his new championship belt?' he asked me. 'Big, ain't it?' Ali called
one of the card girls over to ask how he could get hold of one of
the hats advertising the car retailer that was sponsoring the event.
Somebody had managed to find the Yemeni flag. 'But it's still too
small,' said Ali. Naz was meanwhile telling the world: 'He called me
a child. I showed him I'm a man tonight and I'm going to be king.'

At the press conference after the fight Frank Warren lambasted the
assembled journalists for not previewing the fight in any of the
national newspapers. For Yemeni television Warren's half of lager was
pushed to one side out of shot. Rafael Guerrero, Cruz's trainer,
was asked whether Freddy would now retire. It was time for a bit of
delicate backtracking. 'We think we are going to box with a little
boxer.' 'You said a child,' interrupted Naz, still obviously cut by this
comment. 'OK, I made a mistake. I think he is going to be a world
champion at super-bantamweight. If . . .' There was a pregnant pause
before Guerrero continued in his broken English. 'If God bless him
and give him two or three inches more.' Rafael was warming to his
task. 'I said to Freddy during the fight, "Why you no throw punches?"
Freddy said, "I don't know where he is." In my opinion he's going
to kill Steve Robinson [the WBO world featherweight title holder,
who was ringside].'

Naz interrupted him again. 'I don't want to kill Robinson. I just
want to beat him.' Naz was coming of age all right.

Warren was planning an open-air fight in the summer of 1995
against Robinson. 'It's not professional hype. Naseem is different.
Opponents may be frightened of him, but they were frightened to
fight Ali or Sugar Ray Leonard. But they'll fight him if the money's
right.'

Naz, on the other hand, wasn't talking about money, or comparisons with the legends of the sport, or even making his plans for the
future. There was just one thing on his mind. 'He called me a child.
He had to take the punishment. He knew that I was a man after that.
He knows I'm a man now.'

A Moment's Reflection

The Prince was riding high. The fight against Freddy Cruz was his best performance to date. The tone of the television commentators was changing. They were getting a glimpse of the real substance beneath the hype. They still commented on Naz's circus-like antics, but they now knew there was something there. Cruz had been a serious opponent; he had gone the distance with Steve Robinson for the WBO featherweight title in Cardiff four months earlier. But that night at the sports centre in Sheffield he was demolished. His trainer offered his man as a possible sparring partner for Naz in the months to come. 'He'll make the boy work.' At the weigh-in the Cruz camp had taunted Naz, calling him a child. 'I'm a man now!' Naz screeched in that adrenalin-filled pseudo-American accent that covered his Sheffield accent at times of stress and excitement. Perhaps he was still a boy to the group from the Dominican Republic. Who knows? But then again that might just be the way that boxers talk. A possible world championship for Naz did not now seem that far fetched. Robinson himself was ringside. Still quietly confident. He oozed it in the television interview afterwards. Naz and Brendan were still talking about Naz being a world champion at four weights. Consecutively or simultaneously? It didn't matter any more. They were riding high. A few days later Brendan took me to a little transport café tucked under the M1 viaduct near Wincobank.

I was wondering how the pressure might be building on Brendan, now that the public were starting to recognize that all that Brendan had been saying for thirteen years might have some substance to it. There wasn't anyone in the fight game now who doubted Naz's talent. Were the sharks closing in?

'There's no real pressure. Don't forget, I've been through it all before. The point is that Naz has got his feet on the floor despite his brilliance, and he's only twenty. My favourite boxer of all time, who dragged me out of bed at three o'clock in the morning to watch him, was Muhammad Ali. I think Naz is going to be better than Ali. People say to me, "How can you make a statement like that?" And I say because he can box orthodox, southpaw, he can switch. He's the most versatile boxer around, he's going to be something special.'

I felt like stating the obvious. The funny thing was that everybody was now fairly convinced that Naz was something special. Was Brendan amazed at the change in the attitude of the press and the media?

'Well, nothing surprises me. I've never wavered in what I've had to say about Naz. Let me explain. Reg Gutteridge, the ITV commentator, is of the old school, he's always worked close with the top promoters, who are Mickey Duff and Jack Solomons, and his relations were in the game and they all knew it inside out. But they're very conservative when it comes to boxing. Well, over the years, with my own boxing, and watching my brothers box, and being involved day in and day out with boxing, but never really getting to the top, I kept thinking to myself that there had to be a way of doing boxing that was both graceful and clever and not run of the mill like Henry Cooper and whoever else was produced by England. But watching Muhammad Ali do the Ali shuffle, and watch him in the thriller in Manila and rumble in the jungle, you realized that boxing could be clever and effective, with a very broad appeal. It becomes so international. It gets people out of their bed at three o'clock in the morning. You didn't appreciate at the time how skilful Ali really was. You look back at the films now and you think it was something else. Ali was the master and don't forget he took three years out of his career. But look at where Naz has got to up to now. Just think of what he's achieved.'

Naz might appear to have broken suddenly on to the fight scene, but Brendan remembered all those long years leading up to it. 'In the amateurs, in sixty-seven fights, he only lost five or six. And in these he got robbed. He only worked two or three times in Sheffield as a kid. I remember we went up to one venue and he was about five stone or six stone at that time. As he came up to the ring he was jiving and jazzing about. When he came up to the ring he jumped the ropes and the place erupted. He was probably about thirteen or fourteen years old at the time. Sid Sears was in charge of the school boxing then and he went mad. "What are you doing, humiliating your opponent?"

But the crowd loved it, plus he won. He was brilliant. And Sid Sears came over to me and he says, "If he ever does that again, he'll get barred from amateur boxing." I've been right through boxing since I was a kid, I can understand the attitudes and everything else. I didn't get into a row with him. I didn't fall out with him. But it made me more determined and I passed that on to Naz, and Naz was improving all the time. The only thing to do when people turn round and slag you off is to get better and to prove them wrong. And consequently they must think back now and look at Naz and think to themselves, "You know, he's been telling us that this kid was going to be the world champion for the last thirteen years. He might not have been far wrong."'

But I could sense the resentment in Brendan that they had not listened to him in the first place. 'They couldn't see the talent in this kid who was four stone two pounds wet through. We used to have to put eight pounds' worth of lead weight in his shorts to get him to make the weight. You had to be four stone ten pounds at the time to box. When he got robbed by a decision in a contest, I used to think to myself, "How can they do this to a kid of eleven, twelve or thirteen years old?" But you have to treat this as part of the learning process. I try to make them learn in the gym. I say to the blacks, the blacks will work with the whites to rip off the whites, the whites will work with the blacks to rip off the blacks, the Pakistanis will work with the whites to rip off the blacks, the Irish will work with the English, if it suits, to rip off the Irish or vice versa. Everybody's at it – ripping off everybody else. But don't let it get to you, or don't be surprised by it. That's the lesson, learn from it. Human nature doesn't change, no matter what nationality you are, and once you start to realize this then you'll have a great in-depth insight into what happens with people. Naz has come through now, learning all the time. Learning and studying what I've taught him.'

But I still wanted an answer to the basic question. They had come a great distance together and Brendan had invested a major part of his life in Naz in preparing him and grooming him for a world title, but as that goal approached did he suddenly start to think that it could all slip away, or was he still confident that *he* could steer Naz to the World Championship?

'If we have a row today, which is very, very seldom, because remember he's only twenty and I'm fifty-four, then we can sort it out. Whatever goes off today, tomorrow's a new day, and we carry on. I have the following saying: "To be ignorant is sad. To be ignorant and not know you're ignorant is very sad. For you to know I'm ignorant and not help me – that's terrible." But the minute you start helping me then I've got a bit of knowledge, and I start thinking for myself and start reasoning and pondering, and won't agree with you all the time any more. Given that I've been teaching him all these years and giving him some knowledge, then you wouldn't expect us to agree all the time. Plus you've got outside influences working on him, saying to him, "Why should you give all that money to him? You had to give him £100 when you were getting £400, now you're getting £4000 you have to give him £1000. What's going to happen when you're on four million? You're going to have to give him a million? He doesn't deserve a million. Nobody deserves that kind of money." But as I've explained to Naz, it's not the money. The most important thing about money is the independence it gives you and what you can do with that independence. I've sat down for hours and explained it to him. He says to me, "Well, as an instance, take such and such a fighter you've had. He's done terrible things to you, and I says "Yeah," so he says, "How do you feel about him?" So I says, "When I crack it, I'm going to buy him a house and give him some money." So he says, "How can you do that?" I says, "'Cos I've matured, and I've learnt." People say revenge is sweet; I say revenge is a waste of time, it's time-consuming, it makes people bitter, and really I think life is too short. Of course it's taken me a long time to learn that, to get to this position of knowledge.

'And power,' he added after a pause.

I wanted to pursue the relationship between Naz and Brendan. I asked whether Naz felt a debt to Brendan for getting him this far.

'Well, let me say this to you. I'd be very, very upset if Naz felt he was under any obligation or any debt to me. I would never want him to feel under an obligation or debt to me, and I'm not being cunning or crafty when I say this because I've learned. About eight years ago I had a terrible upset in the gym. I really was in a terrible state, and probably looking back at it now I was going to hit one of my boxers over the head with an iron bar in the gym for what he done on me. I went over and I went into the house and Alma says to me, "What's

220

up with you?" So I told her what so and so's done to me. I couldn't believe it, given all I'd done for him and now what he'd done in return. She said, "I can't understand you getting upset. You've been in the gym for thirty-odd years. You've seen the trouble in Ireland. You've seen the trouble with your own family. You've seen the hassle you've had here, and it upsets me more to see you getting upset." But this particular thing was very serious. Yeah, I was going to kill him. So Alma says, "Listen, think about Jesus Christ in the garden of Gethsemene. You know the story of St Peter, his number one man. Jesus told him that when the soldiers came he would deny him, and Peter said, "No, Master, I shan't do that," and he said, "You will, when the cock crows three times." So Jesus goes over to the corner to pray and while he was praying, the soldiers came and said, "Are you with that geezer?" And Peter said, "No, I'm not." So Alma says to me, "If St Peter done it on Jesus Christ, what are you moaning about?" So from that period of time nothing bothers me. I got over that trauma.'

This seemed like an oblique way to answer the question. A tricky kind of way, suggesting that you cannot foretell what people are capable of doing to you, and you must be prepared for any eventuality. People in a relationship involving debt or obligation are susceptible to all the usual human failings. Brendan had seen enough of these to know that a sense of obligation is no foundation stone for the future.

I asked whether there was anything that could stop Naz from going the whole way.

'Only himself. I always say that to him. Let me tell you that there's no hint of him self-destructing, but anything can happen in life. It's human nature. I've studied human nature for forty-odd years since I was a kid. I can remember things from when I was a kid of four or five that didn't make a lot of sense to me at the time, but I think about them now and I can understand them. I can understand relationships between people, I can understand religion, I can understand relationships between the man and the woman. I've sat down and studied this and consequently it's stood me in good stead because I'm married with five kids. I'm quite happy and I don't have any hassle at home. I have to try to teach Naz some of what I've learned. Take relationships. Naz doesn't have a steady girlfriend at the moment, nothing too serious. I always say to him, "Religion, sex and politics are private and personal, a door closes when a man and woman go behind it into a room, you don't know what they are going to do and, what's more, once they consent to what they do, it's nothing to do with anyone else." Naz doesn't drink alcohol, he doesn't smoke, he has one or two girlfriends he goes around with. At the moment there are no serious relationships, but he's very on the ball about what is happening in his life. I've told you the story about when we went to London and he had to make the weight. I told him that he wasn't eating right, sleeping right, or drinking right. I said to him, "Just because you're knocking everybody out doesn't mean that you've got it all right." And from those days nothing has really changed. Well, me and him handle it in our own different ways. Remember this, I don't know it all, I'm still learning. He's a night person, he becomes active, very, very active, after four o'clock in the afternoon. With Naz, you can forget about the morning. Now, I'm an all-day person because I've learnt to be like that. I get up four or five o'clock in the morning and I'll go for a run. Not every morning. I'll go for a walk sometimes when the place is pitch dark and I'll think. At five o'clock in the morning people see me walking around where I live, and I'll walk and I'll think, and I'll ponder ideas and one thing or another. Some people might think I'm a nutter, but I've learned that this is a special time of the day for reflection. Then I'll come back and have a shower and then go to bed. I'll get up about eight o'clock. I may only have had about an hour or an hour and a half's sleep. But when I get up I've got inspiration about something going through my mind, or something I've seen on television or something I've read, and then I'll try to relate this to do something else in the gym. People say to me that I'm trying to make myself sophisticated and important, but that's not right because I know my limitations and the great part about it is I keep turning out champions. And if you can motivate people and inspire them you must be doing something right. This motivation is a serious business. It's philosophy, it's psychology, it's kidology all rolled into one. Herol Graham always said that I brought the motivation to his boxing, and it took him pretty far.'

If I had closed my eyes while talking to Brendan, and shut out the transport café in Wincobank or the run-down gym just up the road, I could easily have imagined all this talk occurring behind the cloistered walls of some monastery somewhere in the West of Ireland. A million miles from the duckers and divers of boxing, and yet there were those who kept whispering in my ear, informing me and then reminding me that Brendan was one of the biggest duckers and divers of them all.

'But I've got human failings, you know, plenty of them. The fight game is full of highs and lows and they highlight your failings. I had a lean three years after Herol Graham had finished and Slugger O'Toole had finished, and Johnny Nelson had gone on walkabouts. I was just struggling from week to week, so all of a sudden Naz comes through. Naz was the end of my barren three years. I know everybody's going to try and nick him off me. I've got to try and get as much money as I can for him.

'And for myself.' There was a pause again, but only a very short one this time.

'For the money he gets I get. The English are one of the cleverest, if not the cleverest race in the world. People say how can you justify that? Well, I say to them – imagine a little place like this, if you want to be horrible let's say a poxy little place like this, that has controlled a third of the world for two or three hundred years. I've watched the English and studied them. I used to dislike them, with the hassle that we've had in Ireland, even though my grandfather was English. But you have to be on your toes when you're dealing with them. With Naz, first we went with Barry Hearn and everything went well for four or five fights. It was the highest fee in the country for a novice of eighteen. Then I went to Mickey Duff and he offered me six fights a year, trebling the money in the first year. We had three fights with Mickey. Last year Naz went to Ireland and boxed the number eight in Europe, Chris Clarkson from Hull, and knocked him out with the sweetest left upper-cut to the body that's ever been thrown. And he paralysed him. I come from Dublin and fellas were coming up and saying to me, "Naz was looking at his feet when he hit him. He was doing movements with his hands that I couldn't understand. He's something special." And don't forget they know their boxing in Dublin. I says to them I know he's special. I've been teaching him, and what I've been teaching him has sunk in. I've been making myself important, making myself busy, and he's been improving on it, which is marvellous.

'In the meantime we go to the Yemen. Naz's father is very, very wise, because he came from the Yemen like I came from Ireland, and to come to Sheffield, six or seven thousand miles away, and to survive, took something special. He was wise enough to send all the videos of Naz from his schoolboy boxing days to his home in Yemen, so the government invited us to Yemen. I took an advertisement out in the *Boxing News*. It cost me one hundred and fifty quid, the best one hundred and fifty quid I ever spent. I said, "Prince Naseem Hamed, the Arabian Knight, has been invited by the government of Yemen, all expenses paid with a party from Sheffield, and he will fight anyone." We went out there, and he drew ten thousand people at the exhibitions. When we came back we brought the video. We went to see Frank Warren and I showed him the video. He was very, very impressed. He wanted to do a deal, and he came up with the best figures. This was psychology in action. In January '94 Naz boxes a fella he'd already beat, but this time he stops him, a fella called Peter Buckley; he's the only one that went any distance with him. The next fight he boxes Miceli who boxed for the European title. Then he fought Belcastro for the title. We got a good deal from Frank Warren. Everything slotted into place, the trip to the Yemen, the crowd responses, and Naz always managing to produce the goods.'

But Naz was now very hot property. There seemed to be a lot of people who wanted in on the action. 'We had another approach from a former boxer with good connections in the media. He told me that he would get the television interested in him, plus the very best money for him. So after half an hour I says to him, "Right, now the sixty-four-thousand-dollar question. What do you want?" He said that he wanted ten per cent of Naz. So me and Naz went for a walk and talked it over and I asked him what he reckoned. He said "No deal." This guy was asking for ten per cent for what? I'd spent thirteen years training Naz, motivating him, inspiring him like my own. What had this complete outsider done for a slice of the action?'

The boys from Wincobank were on their way. They could afford to act big and dream of the millions just over that next horizon. 'So Naz says to me, "How much do you think I'm going to make, Brendan?" And I says to him, "Forty million quid, if you listen to me." So he says to me, "What are you going to do with your ten million?" I says to him, "I want to buy a house in the South of France, a house in Aden, one in Spain, one in Ireland and I've got one in

Sheffield." He says, "Are ye?" And I says, "Yeah. And all the people that helped me can use the five houses to have their holidays, and I want to buy Herol Graham a house, and I'm going to give him fifty grand." And he says, "You're kidding, after all that's happened?" But I says, "I can afford to be generous with my ten million." Then I says to Naz, "You might think that I'm a Holy Joe or a do-gooder, but the proof will be in the pudding, when I get the money."'

But back to reality. Plans were progressing for Naz's next fight in Cardiff. 'For the next fight Warren sent me up a tape of a fella called Ramirez, he's twenty-eight. He's unbeaten and he's very good, but to be honest he's too much of a danger man for Naz for his next fight. Naz could beat the three World Champions easier than what he would beat this fella. I went up to Naz this morning and I says to him, "We don't want Ramirez, there's nothing to gain from it." The next fight is in Cardiff. Up to the present his opponent is Ramirez, but between me and you since I seen the video this morning his opponent will be changed.'

I then asked about Herol Graham. Herol was Brendan's first big star. How did he compare with Naz?

'Herol's greatest weakness was women. He was a very emotional person, and his choice of women in my opinion was poor. And he got carried away. I was to blame as well. I run after him. But he was brilliant. The other thing was he never worked, he had only boxed. He had a few bits of jobs for a couple of months and everything else, but he never had the discipline of work. I worked on building sites for years. This did me a power of good. You need this kind of work to teach you about discipline, and to teach you about life. Otherwise, you've got nothing to compare your present situation to. You also need a work situation to understand human nature. The most complicated thing on this earth is human nature, and human nature doesn't change. What they were doing five thousand years ago they're still doing now. I'm a great reader of the Bible, and the stories about human nature are all in the Bible, with the parables and the story of the prodigal son.'

I was actually interviewing Brendan at a critical point in Herol's life. Herol had announced his comeback to the ring but was still waiting for the British Boxing Board of Control to give him his licence back. Rumours about Herol and what had become of his legendary reflexes were rife, prompted by the story that he had been knocked out in training. I asked Brendan for his views on the Herol Graham comeback.

'For eight years nobody could hit Herol, never mind beat him. I sold his contract for seventy-five thousand quid to Barney Eastwood. I always said that was my pension money. Herol was ranked number one for the world title at the time. I never had two bob. I was kept on as the trainer at ten per cent. It was costing Herol thirty-five per cent – twenty-five to Eastwood as manager, ten to me as trainer. After Eastwood took Herol over, Herol beat a fella called Robotte in the first round in Las Vegas, on the same bill where McGuigan lost to Steve Cruz. A few weeks later, the atmosphere in the gym was shocking so I asked Brian Anderson who was very close to Herol what the matter was. Brian told me that it was because I hadn't given Herol any of that seventy-five thousand quid. Herol said that I always told him that if I ever made any money out of him we would share it. But I needed this money to give me the protection to do what I wanted to do in the gym because I've always done everything there on a shoe-string. I'd got so much to do at the gym with the kids I was developing, and I'd got kids who had plenty of problems at home that I was sorting out. I was up to my neck in the gym with people's problems. Really I was doing the council's and the government's work, and I wasn't getting paid for it. I went to see Herol and I told him that he was going to get a fortune working with Eastwood, and I wasn't in at twenty-five per cent no more. But he says to me, "If you don't give me twenty-five thousand pounds out of that money then you and me are finished." I was very upset by the dispute because he'd lived with me for a year and a half, for more or less next to nothing, like he was one of the family. So I said, "Let me think about it." A close friend of mine – "Billy Flat Cap" as we call him, or "Billy the Bagman" – told me to offer Herol two-thirds of the ten per cent I was still on as his trainer until I paid the twenty-five off. Herol then beat Mark Kaylor in London, then he boxed Charlie Boston in Belfast. But we had a dispute over money again, this time about the money he was getting for fights, and that was that. Everything stopped. I stopped paying him and he told me that I was too cunning and crafty. I said to him that if I wasn't cunning and crafty bringing up five kids in the fight game then I never would have survived. Our relationship broke down completely. When he fought Kalambay for the European Title, that was the first time I hadn't been in his corner. He lost.

'Eventually, a journalist friend of mine called Peter Markie, a smashing fella, tells me that this dispute is going to kill the boxing off in Sheffield for the next twenty or thirty years if we don't get back together. So he more or less acted as the intermediary, and me and Herol got talking again. So I bit me lip and apologized so me and Herol could get back together again. Then Herol was on his way back. So Herol starts winning again – Ricky Stackhouse, James Cook and Johnny Melfah. In those last two fights, he retained his British Middleweight title and he won a Lonsdale Belt for the Melfah victory, and he gets right up there and he's boxing for the world title. At the time, he had a denture, and he had to take the denture out to put his gumshield in for fights, but after one of his fights his girlfriend at the time saw him without his denture in and started laughing and ridiculing him, so he went and got a bridge put in. It cost about two or three grand. So he used to put the gumshield over it. So when he boxed Julian Jackson for the world title, in the third round as the bell went Jackson hit him. As I took his gumshield out, all his teeth were in the gumshield, so I've got to put it back. He'd already closed your man's eye. The referee went over at the end of that round and he says that he's giving Jackson one more round. I says to Herol, "Now you've got to be careful, hit and get out of the way. Just get through the round." But as I'm talking to him I could see him thinking, "I've closed his eye, the bastard has broken my denture. I'm going to fucking knock him out." He goes out in that fourth round and he doesn't take my advice. Herol commits himself and Jackson hits him with this hook on his chin as he's coming in. He didn't know what happened to him. He was flat before he hit the floor, and I thought, "You fucking stupid bastard." I've seen it all in the fight game. He would have won that world title if it hadn't been for some girl winding him up about his denture.

'Four weeks before the second Kalambay fight he had more woman trouble. He went on to fight Kalambay, but his mind wasn't on the fight. But I tell you, what a fight. He boxed brilliant, he beat Kalambay. But he got robbed.

'So I got the sack. Herol's gone elsewhere to train. Herol is coming up to box Frank Grant for the British title, a step down in class. But he goes down to train in London for this fight. Mickey Duff asks me to go into Herol's corner for the fight. That kind of request always seems to me to be a bit of an insurance policy. If Herol lost and I was in his corner then I would get blamed, even though I wasn't training him. On the other hand, if Herol lost and I wasn't in his corner I'd still get blamed because people would say, "Can't they patch up their differences?" On the night of the fight Herol was like death warmed up. He was like that the week before the fight. When he got into the ring he was knackered and he got knocked out. So then he came back to Sheffield with me and he started training. But there was no co-ordination, it was all gone. It was terrible just looking at him, a real shocker. Amateurs were hitting him, we even had a thirteen-year-old kid landing good shots on him. So then Herol drifted away from the gym and he packed it all in. The story's over. But he's got rid of his money. He's got nothing. Then the next thing you hear is that he's planning to make a comeback, he's going to do this and that and the other. I'm the bastard now, aren't I? Last month I had a little kid in my car, and he says that he wants to ask me something personal. He says, "Did you rip Herol Graham off?" I told him that I wouldn't rip anyone off. But this is what the little kids have heard on the grapevine. So Herol went down to London a couple of months ago to spar and train with Mickey Duff, and he was given a very hard time by a young boxer there. Everybody was saying that he was a tragedy waiting to happen. It wasn't me who said this.

'Meanwhile Herol is watching what is happening up in his old gym. The spotlight is back on Wincobank. Sheffield has produced a new superstar. No one can blame Herol for being jealous of Naz. I hear that he's warned Naz about me, he's told him to be cautious. But Naz just told Herol that he'd been with me for thirteen years, and I'd never done anything wrong while I'd been with him. Naz has heard on the grapevine that there was some dirt on me going around. But nobody's got anything on me because I keep my nose clean, even when I'm abroad. My style is as long as I get something to eat and a lemonade to drink, I'm into bed and goodnight. I put all the money in my trousers, put it under the mattress and put a chair under the door and that's me done for the night. Then I get on the plane the next day and I'm off. Or I put me money down me sock and I'm off to the airport. Nobody has any dirt on me, no matter what they say.'

It had been an interesting lunch. I couldn't help but notice that the style of the language had changed. The density of the expletives in Brendan's speech had increased dramatically while we were discussing the relationship between Herol and himself, and I couldn't help but recall that Brendan had said earlier that he had spent the major part of his life studying human relationships. But presumably in a more abstract sense. The frustrations in trying to understand particular relationships with all their ups and downs and nuances and connotations were plain to see. But he wasn't finished with relationships just yet.

'Let me just finish by adding that there are a lot of people around who would like to spoil the relationship I've got with Naz. But I think that a lot of people are going to be disappointed in this particular case. This time I've got a boxer and me and him are going all the way.'

It Hurts Being This Good

Despite all Brendan's reservations, Naz's next opponent turned out to be Laureano Ramirez. Ramirez had never lost a contest and was then ranked number four in the world. Seventeen wins and one draw beneath his belt, seven of the wins coming by KO. Naz went to Cardiff to meet him, to the National Ice Rink. He got a chilly reception. Steve Robinson, whom everybody was now saying Naz would be challenging for the world title some time in 1995, was a local boy. Boos greeted Naz's entrance. This was a long way from Sheffield. The fight commentators were changing their tune about Naz yet again. 'I feel sure that he's going to be a world champion in 1995,' said Jim Rosenthal before the fight began. Barry McGuigan now hailed Naz as 'an awesome prospect', with 'incredible hand speed' and 'incredible punching power'. 'But he's got to keep winning,' he warned. 'The boxing world is full of pitfalls.' Naz was creating possible pitfalls for himself by predicting the round yet again – the third, he told me.

'Just like the old master Ali,' said Brendan. 'It's not enough for him to win any more. He wants to do it in that particular style. He'll be writing verses next.'

The Flintstones were now old hat, but Ryan, Naz's pal, still came into the ring carrying Naz's WBC international belt wearing the full leopardskin outfit. Brendan, meanwhile, had returned to shamrock green. One of Naz's brothers again had the Yemeni flag. Reg Gutteridge at ringside still had some misgivings for the ITV network: 'Is Prince Naseem Hamed the real thing? He's certainly beginning to look like it.' Jim Watt summed the Prince up nicely: 'He does things that you wouldn't want boys in the gymnasium to do. But he's so good at doing them that he gets away with it.'

This fight was different. The first two rounds were slow. Ramirez was not to be bullied. The leading upper-cut which had finished Ramirez's fellow countryman from the Dominican Republic, Cruz, never managed to catch Ramirez himself. At times it looked as if it was in slow motion, and the crowd booed and jeered. I kept thinking that they should just have felt relieved for Steve Robinson's sake. But no, they wanted a show. However, the third round, the round which Naz himself had warned us to keep our eyes open in, was different. Naz threw Ramirez over. 'Outrageous,' said Reg Gutteridge. The referee, Mickey Vann, thought so too, and gave the Prince a stern talking-to. But the next minute one punch had Ramirez turning away, complaining that he had swallowed his tooth. The next minute he was down. Naz was jumping up and down with a new gum shield that was white in the centre and black elsewhere. He looked like Bugs Bunny on speed. His prediction had been accurate after all. Ramirez looked as if he couldn't remember how he got to Wales.

Afterwards, Prince Naseem Hamed, for the first time, publicly thanked Allah for his victory. 'Allah said to me "That was your round."' Before reverting to form: 'It hurts being this good.' Ramirez looked as though he believed it as well.

Even When I'm Asleep I'm Thinking About Boxing

I had never seen the gym so full. 'Is Naz here?' I heard one kid ask. I hadn't seen this particular boy before. The news was spreading. Eight in the ring were sparring at the same time, six were around the ring waiting for their turn. 'Two in, two out,' said Brendan, directing the flow without even glancing up. The heavy bags were all busy, and there was a little unbroken line of future world champions all shadow-boxing in front of the one cracked mirror laid up against the wall.

In the ring professional and amateurs were all mixed together, as always. One slight, eight-year-old boy called Alex, whose mother is a professional shoplifter, sparred with Johnny Nelson, the European cruiserweight champion. Alex danced excitedly this way and that way around him. His mother had recently been away for six months. Brendan told the boys in the gym that she was away on holiday. 'I bet she comes back with a suntan with two stripes down the middle,' said one nine-year-old. These boys take some fooling. Jimmy Wood, fifty-five and a moneylender, who trains every day, including, he told me, Christmas day, sparred with Ryan Rhodes, the eighteen-year-old soon to make his professional debut. The jabs did not sting Jimmy as he moved relentlessly forward; they ended their short, abrupt journey in loud, deep thumps on the bone in shoulder and forearm.

Jimmy had recently been robbed at home. 'It's common knowledge around Wincobank that I'm a quarter of a millionaire,' he confessed to me. He had told me that he gets a lot of frustration in his particular job, but boxing released it all. 'Plus, I love the competition. All these young 'uns go into the ring with me and they think they're going to fucking bash me up because I'm getting on a bit, but they're wrong.' Ryan's jabs were leaving great red welts on Jimmy's upper arms, but Jimmy was still trying to rush him.

Jimmy Wood. 'The young lads think that they're going to bash me up because I'm getting on a bit, but they're wrong.'

Two men from the *Daily Express* were waiting patiently in one corner of the gym for Naz to arrive for training. 'I'll let you take a photograph of me sparring with Johnny for a quid,' said Alex. It was no deal, said the men from the *Express*. 'Could you lend me fifteen pence for my bus home, then?' asked Alex, even though he only lived up the street. They hadn't the right change, so he got twenty pence instead.

'I'm at this game twenty-four hours a day, seven days a week, week in and week out,' said Brendan, sitting on the wooden steps beside the ring. 'Even when I'm asleep I'm thinking about boxing. People say to me, "Boxing has taken over your life," and I says to them, "Dead right it has." It has to if you're going to get anything out of it.'

I asked him what he still had to get out of the fight game. 'Recognition. For thirty years people have been saying that I'm a nutcase

233

because of the unorthodox system of training I use. I teach time and distance co-ordination, I teach mobility and flexibility, I teach balance. I use music to teach these things – Glenn Miller for Herol Graham, rap for Naz. People thought I was mad for doing this. I have eight sparring in the ring together; people thought I was a nutcase for doing it this way. When I drew lines on the floor and started teaching footwork and movement and started teaching the choreography of boxing, people said I was crazy. I understand that self-praise is no recommendation, but I knew that my ideas were good and I decided then that nobody was going to pinch my ideas off me. But now people are ringing me up from all over the place when they see Naz on the television. They want to come up to the gym to see how I teach the kids to be so good on their feet. After all these years, it's quite funny really.

'You see, I've followed all the great trainers since I was a kid, and all the great trainers are the professors of boxing. You've got to know your subject inside out, otherwise you don't operate. I'm a professor of boxing, a professor of psychology and a professor of kidology all rolled into one. You have to be. I got my fighters through without having the money to develop and promote them. I taught them the art and the skills of survival – in the gym and on the street. I motivated them, I picked them up when they lost and I started all over again. Now I've brought a young lad to the edge of the world championship – in six months he'll be officially the best in the world. I got some help off my friends, but I never had the big money behind me. Nobody can fault the kid, and they're now starting to believe what I've been saying all these years about him. They thought I was a nutcase. Now they've had to change their tune.'

There was just a hint of bitterness in Brendan's tone. Criticized throughout his career. But slowly, month by month and fight by fight, things were changing.

'When I had Herol Graham I came in for a lot of stick. They said that Herol was a defensive master. They said to me, "All your boxers are very defensive, they're boring. They're all limbo dancers, they're not fighters. It's not what the paying customer wants." Another fella criticized me in a different way. He said to me that Herol Graham was already made when I took him on. So I said to him, "OK, Herol may already have been made, but the year before he came to me he got licked in the ABA championships. The first year with me he won the ABA championship and went on, and was unbeaten for eight years until I got the sack." And if this is right, how do you account for Johnny Nelson? Johnny was absolutely terrible at the beginning of his career. He had fifteen fights as an amateur and only won three. And now he's won the British cruiserweight title, he's won a Lonsdale Belt outright, he's become European cruiserweight champion, and he's won a version of the world cruiserweight title – the WBF. How do you explain Naseem Hamed? I've had him since he was seven. I taught him everything he knows. He won seven British titles in amateur boxing and at twenty, when Eubank was still boxing four-rounders and Nigel Benn was still boxing Mexican road sweepers, Naz becomes European champion and beats world-ranked fighters.' But if Brendan was now getting all that he had wanted from boxing, did he think the same was true of his old protégé and friend Herol Graham?

'In my view, Herol will not get his licence back now. The British Boxing Board of Control have brought out a new psychometric test for boxers as well as insisting on brain scans and a general medical. The test is a combination of arithmetic, word association tests, oral skills, puzzles and written questions and answers. It's the psychometric test he failed. To be honest, I wouldn't pass it myself. No chance. I don't think that any of the fighters in here would pass it. The English are a very clever race, you know. They can always shift the goal post when they want to. When they make up their mind about something they'll go ahead and do it. When Herol looked so down in training that was it. Boxing has been my life, but I know that it can be very cruel. Naz won't make the same mistakes as Herol, take it from me. And all the young kids here in the future will learn from Naz.'

Brendan raised himself up from the wooden steps and went over and turned off the music. It was time for the first lesson. He climbed into the ring with a little pair of reading glasses perched on the end of his nose. He was the Irish schoolmaster again. The teacher back in Dublin who had made his life hell as a boy. He carried a cutting from a newspaper. He asked the boys and the men, the novices and the champions, to line up around the outside of the ring. He asked for quiet.

'Can you see this paper? Can you see it? Can you see it? There were fifteen hundred jobs advertised in a car firm in Ontario in Canada. There are sub-zero temperatures in Canada at this time of year. It would absolutely freeze the balls off a brass monkey out there, and there were twenty thousand people who turned up for these fifteen hundred jobs and they queued up in the cold. One fella who was in the queue said that getting a job was like winning the . . . what?'

'The lottery,' answered one of the young boxers. The last time I had seen this young lad he had had his face badly beaten up after a fight on the Prince's undercard at Hillsborough Leisure Centre.

'The lottery,' repeated Brendan. 'Have you got me? Do you know why I'm saying this to you? Never take anyone or anything for granted.'

He pointed at Johnny Nelson. 'He's the European champion, he's a Lonsdale Belt holder, he's got the whole lot. Do you know why? Because he didn't sit on his backside. He's gone out there and done the business. He's getting a living from boxing, he's fighting all over the place. He's just back from Thailand where he fought a big Russian fella – a giant – and he licked him. Isn't that right, Johnny? He's out to Thailand next month to fight again. Then there's Naz. He'll be world champion in six months, and they want him to fight for the world title out in the Yemen. He's a hero out there. His photograph is on the front and back cover of all the schoolbooks. Not even Muhammad Ali had his photograph on schoolbooks. But Naz, born just up the street, has done this. Have you got me? That's what boxing can do for you.'

One boy started talking to the lad next to him. Brendan adjusted his glasses in a schoolmasterly fashion. 'You're not paying attention. Getting a job is like winning the . . . what?'

'The lottery.'

'The lottery. Have you got me?'

He worked his way up one side of the ring.

'Are you working?'

'No.'

'Are you working?'

'No.'

'Are you working?'

'Yes.'

Brendan seemed dumbfounded for a moment. He hesitated.

'Are you? That's marvellous.' But the hesitation only lasted for a fraction of a second.

'But it's like coming in here. This is the only game that you can get . . . what?'

'Killed at.'

'Killed at. Have you got me? It's a serious business, but if you're on the ball in here you've got a better chance out there of getting a . . . what? A job. That's right – a job. And a decent life. Don't forget that either. Have you got me? Now, off you go to the music.'

Naz was not just a hero back in the Yemen. You just had to look around the gym to see that. Herol Graham had got so close and fell so far. When Herol faltered, so did the dreams and aspirations of a whole culture. It was tough out there, and it was just as tough in boxing itself. In fact, there was no way through for any of them. So why bother? But suddenly things were different. You could go all the way with persistence and dedication. It was not just Brendan preaching to them any more. They could see it with their own eyes. In their living rooms. And they had all learned from what had happened. Naz would not make the same mistakes. Brendan had confessed that in boxing these days great skill is no longer enough. Chris Eubank had taught everybody that. A man who had never fought Herol Graham in his prime had made millions from posing and strutting as 'simply the best'. Right from the beginning of his amateur career Naz had been vaulting the ropes and doing hand springs across the ring, and dancing and jiving about. To be noticed, to stand out, to draw attention to the fifty-four combination punches that he could throw in a few short seconds. But which might otherwise go unnoticed. And Brendan had the rest of these kids all practising their entrances as well. Every day lining up by the ropes, and one by one vaulting over them. He was not just teaching them boxing or even the more valuable skills of survival inside and outside the ring. He was keeping the dream alive.

I had learnt a lot from my visits. I was just about to leave. Naz was chatting to the men from the *Daily Express*, Alex was asking two fans, who had wandered into the gym for Naz's autograph, for his bus fare home. Jimmy was still up there in the ring going forward, with something to prove. The rest of the lads were practising their ring acrobatics for the day when they too would be criticized by the ringside commentators on the television in your living room for being the showmen and the show-offs of the boxing world.

Brendan pulled me to one side for one last confidential word. 'Let me give you a tip. You've come down here to learn about boxing, right? Now take it from me, if you want to see how I go about making a kid the best in the world, then you've left it too late with Naz. I've got a kid here called Daniel Teasdale. He's only twelve now, but I've had him since he was six. But he's brilliant. He can hit and he can fight, and he's got plenty of guts. That's one thing you've got to have in this game. And he's dedicated. He comes in here every day. And if I tell him to jump, he just asks me, "How high do you want me to jump?"'

Brendan took a sharp intake of breath. I could sense what was coming next. I almost ducked. 'Daniel has got as much talent as Naz when he was that age. He's going to be a world champion at four different weights. At least. Have you got me? Now what you'll have to do is come down to the gym a couple of times a week for the next eight years, and then you'll see how it's done.

'We can start tomorrow if you like.'

No Occupational Fear At All

It was the new year. The year it was all going to happen. Naz was to fight the Mexican Armando Castro in Glasgow in the WBC International Super-Bantamweight title defence in January 1995. Castro was another world-class fighter, it was said, and he was being billed as yet another serious threat. In his previous fight Castro had boxed for the WBO Bantamweight title and had lost on points to Alfred Cotey. But most of Castro's fights were at a lower weight – flyweight or super-flyweight. He came into the ring looking heavier for the fight, but flabby. The extra weight did not suit him. Naseem on the other hand was lean and keen. 'More fat on a butcher's apron,' said the fight commentator.

Naseem backed him up from the opening bell. Castro's reputation counted for nothing once that bell sounded. Reg Gutteridge, sitting ringside, said that Naseem had 'no occupational fear at all'. Castro beckoned him on. This gesture looked faintly ridiculous. Naseem landed a jolting left hook which caused Castro's legs to stiffen. The punch was bang on the chin. One of Naseem's sparring partners had earlier described to me how when one of Naz's punches lands spot on, it feels like an electric shock. To make this account more credible the young sparring partner told me that he knew what a real electric shock felt like, and he described in detail how he had once climbed an illegal electrified fence in somebody's back yard in Rotherham to look at some birds, feathered birds, and had received a few volts for his efforts. 'It were fucking horrible,' he told me. I looked at Castro's face and I knew that the young sparring partner's description was accurate. Castro had the expression of a man stuck on a fence out the back of somebody's house, somewhere in Rotherham, with a few unexpected volts zipping through him. Naz was now giving an exhibition of a flurry of two-handed punches. The kind of exhibition he gives at the end of each round in training when Brendan calls 'ten

239

seconds', when he's in the ring working with John, Brendan's son, on the pads. You see John slumping in the corner between rounds after this barrage has temporarily ceased, and he has the pads to protect him. 'I feel sick,' said John after the blows stopped raining down on his pads, although admittedly he had experienced twelve rounds of this. After this painful exhibition Castro was still trying to beckon Naz on. It was not just ridiculous any more, it was pitiful. Castro's legs still hadn't recovered, they were hardly holding him and he clearly had no ability to balance left in him. His wild, swinging punches were propelling him across the ring to more punishment.

In the second round two punches, one immediately after the other – a beautiful right upper-cut and a left hook – put Castro on the deck, but this was judged to be a stumble, or a shove. Still Castro motioned Naz forward. You almost wanted to avert your gaze. It was all over in the fourth. A right hook had Castro on his way, his backside held up by the ropes. The referee stepped in. Naz thought it was all over and did a somersault, but the referee just gave Castro a standing count. It was stopped a few seconds later, and the official somersault followed. The President of the Yemen had now promised Naz a Mercedes sports convertible to go with the gold Rolex. Naz told the viewers in his post-fight interview, 'I'm definitely getting it. I know that. I think he wants to give me three after this fight.' For a moment Naz sounded like a young boy again, dreaming of Christmas.

I talked to John after the fight, the man who knows what these punches from Naz can do. The man behind the pads for the last ten years. I asked for his assessment of Naz's performance. 'Castro came here with a good reputation. In his last fight he fought Alfred Cotey. Cotey was bashing him all over, but he never looked as if he was going to stop him. The reports in the boxing papers were all about "Iron Chin Castro". Castro got hit with everything in the fight against Cotey, but he never got rocked and he never looked as if he was going to get stopped. Tonight was completely different. It was all over in the first round really, it turned out to be an exhibition fight for Naz. Naz did with him what he wanted. I don't think Castro can believe it. The press conference was quite funny. His manager and trainer were Mexican but they all lived in California. Naz was saying at the press conference that he would knock this guy out in four rounds. The manager with the baseball cap was saying, "You're nothing but a clown. Armando's going to do this and he's going to do that." It was really funny, it wasn't nasty. It was all done in good humour. Naz wanted to put his purse on the fight to test the manager out. At the weigh-in, the manager looked at Naz and said, "Is this him?" They were looking at him and seeing that he hasn't got a mark on him. Not like the Mexican fighters you see. Naz doesn't look like a boxer, he looks more like a pop star. They must have thought that Naz's record was based on somebody getting him dead bodies to beat up in the ring. I think they've probably changed their mind about that now.'

I asked John to talk me through the fight. 'Castro came out on a suicide mission tonight. He was swinging everything. Naz just leaned back and went bump, bump, bump. Naz did with him what he wanted. He stepped around and made him look foolish. The kid was swinging wildly, Naz just bashed lumps off him. I don't think that the kid laid a punch on Naz. It looked as if Naz was going to stop him three or four times before he finally did. Naz had him with his backside on the ropes, the kid was more or less gone. If the ropes hadn't been there the kid would have gone down. Castro basically just followed him around for three rounds, getting bashed up. It's another big stepping stone for Naz.'

John and Naz have been inseparable for the past ten years, as friend and assistant trainer, the man with the pads in the ring, the man who takes all the punishment as Naz gets stronger and stronger. John is very sensitive, though, if you refer to him as Naz's trainer. 'I'm always in the corner with my dad. I'm not the trainer. My dad's the trainer. My dad does all the talking between rounds in his fights. I'm there in the corner as well, but I'm more at the side sort of thing. My dad will be saying, "Deep breathing, Naz," "Steady up," "Do this, do that." I'll just comment on anything that I've noticed during the fight, but I won't talk over my dad. If my dad says "Deep breath," I'll just say, "You're busting him up, Naz," "You can see that he's going," or "He doesn't fancy it." I don't want to distract him, I just want to encourage him between rounds.'

Naz was part of the Ingle clan in Wincobank. 'Naz wasn't the kind of kid who went to watch Sheffield Wednesday on a Saturday afternoon. He'd come down to our house and we'd spar together when he was eleven or twelve. We'd just do play acting of the great world title fights. I would pretend that I was Barry McGuigan and he would pretend . . . well, that he was Prince Naseem Hamed. It was funny. He never played Sugar Ray Leonard or anybody like that. He always wanted to play himself. He would be all out to try to stop me. All our play fights would go to the last round. "Prince Naseem Hamed needs a stoppage to get Barry McGuigan's world title." That sort of thing. He'd be dancing about. He always liked to call himself the Prince.'

I asked where he had got this nickname from.

'My dad's got all these old records. Naz heard the "Rich Maharajah of Magador".' John asked me if I knew it, and then started to sing it for me. '"There was a rich Maharajah from Magador. He had ten thousand rupees" . . . or women, I can't remember which, or maybe more. "He had diamonds and pearls and the prettiest girls, but he never knew how to do the rumba." Naz always liked hearing about maharajahs and princes. When he had to pick a nickname, that's what he went for. He knows all my dad's old records. He knows all the Irish rebel songs that my dad likes to sing. He likes the Dubliners' "Whisky In The Jar". He knows all the Inkspots' records word for word.'

John was twenty-seven. Like Naz, a lot of his growing up had been done in the gym. I asked about his relationship with Naz. 'We're like brothers, really. He's always been part of our family. Sal, Naz's dad, knew from the beginning that he could trust us to look after him. Naz's family only lived a few hundred yards up our road. I'm six years older than him, but we always hung about together. When we used to go up to the Pinegrove or wherever, I could see some people thinking, "What's the crack here?" You know – I was eighteen and he was twelve. I suppose that it looked a bit odd sometimes. But it was never as if I was dragging him around, he was always on equal terms with you. I didn't know whether people thought that I was a bit immature knocking around with a kid, but he never seemed like a kid to me, or anybody else who knew him well. It's funny looking back on it now, because it's quite an age difference when you're that sort of age. But that's how it's always been.'

I asked about Naz's singular determination to win – to be the world's number one. How long had he been that determined, that focused? 'He's always been the Prince and he's always been determined to win – be it pool, tennis, football or whatever,' said John. 'We've had some classic pool contests over the years, but he's always got to be number one. The match always has to go on until he wins. One of the reasons that I'd never box is that you have to be one hundred per cent on top of it. It's no good getting into the ring and having doubts because you haven't run today or whatever. There's no place for doubt in the ring. Naz never has any doubts. To me it's not the be-all and end-all to win. That's why I couldn't be a boxer. If I'm playing table tennis and I lose I think to myself "So what?" That's no good if you're a boxer. Naz has got a different sort of mentality to me – to him winning is everything. He's very focused. Before his fights his dad and his brother, Raith, come in and talk to him in Arabic. They're all shouting in Arabic and building him up. When you take him on the pads and his dad comes in, he hits those pads with a real vengeance. His dad never interferes, he just gees him up by saying things in Arabic. I honestly think that Naz is a throwback to the gladiators. If he could go back in time he would have loved it in the Coliseum in front of a hundred thousand people. He'd have no fear, he'd revel in stuff like that. He's a one-off, a born winner. And when you look at what he did tonight you realize that he's only interested in winning good style.'

I Hope He's Nice and Safe

Brendan Ingle always likes to point out that boxing is the only sport where you can legally kill your opponent. Sometimes when you watch it you can get carried away with the balletic grace and the superb skill and the almost choreographed movement, and forget all about the fact that the two guys in that ring are trying to knock each other senseless. All the talk about Naz and his fifty-four combination punches in twelve seconds with eight different foot movements and ten different hand movements makes him sound at times like a ballerina. You can forget that boxing is a serious business. Sometimes you need to be reminded. And boxing has the habit of doing just that.

A recent clip of Muhammad Ali appears on the television in some documentary or other. You see him trying to pick up a little black child to kiss as he is led through a crowd of well-wishers. You are drawn to the agonizingly slow movements, exaggerated by the tremors of Parkinson's disease. That beautiful face unmarked on the surface by the years in the ring still smooth, but now fat and bloated. The rumble in the jungle, the thriller in Manila all left their mark all right. The child he has picked up looks terrified as Ali tries to draw her close. The well-wishers look on embarrassed, hoping that Ali himself will not notice the child's discomfort as she is drawn so slowly and so shakily to a face that was once the most famous face in the world. Boxing had made him what he was then, and it made him what he is now.

'Never forget,' said Brendan Ingle, 'this boxing is a serious business. Just ask Michael Watson.' And he passed me a yellowed clipping from a newspaper showing Watson in a hospital bed with tubes and wires keeping him alive. I had only met Michael Watson once, in a nightclub in Sheffield. He was being shown the City of Steel and his companion pointed me out as a local but not very significant landmark, a kind of predictable figure at Sheffield's ultimate nitespot. 'He's a writer,' said his guide. 'A journalist?' enquired Watson. 'Yeah, sort of,' I replied. 'Oh,' he said and walked on. This wasn't done in any rude sort of way, it was simply the end of the exchange. He had met me, I had met him, and that was the end of it. He didn't want to talk to a journalist on his night off, and who could blame him? When I later saw the photographs of him in that hospital bed it was hard to recognize him. But then again it was only a cursory sort of meeting. The little sign at the Wincobank gym said it all: 'Boxing can damage your health.'

And now boxing was up to one of its old tricks again. Gerald McClellan was the latest victim of the serious business that is boxing, at the hands of Nigel Benn in his WBC Super-Middleweight defence in February 1995, in a fight which was already being described as a classic. As much a classic as Sugar Ray Leonard against Roberto Duran in Montreal in 1980, as much a classic as Sugar Ray Leonard against Thomas Hearns a year later in Las Vegas. It was a real war – what the punters pay to watch. But real wars unfortunately have real casualties. And Brendan Ingle had been right there in McClellan's corner to see it all first-hand. He got twenty nicker that night for the job of 'handing up' in the corner – passing up the stool and spittoon between rounds. He was sitting ringside with Frank Warren when Ernie Draper, 'the whip' – the man who brings the boxers to the ring – asked him to go to see Ernie Fossey, the matchmaker. Fossey asked him to be the 'bucket man' for McClellan for the night. But Brendan told me, 'I would have paid for the privilege of working there that night to witness the greatest fight I've ever seen in a British ring. I must have watched over one hundred thousand fights, and that was the greatest of them all. It was worth a million pounds to experience the way them two fought that night.'

He told me that he's had that twenty-pound note framed – as a memento of the greatest fight of all. Unfortunately, that battle in the ring led, several hours later, to the Royal London Hospital, to neurosurgeons fighting to remove a clot from McClellan's brain.

But how can those involved justify this savagery? 'Look,' said Brendan. 'In my opinion the fight should have been all over in the first round. McClellan put Benn down, and the count lasted a good fourteen or fifteen seconds. The ruling is if you get knocked out of the ring and finish up on the floor outside you get twenty seconds to get back in, but Benn was only knocked on to the apron of the ring. McClellan put so much effort into the first round that when he got back to the corner he was gulping for air. McClellan chased Benn from pillar to post in the second round, and he was throwing bombs at him, but Benn was fighting back. After the third round, if either Benn or McClellan had thrown their hands up and said, "I surrender," nobody could have complained. Everybody had got their money's worth by then. But the battle went on and on and on. I couldn't believe the punishment that was getting dished out and how hard they were hitting one another. But I think it was a clash of heads that did the final damage. Benn caught McClellan with his head just under the eyebrow. Just feel that spot – it's a very tender spot, and just under there is the brain. That was the straw that broke the camel's back. McClellan went down on one knee. Some people thought that McClellan had spewed it – packed the fight in. But I knew that he didn't know where he was. It was a life and death struggle that night.'

I asked whether this really was boxing at its best. Or was this boxing at its very worst? Brendan did not need to think about the answer. 'It was boxing at its most sophisticated, crude, barbaric, enchanting, skilful – all at the same time. Boxing is a serious business. I teach my lads how to take precautions – how to survive in the ring. But I remind them that they're not playing marbles in there. That fight was what life is all about – it was Benn coming back from the brink of nearly getting killed, and surviving. It was McClellan coming back from the brink of nearly getting killed and surviving. And then there was that clash of heads, which was so sad and so unfortunate. It was like Muhammad Ali and George Foreman in Zaire, when Ali took all the bombs that Foreman had to throw at him and then came back and won. Just remember: you don't begin to live until you begin to die. That's well worth remembering.'

I wanted to say, 'Try telling that to the neurosurgeons who had to operate on Gerald McClellan that night,' but sometimes it's prudent to keep your mouth firmly shut. All I did know was that with Ali, Watson and now McClellan, the list of casualties from these classic battles was growing.

And then there was Naseem, or rather Naseem's opponents. They were flown over from South America or Italy, or whichever country can produce small, hard men with creditable records who can take a few knocks, and Naseem was knocking them senseless. Gone were the days of Herol Graham, the limbo dancer they called him, the man who could on occasion hoist his opponent over his shoulder and on to the deck. Gone were the bobbers and weavers, the ordinary lads who grew up in the Wincobank gym, who had been taught how to survive in the ring and out of it. Naseem was more than a dancer, and he was doing more than surviving. He was hot property, and he was knocking their lights out – usually within three rounds. He was starting to resemble a cobra in stance.

His next opponent was Sergio Liendo, from Argentina. Naseem was back in Scotland wearing Armani shades and a tartan – Mr Cool, milking the crowd for all he was worth. Under the tartan he had his leopard thongs. Gerald McClellan was on everybody's mind. Brendan had commented at the weigh-in that Liendo wasn't marked. 'That's a good sign. So he doesn't get knocked around a lot.' Although Liendo was only twenty-five, he had had fifty professional fights, with forty-two wins. Brendan also pointed out the fact that because Liendo fights so often it must mean that he doesn't get involved in wars. 'You need time to recover from wars,' he said. I thought that was something of an understatement.

The fight was over in less than two rounds. A perfect left hook from Naz put Liendo on to the floor. His legs had gone completely, but the Belgian referee signalled for him to box on. Another left hook put him down for a second time. This time he landed very heavily. Jim Watt in his commentary for ITV said quite accurately that this second left hook was totally unnecessary, as the fight should have been stopped after the first. Liendo was lying very still in the ring. The doctor scrambled in. The Master of Ceremonies hurried over to Liendo's corner to fetch a stool. These were agonizing seconds for the boxing world. Even Naseem, pumped to the hilt with the adrenaline of victory, realized that something was wrong. The television commentator tried to reassure the audience at home by pointing out that the doctor wouldn't let Liendo stand up 'until he's quite capable of doing it'. But how the doctor would know this until the boxer actually tried was not explained. Eventually, Liendo was helped unsteadily to his feet and assisted by Brendan Ingle and others back to his corner. There was a quite audible sigh of relief around the arena. This was the first time in fifty-one contests that Liendo had ever been counted out.

247

Naseem hugged him, and a little smile appeared fleetingly on Liendo's face. That smile somehow told you that everything was going to be all right. Naseem held up the hand of a gallant loser. 'I hope he's nice and safe,' said Naseem in his television interview from the ring afterwards. Naseem was presented with his WBC International Super-Bantamweight Championship belt. It looked like a massive version of a cheap plastic watch that a child might whine for on a Saturday afternoon in a bargain shop. It was a lurid green colour.

The Scottish crowd were roaring their approval. It had not been a war, but the destructive power of that left hook had been 'awesome'. It was Mick Mills' favourite word. Awesome. In his opinion, pit bulls were awesome, Herol Graham had never been awesome, Naseem now clearly was. The crowd was singing 'Flower Of Scotland' – 'When will we see your likes again.' Naseem, already a Yorkshireman and a Yemeni, was now also an honorary Scotsman.

Liendo was helped slowly from the ring. The man who had never been stopped in fifty-one contests looked very shaky indeed as he was led by his trainer slowly but not very surely back to the dressing room.

Reach for the Sky

Enrique Angeles was no has-been. He was twenty-one, the same age as Naz. He was Naz's next challenger for his WBC Super-Bantamweight Championship. He had lost four out of his thirty fights, but significantly he had lost the Mexican Championship the previous November. They were to meet at the Royal Bath and West Showground in Shepton Mallet. It was part of Frank Warren's grand strategy to make Naz better known the length and breadth of the country – over to Wales, then up to Scotland, then down to the West Country. This was the boxing Grand Tour. ITV had been making Naz a star, but now Naz had suddenly deserted ITV for Sky Sport. 'Big Time Boxing on Sky Sport', was the new slogan. This was the big time all right. Miles from Sheffield and the venue was packed. But what was most surprising was the age of the audience. Naz was starting to hit the youth market. Here comes the hot-stepper. It all seemed to be working.

'They breed them tough over in Mexico,' said the commentator on Sky television about Angeles. It was better than the usual Mexican road sweeper quip. After all, there seem to be only two clichés about Mexicans in the fight game. Either they are as hard as nails, or they sweep the roads. Only two roles to play, often both in the course of a long evening. Barry McGuigan said that he wanted to see Naz severely tested. 'I'd just like to see him hit on the chin.' Naz's entrance was even more dramatic than usual. Something went up in flames at one side of the auditorium, and Naz suddenly appeared out of the smoke. 'Absolutely fabulous,' said the commentator. Even Angeles was smiling, but as usual the smile did not last that long. The little southpaw from Mexico was flung over and then cut in the first, and knocked out in the second. It was the right hand that did it. The mouth was at if again, after the KO. 'When I say I'm supreme, people just laugh. That was a beautiful workout. Baby, he couldn't take it.' Brendan was patting him reassuringly. The TV commentator played the final punch back to him. 'Oooh, what a beautiful right hand.' It was as if he was talking about somebody else's punch. 'He's got so much juice and you haven't seen any of it yet,' said Frank Warren. 'A legend's going to be coming soon,' said Naz.

Three days later the surroundings were more mundane, the atmosphere less charged. Naz's fake American accent, the tone of hyperbole, pumped and fuelled by adrenaline, was a fading echoic memory. Brendan and I were back in the transport café in Wincobank. Brendan, the vegetarian, ordered the usual meat and two veg without the meat. 'In the fight against Liendo, the referee should have stopped it,' said Brendan, shovelling the gravy over the imaginary meat. 'But that's being wise after the event. If the referee had stopped it and the fighter was still stood up, the referee would have got some real stick. So he gave Naz another crack at his opponent, and then it was all over. So everybody starts slagging the referee. Sometimes you just can't win in this game.'

Brendan took a long sip of his glass of water. 'But Naz is getting better all the time. He's better than Muhammad Ali when he was twenty-one.'

We were back to the Ali routine again. I had heard it so many times I could recite it myself. I sometimes wondered what the point of it all was. Who was the crafty Brendan trying to convince? Was Brendan, the Professor of Kidology, some sort of dedicated behaviourist using classical conditioning to connect those two names – Ali and Naz – in trial after trial, at the ringside, in the café, so that through time by mere association we would quite unconsciously produce the same responses to the name Naz, as we all had once done to the name of the great Ali?

'At twenty-one,' said Brendan, 'Muhammad Ali could box orthodox, and he could shuffle. But Naz can box orthodox, he can shuffle, he can box southpaw, he can switch, and he can hit angles that Ali couldn't. The fans are recognizing Naz's talent. At Shepton Mallet in the middle of nowhere the fans at the show were from six to sixty. They came from all over Britain. Naz's tour has been working. Frank Warren has done a great job promoting him. The last fight was Glasgow, and in Shepton Mallet there were two coaches from Scotland. Frank Warren and myself are working as a team, and Naz will get well looked after by the pair of us.'

250

This was still Brendan's regular lunchtime haunt. We were joined by Tony, a lorry driver and devoted boxing fan. They were all boxing fans in there. Brendan spreads the word, down in the café, across the street, up in the corner shop. Up in the corner shop live Naz and his family.

Brendan paused for another sip of his water. 'Naz became a millionaire last week.' It came out in a matter-of-fact way. I suppose that it had always been a milestone down in St Thomas', a milestone somewhere in the distance down that long, winding road of self-denial and punishment, and standing man-to-man and toe-to-toe. They were all going to make a million pounds one day, and become world champion the next. Or vice versa. The plans and dreams sometimes got a little confused that far ahead. Now Naz had really done it. Or had he? Was this still a paper promise? Tony, the lorry driver, had no such doubts.

'Not bad, is it, at that age?' said Tony. 'Getting up at nine o'clock in the morning and coming back a millionaire at four o'clock. Not bad, is it, for a lad that age?'

I asked how it had all happened so quickly. Last year in the café in Mansfield with Brendan's promises of the millions to come ringing in Naz's ear, even ringing in my ear I had heard them so often; this year in the café in Wincobank hearing that it's already happened? I couldn't see any obvious signs of change, except perhaps that Naz was less obvious on the streets than he had once been. Brendan took up the story. 'A week before the Shepton Mallet fight we were doing a press conference down in London. ITV were all set to do the show. Warren gets a phone call, as we're all sitting down. He gets up and he goes out and he comes back. You could see by the look on his face that something had happened, something good.'

Tony gave the sort of knowing look as if he too could read Frank Warren's body language at a glance from a distance, in Tony's case a considerable distance as he wasn't even at the press conference.

'So,' said Brendan, 'I says to myself, "What's happening here?" So off we shot. Frank didn't tell me what the crack was, but he said that he would ring me that evening. When I came in there was a message on my answer machine. It said, "Sorry I missed ye. Get on the six o'clock train in the morning. We're meeting at" – I forget which hotel it was – "twelve o'clock." When we went into the hotel, all the back wall was lined up with Sky posters. Frank Warren calls me over and tells me that he's just done a multi-million-pound deal with Sky. He says that we've moved lock, stock and barrel from ITV to Sky. I says, "You're kidding." This was a bit of a shock. ITV had been building their big fight night specials on a Saturday night around Naz. But we'd just gone. Warren had done a fifty-million-pound deal with Sky. And Naz had made it big.'

'And what about the man who put him there, Brendan?' quipped Tony. 'Don't be telling me that you're not doing all right out of this deal with Sky. You'll be driving down here in your Roller next.'

Brendan was spooning up his gravy with his fork, pretending he hadn't heard him. 'Frank Warren sent me a tape up of the man Naz was to fight. What do you call him? Eagle?'

'Angeles,' said Tony, helping out, leaning over the shoulder of the trainer and manager who brought kids from nowhere to the edge of the world stage, who analysed their every opponent, dissected them, diagnosed their every failing and weakness. 'Enrique Angeles,' said Tony again, as if Brendan was hard of hearing.

'Enrico Angles,' repeated Brendan.

'Enrique Angeles,' corrected Tony. 'Angel – Angeles,' changing the stress on the surname.

'Angeles is about five foot seven and clever with it,' said Brendan. 'Only stopped once with a cut. He's a fella who's handy. So you've got to be on the ball with a fella like that. So Naz and me watched the tape. We only watched two rounds and Naz suddenly got up and said, "I'll knock him out. I'll knock him out in three rounds." I told Naz that I thought he'd knock him out in five rounds, because Naz was training well. He was hitting terrible hard, but I thought that three rounds was a bit optimistic. Then the week before the fight I lost my voice.'

'At the Tony Booth fight,' chipped in Tony, 'for the Central Area Title. Brendan was shouting a lot and coaching from the corner as usual. A good night's boxing. The real bread and butter stuff.'

'The ceiling was low in the hall, the smoke was hanging,' said Brendan talking over Tony, who was sitting there reliving the night at the Tony Booth fight, tensed up, ducking and diving at the side of Brendan's plate. 'I lost my voice. So Naz gets the cold as well. One or two in the gym had got it – whether they had all got it off me I don't know. So I ring Frank Warren up and I tell him. Frank Warren says that it'll be all right. I'm massaging Naz every day. I took Naz down to Shepton Mallet on the Wednesday. He trains at half past twelve in the health suite with good carpet on the floor. Good thick carpet. He worked on the pads. He was hitting terrible hard. At the weigh-in Naz was bang on the weight at eight stone ten, the other fella was two pounds under. Naz was getting even cockier. He said he'd knock him out in two rounds now. He's holding up two fingers saying two rounds. "In two rounds he'll be down," he was saying to everyone present. The night before the fight Warren took fourteen of us out for a meal. My son John stays behind to look after Naz. Coming back through Bristol at a quarter to one on the morning of the fight, who do we see walking through the centre of town? It was Naz and John. It's a Friday night – everybody's out drinking and celebrating. It's like Dodge City down there, and there's Naz strolling through the town as if he hasn't a care in the world. He said he was hungry, he wanted some chicken and rice to eat. We tried one restaurant but they didn't sell chicken, so we had three Cokes instead. Naz got mobbed while we were waiting for the Cokes. The fella behind the bar wouldn't take the money for the drinks. The Cokes were on the house. That's how big Naz has become. We can even walk into a restaurant down in Bristol and get all the drinks on the house.'

'But it's not as if you were drinking champagne,' quipped Tony. 'It was only Cokes they were giving you. If that had been Sheffield they'd have given you champagne.'

'But me and Naz don't drink. We wanted Cokes. It would be no good them pouring out champagne for us, if we don't drink the stuff.'

Brendan took one last mouthful of vegetable. 'Eventually we found a restaurant that sold what he wanted. We sat down and he got mobbed again. "What are you going to do, champ?" and all this crack. You could see some of these fans thinking that this guy's fighting tonight, but what's he doing out at half one in the morning? We didn't get back to the hotel till half two.

'The next morning Naz got up early. I couldn't believe it. He likes to sleep in the mornings. He must have been excited. He went into a betting office that afternoon. The place stopped dead. He asked them what the betting on him was. He tells all the punters in the betting office that it's going to be all over in two rounds. He didn't put a bet on himself. Call it cheek, call it confidence, call it whatever you want.

I've never seen anything like it. Muhammad Ali never done that. Even Ali didn't go that far.'

I was sitting there over lunch, salivating all over my food, manipulated by the great behaviourist beside me.

'They laid on a big limousine on the night of the fight to pick him up from the hotel. Naz was so relaxed. This reporter from the *Sun* couldn't believe his eyes. He saw Naz with a big plate of chicken and Branston pickle sandwiches an hour and a half before the fight. He asked me what I thought. I told him that I belong to the old school – a fighter shouldn't eat just before a fight – but I told this reporter that Naz is just different. Most boxers look as if they're going to the hangman before a fight, but Naz is dancing and playing music. Frank Warren came in and just waggled his head. He couldn't believe it. I've known Naz to train from half past eleven at night to two o'clock in the morning. That's how different he is. Most boxers get up to train at dawn, but Naz is different. And it works for him. Then after the sandwiches he goes into that ring and still bashes the fella up. Angeles was here to fight, but all of a sudden Naz steps out that way – it's not a straight right, it's not a right upper-cut, it's not a right hook, he just steps out that way, and then whaaaaaaaaang.'

Brendan's hand holding his fork coursed through the air and a large dollop of gravy landed on Tony's shoulder. I was the only one to notice it, but I kept quiet.

'He broke the other fella's nose, bust his eye and cut his mouth in the first round,' added Brendan in a matter-of-fact manner. 'So you could say that the fella had been through a thrashing machine.'

I interrupted Brendan to suggest that he had meant to say a 'threshing machine'. I felt that I had to do something positive after I had failed to mention the gravy. There was a slight pause during which Brendan looked at me quizzically. 'No, a thrashing machine is what I'm talking about. He got thrashed. So it was a thrashing machine.'

Tony was nodding in agreement. 'Brendan is the world-famous trainer, after all. He's seen a few boxers that have been through thrashing machines. He should know what he's talking about.' I was forced to agree.

'After the first round,' Brendan continued, 'Naz said, "Just watch this, he's going in this round," and bang it was all over. He's unbelievable. He reminds me of Muhammad Ali, Joe Frazier, Archie Moore,

Rocky Marciano and Sugar Ray Leonard. Naz is all of them rolled into one. In the thirties there was a fella called Henry Armstrong who was featherweight champion of the world, went up to welterweight and won the welterweight title, dropped down to lightweight and won the lightweight title, and drew for the world middleweight title. Naz is going to go one better than this: he'll win from bantamweight up to the ten stone welterweight. Whatever he wants to win at he'll do it.'

'He's already the greatest in Sheffield,' Tony added, a little unnecessarily.

'This time last year,' continued Brendan, 'down in Mansfield, I told him that he was going to be a millionaire in one year. So now he's a millionaire. Can money change people? It probably can, but at the moment it hasn't changed him. He still lives with his family, but he's just about to buy a big house in Dore in Sheffield. But he's cracked it financially. He's a household name. He's in the Audi ad in the papers. Let me tell you something – I've just bought a fax machine and a mobile phone. Well, to be honest, a fella up in Scotland gave me the mobile phone, and I've given it to my son John. But the fax machine has changed my life. People were always making deals by telephone, then changing their minds. When somebody makes a deal now I tell them to fax it through to me. The people from Audi faxed through a deal for Naz to run around in a top-range Audi taxed and insured for twelve months. But what they don't know is that Naz has been banned from driving for speeding, so I didn't tell them. So I told them that I needed to think about the deal. When they rang me back, I told them that he was getting a Mercedes off the President of the Yemen in the next few months. There was a pause on the phone. So I said, "Look, this fella's better than Muhammad Ali. Give him five times that and he'll endorse the car. And better still, he won't drive the Mercedes around." What he didn't know was that he couldn't drive the Merc about anyway, because he was banned.'

We were all laughing now, even if the tone had become that much more conspiratorial. Tony had to leave and went back to his lorry full of the gossip about the fight game. Brendan was now leaning right across the table. 'People say to me, "That Brendan Ingle is a crafty bastard. That Brendan Ingle is a con man." But you have to be crafty in this game,' said Brendan. 'Audi wanted to take an option on Naz for the following year as well. Naz is on his way to London, so I ring him up on his mobile and I says to him, "Whatever you do, don't sign nothing. Stick the price up." So he did, and they went up to my figure. A computer games firm are just about to do a deal with him now. The lad's raking it in.'

But all of this talk about money was attracting the attention of the other diners in the café. Brendan was getting uncomfortable. 'Come on, we'll sit in your car and I'll tell you the rest.'

We sat parked outside the little café in Wincobank, Brendan stuck in full flow. 'He's a celebrity now. He went over to Blackpool the other night for a celebrity night with some cricketers and Frank Bruno. They paid all of his expenses and gave him two grand plus VAT. At Bradford the other night at a formal do he was the guest of honour. He sat down, ate a meal, signed a few autographs and got a grand plus VAT. He's got a licence to print money.'

But you can't go anywhere in Wincobank without Brendan being recognized. A well-rounded lady was peering in through the side window. Brendan immediately recognized her.

'*Hello!* How are you? What are you doing with yourself?'

'I'm still working for the housing department. This is Terry.'

'Hello,' said Terry. 'I've seen you loads of times on television.'

And so Brendan and his old friend proceeded to reminisce about old times for the benefit of Terry and myself. 'I had fourteen boys and girls with me on this council scheme and they were all nutters. I had this girl and all she ever said was "Go and get fucked, you Irish bastard." I was teaching them a little bit of gardening, and a little bit of this and that, and sometimes I'd take them down to the gym to teach them some more survival skills. I'd let them put the gloves on, and I'd teach them how to get by. Kids would come in sexually assaulted by their parents, kids would come in sexually assaulted by their neighbours, and I'd think to myself I'm supposed to be teaching bleedin' gardening skills, me. This lad comes over to me and says I was painting under there, and this fella comes over and grabs me by the testicles. I told him that in future if anyone tried to sexually interfere with him just tell him to "bollocks" and run off. I've been teaching survival skills for years.' We all laughed, and then Terry and Eileen continued their journey under the fly-over on their walk from Rotherham to Wincobank.

256

On the way back to Brendan's house an old-age pensioner signalled with his walking stick for us to stop. He wanted to thank Brendan for something. I assumed that it was for the glory that Brendan had brought to this small part of South Yorkshire with Naz on the verge of his world championship. But I was wrong. 'This man here rang me up,' said Brendan, 'because these kids were creating a nuisance outside his house. I got this kid at the top of the road by Naz's shop and I said to him, "What do they call you?" So he says, "so-and-so". So I says, "Watch me lips. We're all fucking going up to your fucking house and we're all going to kick up fucking hassle outside your bastard door, and when your mother and father come out I'm going to tell them, 'Fuck off.'" The kid is only eight or nine and he's shocked, but you have to be able to speak to them in a language they understand. I says, "Now, I'm not going to do that – this time." The other kids are laughing because they know me. I says, "Get the fuck out of it, the whole lot of you, and let me enjoy my fucking Sunday night in peace."'

The old-age pensioner was chuckling and beating his walking stick on the pavement. 'Brendan's got a way with the little tearaways. It's just as well somebody has.'

The Parting of the Ways

I watched Naz against Juan Polo Perez on the big screen at the Pinegrove Country Club in Sheffield, the country club for the common
man, the country club built on the site of a former rubbish dump.
Naz used to be a regular here until very recently. This was where he
would come to relax before a big fight. You would see him in the
sauna, or on the video games in the children's room. But no more.
Naz was now officially the WBO number one challenger and was
ranked number three by the WBC. He was a star. He no longer
frequented the club.

His fans had turned up to watch him on the big screen in the
members' bar, before the disco. Perez was billed as 'the stiffest test
yet'. Naz had died his hair ginger and in the pre-match build-up was
shown driving around Sheffield – 'just chillin'' in his words. Alma,
Brendan's wife and promoter of most of Naz's early fights, was saying
that Naz had become more like a pop star – 'a pop star and an athlete
rolled into one. Herol Graham despite his massive popularity at his
peak really only appealed to boxing fans. Naz has cornered the youth
market.' Down in the Royal Albert Hall the fight was a sell-out. Perez,
at thirty-one, was a battle-hardened former World Super-Flyweight
Champion. Down in London they were saying that Perez 'had mixed
with the best around and that he had fought nine world champions'.
'Wait until he meets young Naz,' said Gerry the barman, the man
who drove the Roller on the side. 'He'll wish he'd stayed in Columbia,
or wherever he's from.'

Naz was predicting a win in four rounds. 'I'll chase him for three
rounds and beat him in the fourth.' Gerry secretly reckoned that it
wouldn't take Naz that long to catch up with him. There were some
side bets being laid at the bar. Nobody was betting on the outcome
of the fight, only about which round the fight would end in, and
therefore at what exact time the disco would start. Gerry pointed out

that Naz's eighteen professional wins so far had lasted an average of three and a half rounds per fight. He was suggesting that the sensible punter interested in averages should therefore go with the law of averages and Naz's most recent recommendations. But the punters up in Pinegrove members' bar were not that sensible. Or gullible. They all wanted to go for the second round. Gerry thought that Perez's build-up on Sky might help. So he turned the sound up. 'This man may take more stopping than most,' said the commentator for Sky Sport. Furthermore, Perez had only been stopped twice in thirteen years. But the punters were not convinced. Gerry was still trying to rustle up some mugs to go for the fourth-round knockout when the organ music and the fireworks signalling Naz's entrance commenced.

Of course, Gerry and the rest of the gang were dead right. Perez went down three times in the second round. Naseem was seen growling at his opponent after the second knock-down, taunting him to get back up. 'They can't take the punishment,' said Naz afterwards. 'I'm blessed from God. It's a gift.' The referee, Mickey Vann, was less impressed. He criticized Naseem's behaviour after the fight. 'At the end of the first round I pushed Naseem towards his corner and told him that showbusiness stops when the bell rings. And I didn't like it when after knocking Perez down the second time he snarled at him to get up. This is a dangerous business and Perez could have been badly hurt. I won't have fighters behaving like that.'

Naz moved up to number one challenger in the WBC rankings after his victory. 'There's no stopping the lad,' said Gerry. John Montano of the World Boxing Organization seemed to agree with him. 'The kid is an original. So fast, so strong. At his weight he looks unstoppable.'

Gerry had only one regret. 'By the time he gets back to the Pinegrove he'll be well used to Rollers. I wanted to be the first to take him out along the streets so that he could wave like royalty. I guess I've missed my chance.'

Gerry had missed his chance. He opened the *Radio Times* and pointed to the advert inside. 'He's a bit too big a star for this place now,' he said. Suddenly you couldn't get away from Naz. He was on the hoardings alongside the top-of-the-range Audi A4 with the slogan 'They're both the most powerful in their class'. 'If you see either of the above, exercise due caution,' read the advert. He was in every magazine and every newspaper you picked up. A deal had been struck with the Joe Bloggs clothing company. They were preparing the Naz collection. Boxes of Joe Bloggs clothes lay in Brendan Ingle's front room as testimony to the commercial interest in the young lad he had discovered scrapping by the school railings. Computer games companies, manufacturers of sunglasses, video production companies wanting him to make fitness and exercise videos were queuing up with their lucrative offers. A fan club had been set up in Sheffield. A lot of young girls were joining it. It was much harder to get to see him.

He was being sucked into the maelstrom of commercial success. Brother Raith explained: 'We monitor all the commercial activities for him. They must not conflict with his boxing career. Everything has to be worked out around his training schedule. We all know that it could get out of hand. Everybody wants him. This week, for example, he is booked every day. On Monday he does an interview with a girl from an Asian TV channel magazine, plus the *Daily Telegraph*. Then on Tuesday there's an all-day fashion shoot in the gym for *Nineteen* magazine. On Wednesday the photographer from the *Sunday Times* is coming up to Sheffield. On Thursday there are talks with a production company that makes fitness videos. And on Friday the Asian TV people are back. We're building an empire around him. He is twenty-one now and basically he doesn't have to work another day or fight another fight to be financially secure for the rest of his life.' Naz was spending more time down in London, when he was not in strict training for a fight. 'That's where all the commercial activity is,' said Brendan a shade wistfully.

I went back to the gym in early August 1995. It was unexpectedly quiet that morning. There were just two boys training, probably no more than nine or ten years old, with Brendan seated as ever on his favourite wooden steps beside the ring. I caught him a little off-guard. I could almost sense the sadness that morning, despite the fact that after all these years he had been proven right with his unorthodox methods and his idiosyncratic approach to the hardest game of them all. He was going to make a packet after all these years in boxing. Alma apparently was even suggesting that they should at least discuss moving away from Wincobank. 'But why should I?' said Brendan. 'I'm happy here.' In that dusty gym based on years of scrounging and favours from friends, and thirty-five years – a lifetime – of ducking and diving to keep the whole thing going.

I asked straight out if Brendan missed the lad he had spent the past fourteen years with. It was one of the very few times I heard Brendan hesitate. 'Well, well, no, not really, you know. No, not really. I don't think that anyone has the right to pinch anybody else's life.'

It seemed a curious thing to say.

Brendan continued. 'We spent a lot of time down here together, working together over the years. And it's paid off – that's for sure. But you worry about him. He's a major star now, and we do get some funny phonecalls these days. There are a lot of nutters out there. You just worry about him sometimes. I've taught Naz all he knows – all the combinations and all the punches, all the fancy footwork and all the technique.'

There was a long pause before he continued. 'Perhaps most important of all, I've taught Naz the personal and social skills to get by in life – to survive in the ring and out of it.'

Brendan shouted 'Time!' at the two young boxers. He looked back at me. 'I just hope he remembers all I've taught him over the years.'

That night I was back in Sheffield's ultimate nightclub. Mick 'The Bomb' Mills and Alan, who is nearly sixty and works in the demolition business, were comparing hand sizes. Then they started comparing how many calluses each of them had on their respective hands. Alan had more. 'I'm used to hard work,' he said. I declined to show mine. Mick took up a boxing stance. 'I was once.' Mick's physique had ballooned since I first met him. He was doing a lot of weight training these days, rather than sparring and running. His arms and shoulders were massive. He said that the weight suited him. 'Even when I was cock of the street back in Dalton I always wanted to be big with it. Now I am.' I asked what he thought of Naseem's success. 'Good luck to him, that's what I say. But he's an arrogant little bastard. Mind you, he always was, but he's definitely got a lot worse lately. I saw him at the bar the other night, five foot nothing, trying to push through. He was saying to people, "Do you know who I am?"'

And sure enough, across the crowded floor of the nightclub I could see Naz and Johnny Nelson edging to the bar. It reminded me of the nights I had watched Herol Graham and Johnny in the very same club. Everybody in Sheffield was dressed up for their Thursday night out in summer – in their linen suits and white shirts and ties. Naz was wearing a leather waistcoat with his bare chest visible. If he'd been anybody else he would never have got in dressed like that. He was trying to get to the bar and clearly saying something to the guy next to him. Mick nudged me as if to say, 'What did I tell you?'

A girl in her early twenties came up to me and asked if that was Prince Naseem Hamed by the bar. She said her friend had said that it was, but she wasn't sure. 'He's far too little. I've seen Prince on the telly, and he's right big.'

Naz's world title challenge had now been scheduled for the following month.

Don't Tell Me What To Do, I'm the Champ

There was less than a month to go to the Prince's world title challenge. The gym was busy, but there was no Naz. The Saturday before he was right there in everybody's front room, ringside at the Bruno fight against Oliver McCall, shouting his encouragement with Nigel Benn beside him. You could see the two of them bobbing up and down like puppets on a string as Big Frank the muscle machine kept grinding forward. When Big Frank landed a punch it was as if the puppeteer was having convulsions as the two of them jumped out of their seats, their heads bobbing this way and that. You couldn't tell what they were shouting, but it didn't require much imagination to guess. The encouragement is always the same whether it comes from a world champion or the know-all in the second row. 'Work off the jab.' 'Hurt him.' London with all its gaudy attractions was where the action was, and Naz was soaking up his new-found fame miles from Sheffield. John Ingle summed it up for me. 'Chatting up the birds is a bit of a contest, it always has been with us. With Naz now it isn't even hard work. They're falling over. I was in this nightclub with Naz the other night and we were sitting opposite this guy who was touching up these two birds at the same time. We couldn't believe it, we were really shocked. Then Naz gets up to go to the toilet, and this other girl sitting with her back to me turns round and says, "Do you know him, then?" I told her that of course I knew him. She says to me, "Have you got plenty of money too? Can I come and join you?" Then there are all these other people who hug you as if they've known you all their lives. It happened when we went into Stringfellow's, and Peter Stringfellow came up and put his arms around Naz. Naz hadn't a clue who he was. It's unbelievable down there.'

But now, with just over three weeks to go, Naz was back home and well away from all such distractions. He just wasn't in the gym. He had promised to turn up for some photographs, but there was no sign of him. His brother Raith explained that he was watching television and didn't feel like training or posing for photographs. Brendan as usual was making himself busy, running around because a lift had fallen through for two of his boxers and he was preparing to drive them down to Stoke for a fight. 'Naz will be here in a minute,' he said apologetically as the Peugeot raced down Newman Road. A little knot of fans waited expectantly outside the front door. One little black girl, whose nickname was Don King, had her autograph book ready. I asked the little white boy who was with her what he thought of the Prince. 'He's right cool. He acts a bit arrogant when he's in the ring, but he's got a good talent. I like him being cocky. It's cool. I wish he didn't stand over some of his opponents when he's knocked them out, but I like the way he comes into the ring, and the music. I like Frank Warren, too. He lets me sit in his limo.'

They maintained their lonely vigil at the door, waiting for the Prince to get bored with the telly or even for the man with the limo to turn up unexpectedly. But it was a damp night in Sheffield, an early misty autumn, a dreary night to be hanging about outside a rundown gym.

Jimmy, the fifty-five-year-old moneylender, was inside training, as always. He stood in the ring sparring with a big Asian heavyweight, who was hitting hard. I wanted to encourage Jimmy. 'Work off the jab!' I shouted and left it at that. There was no way that Jimmy was going to hurt him; he just had to stand there soaking up whatever was to come. And it was coming hard, fast and brutal.

I went into the changing room. A young lad called Michael was getting dressed. I had seen Michael, who was about fifteen, a number of times down in the gym, but I had never talked to him before. He had always seemed very quiet. I asked him quite casually how his boxing was going.

'Very well. I'd say I'm the best amateur in here. I'm the South Yorkshire Bantamweight Champion, South Yorkshire and Humberside Champion and North Eastern Counties Champion. A lot of people in the gym say that I can be better than Naz. Naz himself says that I'll make a world champion easy.'

You had to admire the confidence with which all this came out. It was an uninterrupted flow, a torrent of self-belief and self-confidence, rehearsed and fluent, like the recital of a catechism. There was no room for doubt, no hesitation for second thoughts. This was what Brendan, the dyslexic schoolboy who feared the priests who ruled the classroom back in those Dublin slums, gave these boys up in Wincobank. I asked Michael about his amateur record.

'I've had twenty-nine amateur fights. I've won nineteen.'

'That's pretty good, is it?' I enquired, doing a quick calculation which told me that he had won about two-thirds of his fights.

'I'm not too pleased with it, because I could have won more. It was my own fault when I lost because I'd not done enough on the night.'

I asked how often he trained.

'Five days a week. I come straight from school in Rotherham. My dad comes here a lot with me and he talks to me about boxing all the time. He's hoping that I'll be better than Naz one day.'

I asked how he compared with Naz.

'Naz was still an amateur when I first came down. He always had an outstanding talent compared to a lot of people in the gym. He's got a very good amateur record. He fought sixty-seven times and only lost six, but he reversed the decision in three of them – when he boxed them again Naz won. ABA officials were biased against him because of his flashy entrance. He used to flip over the ropes even then. They didn't like it. When I first started boxing with him it was very hard, but now after six years of watching him and training with him I can say that he's still hard to hit, but you can catch him with the odd punch. I've never hurt him, but he's hurt me. He hurts everybody. He hits hard, very hard. He hits like a middleweight.'

I told Michael I wanted to know if Naz had any weaknesses.

'Not that I know of. When I've caught him he's told me that it does hurt, but I don't think it does, because he doesn't show it at all. Naz is going to be world champion this month. Naz has shown us all what you can do if you put your mind to it. You see somebody else doing it in the gym, so you know you can do it. I've been training here since I was nine. I know that I can be a millionaire just like Naz. In fact, I'm hoping to make a lot more than Naz. Naz always says that he'll be a legend one day, but I'm hoping to be bigger than Naz from start to finish.'

I then asked the sixty-four-thousand-dollar question. Why wasn't Naz training that night?

Michael just shook his head. I wasn't trying to imply that this might be Naz's fatal weakness, the crack that appears within all truly talented individuals who recognize their own talent early on. The weakness that spreads when the ego takes over and tells the rest of the individual that they truly are one in a million and that hard work and the daily grind is only for the ordinary, for the average, for the mortal. But perhaps I was thinking it.

Jimmy had now joined us. As usual I found my eyes being drawn to those big red welts on his shoulders and forearms. My own arms ached in sympathy. Jimmy had his own explanation of why Naz did not appear to be around the gym quite as much. 'He doesn't seem to need to train as much now, he's naturally fit. But I've seen him come in at eleven o'clock at night to train, when I'm on my way back from the boozer. That's why you don't see him. There's only one Naz. He's an individual. He trains at funny times, times that suit him. He may miss the odd day, because he's so good. But you have to be careful, no matter what talent you've got. If it doesn't catch up with him now it'll catch up with him one day. In my view you have to train every day. I've no natural ability, all my ability comes from training. But I'm very tricky for my age. I can bash up some of the young lads who come down here. Ryan Rhodes is the only one I detest boxing. He's too strong. He fucks me about. He's three stone heavier than me. I'm nine stone seven and he's twelve stone.'

Jimmy's calculations were a bit off, in fact more than a bit off for a moneylender, a man who should be good with figures, but I didn't feel like correcting him. I had too much sympathy for a man with arms so red.

'Naz is very tricky as well,' said Jimmy. 'He's a different man in the ring from outside it. He likes to get into that ring and think he's the master, that he's the fucking king. He likes to think that's his fucking territory. I once kissed him in the ring. I do it to them all. I'm right fucking good at it. I like to go bang, bang, bang and then kiss them. It does their head in. Then I land the big ones. It puts them off, you see. Naz hates it. He hates me kissing him when we're sparring.'

Jimmy said he wouldn't be going down to Cardiff to watch Naz bid for his world title. 'If I go down to Cardiff for the fight I won't be able to train on the Saturday afternoon or the Sunday. I train seven

Ryan Rhodes – the boxer. 'Ryan is the only one I detest boxing. He's too strong. He fucks me about,' says Jimmy the moneylender.

days a week, every week. Why should I miss my training just for a world championship? Anyway, I can watch Naz taking the title on the TV.'

I asked Jimmy how fame had changed Naz. 'He's an idol to the kids around here. Some big company is now making statues of him and selling them. The kids around here love him, but I wish he was a bit more responsive to people. It's easier to be nice in the long run. I don't speak to him these days until he speaks to me, which is a pity. I used to take him to some of his amateur fights. Me and John, Brendan's son, took him to his last amateur fight in Manchester. He was fighting this lad called Brody who had just won a silver medal in a multi-national championship. He was the Irish idol. Naz comes out with his leopardskin sombrero with all the tassels. All you could hear was "Fucking black cunt" and "Black bastard", as we were walking Naz to the ring. He vaulted over the ropes, as usual. He's not supposed to do that sort of thing, of course, in an amateur fight. The referee called the two fighters together, and then bang – in thirty-two seconds Naz had knocked him out. The Irish idol was on the deck. I've always admired Naz's talent, but he's very arrogant these days, very arrogant.'

We chatted for what seemed like hours, as I waited for Naz to arrive. He never did come. He trained the following night, and the photographer went back to the gym and caught him. The photographer asked if he could take a photograph of Naz sparring with Jimmy, the ring regular from way back. But Naz was adamant. 'Get out,' he said to Jimmy. The photographer tried once more. 'Don't tell me what to do, I'm the champ,' said Naz.

'For a second,' said the photographer afterwards, 'I thought that Jimmy was going to cry.'

My Destiny

It was the Sunday before the big fight and I was back in the gym. Billy the Bag Man was looking for a lift down to Cardiff. He had bad circulation and didn't fancy driving all the way to Wales. Brendan and John and the man himself were going down on the Wednesday, so Billy couldn't get a lift from them. Billy had five hundred quid on Naz to win. 'To make two hundred and fifty. It'll buy the shopping for a few weeks,' he said. Naz may have been getting hundreds of thousands for the fight, but everybody was trying to make something out of what they had learned over all those years, watching what was going on in the gym. Naz wanted to spar with Johnny Nelson. 'Steve Robinson is boasting that on the day of the fight he's going to be up to nine and a half stone. Johnny is nearly fifteen,' said Naz. 'I'll show you what difference a few extra pounds makes.' Everybody laughed. 'No sparring,' said Brendan. 'Twelve rounds on the pads.' Naz was putting on his bandages. He had a t-shirt on with 'All I have to do is turn up' written on the back. Brendan had forgotten his glasses. 'What does that say?' he asked me. I read it to him. 'The cheek of the lad. Some call it arrogance, I call it confidence.' Brendan kept repeating the slogan on the back of the t-shirt. 'All I have to do is turn up.' He was chuckling to himself.

I asked John Ingle how the betting was going. 'This lad in the gym said to Naz, "Is it all going to be over by the sixth round as Brendan says, because I've put a lot of money on it?" And Naz turned to him and said, "It's all going to be over in four. Put some more money on the fourth round and get your money back." There's nobody in the gym who fancies Robinson's chances. He's going to get bashed up.'

In the weeks before the fight there was a lot of serious speculation in the press that Robinson was considering pulling out. He had been fined for breaking his contract with Barry Hearn; his prize money for the fight would just about pay off the fine. Not surprisingly, he was angling for more money. John took it all with a pinch of salt. 'The fight has to go on. If Robinson pulls out they'll strip the title off him. As a man without a title he won't get anything anyway. He has to fight.'

Robinson appeared in his interviews as a modest character with a quiet dignity, in stark comparison to the rising star he was to face. Robinson had always seemed a boxer of fairly average form, until fate gave him that one chance to take the world title. The story goes that one Thursday some two and a half years ago Robinson was just finishing his lunch when his trainer Ronnie Rush telephoned him to offer him a fight. The fight was on the Saturday, for the world title. Ruben Palacio, the Colombian due to defend his title against John Davison, had been found to be HIV-positive. Robinson's two previous title shots were for the vacant Welsh super-featherweight title, which he lost, and the vacant PentaContinental featherweight title, which he won. A world title shot was to say the very least a step up in class and prestige. Robinson, so the story goes, had not sparred since his last fight against Mehdi Labdouni in Paris two months earlier, which he had lost on points over eight rounds. But he had kept himself fit in between his part-time job as a storeman. He took his chance up in Washington in County Durham and won the world title over twelve rounds. Up to that point in his career Robinson's form had hardly been sparkling. Out of twenty-three professional fights he had won thirteen, lost nine, and drawn one. In a busy few months in the latter half of 1990 he had lost four fights out of five. Hardly world championship class. But suddenly he was there. Recognition, however, was slow to come to the new champion, but it did come almost grudgingly in a series of successful defences of the title. It really took seven successful defences against classy opposition such as Colin McMillan, Paul Hodgkinson and Duke McKenzie to make Robinson the People's Champion down in Wales. A strong, quiet man worthy of admiration and respect, a man who had battled to get where he was. A man who had been given just the one chance and had grabbed it.

Naz's arrogance was getting the Welsh crowd focused on their man; his conceit was helping Robinson become a real man of the people. Some papers were predicting trouble at the fight. The last time Naz had boxed in Cardiff he was greeted with a cacophony of noisy booing. Some pundits were predicting a lot worse for this fight. I chatted to

Mick 'The Bomb' Mills the night before in the club where he worked. He was looking a little aggrieved that he hadn't got a complimentary ticket for the fight. He was predicting mayhem. 'There's bound to be trouble. They'll be scrapping in the streets down in Cardiff. Don't wear that bloody orange jacket again,' he said, recalling my sartorial elegance at the bare-knuckle fight in the park some time before. 'You'll stand out a mile. You'd better get dressed for a scrap this time.' Brendan had taken his own precautions. 'I took Naz on a walkabout down in Cardiff last week and he was mobbed everywhere he went. I personally think he's very popular down there.'

Robinson had had some luck running for him when he'd got a shot at the title. But up in the gym in Sheffield the consensus was that his luck was running out. John Ingle had no doubts. 'We watched him when he lost to Labdouni and he's no better now than he was then. He's just ordinary.' But no matter. The tickets were going like hot cakes because the punters wanted to see the 'Naz fella', as Brendan sometimes likes to call him, the man of the moment, in action. 'A friend of my dad's from Liverpool phoned up the other day for thirty ringside seats and sent a cheque for three thousand pounds,' John told me. The fight was being billed as 'A bridge too far?' 'Well, it's too far down to Cardiff with my bad circulation,' said Billy the Bag Man, presumably seeing the funny side of it.

All the planning in the gym was for the months after the fight. 'Sugar Ray Leonard won world titles at five different weights,' said Brendan. 'The Naz fella is going to do the same. Leonard won world titles at welterweight, which is ten stone seven pounds, then at light middleweight, which is eleven stone. Then he moved up to middle-weight, which is eleven stone six pounds, when he beat Marvin Hagler. Then up to twelve stone, which is super-middleweight. Then up to light heavyweight at twelve stone seven pounds. He won world championships differing at over two stone. Naz could win world titles from bantamweight eight stone six pounds, super-bantamweight eight stone ten pounds, featherweight nine stone, then super-featherweight nine stone four pounds, and then lightweight, which is nine stone nine pounds. With the will power he's got he could be champion at all five weights. Over the next year he's going to be worth forty million pounds.'

I watched Naseem work a full twelve rounds in the ring with John

Ingle on the pads, with Brendan, Naz's father Sal, and Johnny Nelson beside me. The doors were locked to keep out the reporters and the fans and the hangers-on. The heater was on, turned up full blast. So too was the music. It was like a sauna in there. 'Naz's punching is just awesome at the moment,' said Johnny. 'He really hurts you.' John had told me earlier that he reckoned that by the time he was thirty the joints in his elbows would have seized up from the punishment he receives holding those pads. 'It's like getting an electric shock in your joints every time Naz hits you,' he had said. Naz was enjoying himself beckoning to John like a belly dancer, calling him closer, before pounding the pads. Every round ended with a ten-second countdown and a flurry of venom on the pads. Between rounds Naz gobbed down the back of the ring, as if he was marking out his territory, and stalked arrogantly around his little kingdom between the ropes. I remembered that Jimmy, the moneylender and inveterate trainer, had told me Naz likes to be king in there – the king of the jungle.

'Come on, John!' shouted Sal. 'Get stuck in!' 'I'm in front,' shouted John. 'I don't want to get knocked out while I'm in front.' Sal and Johnny Nelson were laughing uproariously. Brendan was deep in thought. 'Phenomenal punching,' he said to nobody in particular. 'Phenomenal.' The rounds went on and on. Naz did not slow down or tire. The newspapers had an angle on this fight. It was the glitz and glamour of the Prince versus the good old-fashioned hard work of the champion. I felt like ringing up some papers and pointing out to them that the word 'glamour' is not all it seems. It was used in the Middle Ages for learning in general and hence, by superstitious association, for magic. But, standing there that morning reflecting on the glamour of the Prince, the older meaning of the word was clear to see. 'He's magic,' said Brendan, as if he could read my thoughts. He said it in that same unfocused way, as if an inner thought had managed to find its way into the public domain, as if an inner thought had found an ancient idea and articulated it there and then. 'Just magic.'

Brendan wanted Naz to shadow-box the eleventh round, to give his son John a rest. 'No shadow-boxing!' shouted Naz. Twelve straight rounds on the pads in something like a sauna. John slumped to the canvas, exhausted and beaten. Naseem made some pelvic thrust movements against the corner post, in a ritualistic victory display straight

272

from the savannah, or the great American Plains. Or the jungle. Naz wanted to go on, he wanted to spar. 'You've done,' said Brendan. 'Don't do any more.' Any doubts I had been entertaining over the past fortnight that here was a man who may one day find the daily grind of training and sparring too monotonous had long gone. Here was a man who enjoyed demonstrating his power and his potency. Training allowed him to do that just as well. 'I'm hot,' said Naz.

In the build-up to the fight, Robinson seemed quietly confident. 'I've had six weeks to prepare, which is plenty of time for a world title. There's no way he'll beat me in four rounds like he's saying. I'm confident that I'll stop him and I'm prepared to go the distance.' The *Guardian* had an interesting photograph of Robinson on the day of the fight. It looked as if he was trying to uproot a tree. It seemed to imply that this was going to be Robinson's tactic, his game plan, the ace up his sleeve. Solid strength-sapping clinches; the clown prince was going to be crushed to death. The subtext in the photograph focused on Robinson's strength. But I just thought of Johnny Nelson and the incredible physique of that fighter rocked by the little man who liked to stalk the ring, and I thought that this was no game plan at all.

According to John Ingle, Naz won the fight at the weigh-in. 'It was like Muhammad Ali predicting that he was going to knock the bear, Sonny Liston, out in five rounds. Everybody used to laugh except the guy he was talking about. Naz got to Steve Robinson at the weigh-in. He was looking straight into his face and saying, "Steve, you're going to get beaten." It wasn't done in a nasty sort of way, it was just done in a matter of fact way. The cold stare of Naz can be quite intimidating. I could feel Steve Robinson crumbling inside as Naz was saying it. I said to Johnny Nelson, " Look at that, he's gone already."'

On the night of the fight, on 30 September 1995, Naz had a long walk through the partisan Welsh crowd at Cardiff Arms Park, protected by the security guards and his cornermen. The crowd were chanting, 'Hamed, Hamed, who the fuck is Hamed?' Somebody hit him on the side of the head with a plastic water bottle top. Naz thought that somebody had spat on him. 'I could see something white flying through the air. I thought somebody had gobbed on him as well,' said John afterwards. John said that he could feel the Robinson fans spitting on the back of his head and the back of his jacket on that long walk to the ring. 'The back of my jacket was soaked by the time I made it to the ring.' The fans fuelled by nationalist pride and the slow build-up of media hype were swearing at Naz, sneering, hissing and spitting. 'Hamed, you're fucking dead!' 'Fuck off back to Sheffield!' The venom came bursting out from both sides of that long narrow aisle. Then it was the turn of the local boy, the People's Champion, the man who had started to crumble at the weigh-in. Robinson appeared to emerge from the flames of Hell. It was the same sort of entrance that Bruno had practised in his fight against Oliver McCall. It was the same metal floor to walk across. I didn't think it suited Robinson's personality. Every fighter now has to have the big entrance, regardless of character. I wondered if this metal bridge was the bridge referred to in the poster. To fuel Welsh nationalist pride, he was led in by a goat. The semiotics of the situation made the whole thing look like something to do with the devil, Beelzebub. Robinson's personal Hell, perhaps? He came in with polythene wrappers on his feet, and for a second it looked as if he was going to box with his feet wrapped to protect himself from the cold, wet night in Cardiff. Naz had gone for the Tyson look – rough sweat top with the neck hacked out. I kept thinking that Naz was smiling uncontrollably during the introductions; it was almost as if he couldn't contain his glee. Boos interrupted his introduction. It was like this the last time he'd boxed in Cardiff. It was cold. And I kept thinking that the cold might be a bigger challenge for Naz than Robinson himself.

Naz pursued him from the opening bell, taunting him. Robinson covered up in a peek-a-boo style, inviting him in. The first round, unlike all the rounds that followed, was quite even. At the start of the second round, Robinson came out fighting and cheers went up from the audience – those sitting far away couldn't really see that his punches were missing. Naz was smiling again. One punch jolted Robinson's head, but this was followed by a shove which put him down. Robinson got up from the floor, his head stuck for a second up Naseem's leopardskin skirt. It looked like the ultimate degradation. Naseem was goading him and Robinson attacked, flushed with rage. In between rounds you could see John Ingle smiling – a sure sign that things were going all right for the challenger. In round three, Robinson tried to attack again but Naz was still smiling. He could afford to – he was bamboozling him. Robinson just looked confused. In round

'Steve Robinson is only a stepping-stone to me becoming a legend.'

four the audience tried to bolster their man. The shout went up: 'STEVO!' 'STEVO!' Robinson still maintained his peek-a-boo stance. He had always said that he thought Naz might make him look a bit stupid in the early rounds and this was one prediction that was exactly right. In round five Naseem was still taunting him: 'Go on, try hitting me to the body.' 'Who's stronger now?' Naz danced with his hands down by his sides. Some statistics after the fight suggested that by this point Naseem had landed eighty-nine punches to Robinson's thirty-one. But most observers would reject this second figure as a gross over-estimate. Robinson was sticking to some game plan, steadily advancing behind his high guard. But Naz kept switching positions, flicking in combinations, dodging out of the way, taunting him, goading him. By round five Robinson's guard was beginning to drop. Naz's punches were sweeping in right through the guard. In round six Naseem produced a four-punch combination and a right upper-cut. Robinson's face was swollen and it looked very painful. I remembered John Ingle telling me, in a matter of fact sort of way a week before the fight, that Robinson would be bashed up. And that is exactly what was happening. But at least he had survived the four rounds predicted by Motormouth in the build-up to the fight.

Of course Brendan Ingle had seen it all before when Herol Graham had out-boxed Julian Jackson in Spain. Graham had out-boxed his opponent for three rounds and then Jackson had landed just one punch, but enough to undo Graham. But Robinson didn't look as if he had that punch inside him. At the start of round seven Robinson came out dancing but Naseem was by now just playing with him. Robinson moved forward and missed. Brendan pulled Naseem back to the corner at the end of the round. In round eight the fight was slowing. Then suddenly a ferocious left hook put Robinson down. 'Right on the button,' said Brendan afterwards. Robinson looked as if he might have slipped in some water – his legs left him violently. There seemed to be a delayed action in the whole thing. It was the first time Robinson had been stopped in seven years as a professional. You could only feel sorry for him. He was a decent, dignified champion, humiliated on the night. The applause was subdued, grudging, even.

When it was all over Naseem went over to Robinson's corner and hugged him. In the ringside interview he complimented the defeated champion, the champion he had just humiliated. 'He was so strong, I hit him with everything.' But there was a sting in the tail. Naseem had hit him with everything and Robinson had avoided none of the punishment. 'I was amazed, with his chin,' said the new champ. It looked as if Naz's new status was slowly sinking in. 'You know who's world champion, don't you?' he told the millions of viewers sitting in their armchairs back at home. Brendan, the old pro who had seen everything, spoke almost dolefully. 'Robinson fought like a champion, he had plenty of heart.'

The Prince had finally done it. And so too had Brendan Ingle and the gym for limbo dancers up in Sheffield, the gym for waifs and strays, the gym a seven-year-old Arab boy had been invited to one day and who had stayed for the next fourteen years. The gym where boys are taught to jump the ropes so that they too will stand out when their chance comes. The gym where the science and art of boxing is taught with a series of mysterious circles and lines on a floor that is musty from the dried sweat of the years. The gym where the Irish blarney resounds from floor to ceiling, talking them all up to be champions. The gym where the sing-song Irish lilt constantly reminds them all of how hard life is outside those doors, and how hard they will have to work in that dark, dank place. The gym where the kids and the 'nutters off the streets' learn about life and all its pitfalls. The gym where Jimmy the moneylender and Prince Naseem Hamed, the champion of the world, train together. The gym where Herol Graham once boxed beautifully and avoided being hit, until his time came. The gym where Mick 'The Bomb' Mills hits everything that is put in front of him, including me, before I learned my lesson and left the gym to those who really needed it.

The new champion of the world was still at it back in the ring at Cardiff. 'I'm not changing my name to King just yet, I'm staying as Prince. I'm just too good.' Naseem had always said that beating Robinson would only ever be a stepping stone to becoming a legend. But as one of the Sunday papers wrote on the morning after the fight, 'After this you begin to wonder.'